22.

Beyond Slavery

Frederick Cooper

Thomas C. Holt

Rebecca J. Scott

Beyond Slavery

Explorations of Race, Labor, and Citizenship
in Postemancipation Societies

The University of North Carolina Press

Chapel Hill and London

© 2000 The University of North Carolina Press

All rights reserved

Designed by April Leidig-Higgins
Set in Quadraat by Tseng Informations Systems, Inc.
Manufactured in the United States of America

The paper in this book meets the guidelines for
permanence and durability of the Committee on
Production Guidelines for Book Longevity of the
Council on Library Resources.

Library of Congress Cataloging-in-Publication Data
Cooper, Frederick, 1947–
Beyond slavery: explorations of race, labor, and
citizenship in postemancipation societies /
Frederick Cooper, Thomas C. Holt, Rebecca J. Scott.
p. cm. Includes bibliographical references and index.
ISBN 0-8078-2541-7 (cloth: alk. paper) —
ISBN 0-8078-4854-9 (pbk.: alk. paper)
1. Freedmen. 2. Race. 3. Citizenship. 4. Slaves
—Emancipation. I. Holt, Thomas C. (Thomas
Cleveland), 1942– II. Scott, Rebecca J. (Rebecca
Jarvis), 1950– III. Title.
HT731.C66 2000 326′.8′0973—dc21 99-053083

04 03 02 01 00 5 4 3 2 1

Contents

Illustrations and Maps

Acknowledgments

This book is the fruit of a long collaboration that has been through many phases. Its prehistory includes an undergraduate course on postemancipation societies co-taught at Harvard by Fred Cooper and Tom Holt, sometime in the dimly remembered 1970s. Its history, however, begins when Cooper, Holt, and Rebecca Scott were all at the University of Michigan starting in 1982, and it is to this institution that we are most grateful for providing the support and the atmosphere in which our project took root. There, Holt and Scott began a graduate seminar on postemancipation societies, and after Holt moved on to the University of Chicago, Cooper and Scott continued teaching it. At Chicago, Holt developed courses on related subjects, some of them in cooperation with Julie Saville. On two occasions, Chicago and Michigan students participated in joint conferences held at the Center for Afroamerican and African Studies (CAAS) at the University of Michigan, at which seminar papers from the courses served as springboards for discussion and at which colleagues — including Harold Woodman from Purdue University, Fernando Picó from the

University of Puerto Rico, Robin D. G. Kelley from New York University, and Fernando Coronil from Michigan—provided comments and suggestions.

Our biggest debt is therefore to our students and colleagues for providing so much intellectual stimulation. We are also grateful to CAAS, as an institution and as a collectivity of faculty and staff, for offering generous support in many forms, including assistance from a major Ford Foundation Grant to CAAS. Starting in 1987, the three authors were the recipients of a grant from the University of Michigan's Presidential Initiatives Fund, which in turn was supported by the Kellogg Foundation. We are grateful for their support. This grant gave our collaboration a formal structure—the Postemancipation Societies Project—and considerable logistical support. Above all, it financed the compilation of a bibliography of primary and secondary sources for the comparative study of societies after slavery. The current book grew out of reflections and conversations among the three authors as we taught these courses and worked with our graduate students on the bibliographic project. The latter is on the verge of completion and will be published in 2001 by the University of Michigan Press as *Societies after Slavery: A Select Annotated Bibliography of Printed Sources on the British West Indies, British Colonial Africa, South Africa, Cuba, and Brazil*. Numerous graduate students helped to find and annotate the bibliographic entries, and their work has informed the present book as well. Neil Foley, who administered the Postemancipation Societies Project in its early days, and Aims McGuinness, who guided it in its final stages, have been particularly important to the entire enterprise. The staff at CAAS, particularly Evans Young, have made collaboration easier, and the directors of CAAS— this project has continued through the tenures of five of them—have been extremely supportive. The Rackham Graduate School and the Office of the Vice President for Research stepped in at crucial moments with continuing funding for the project. Jeanette Diuble provided help beyond the call of duty in collating drafts and typing in corrections, both for this book and for the companion bibliographic volume.

The graduate seminars on postemancipation societies produced the kind of detailed research that makes overviews and comparisons possible. Among our former students, Pamela Scully, Neil Foley, Christopher Schmidt-Nowara, Ada Ferrer, and Laurent Dubois have themselves now published books on related subjects, and their work has informed our thinking in this one. So too with several dissertations in the general area of postemancipation studies, including those of César Solá-García and Hollis Liverpool at the University of Michigan. Our own work has received valuable criticism from students, individually and in seminars. A version of the introduction was presented in 1997 to a workshop at the University of Chicago titled "Triangular Exchanges: Mapping the Atlantic World," where it received valuable and constructive criticism.

Fred Cooper would like to acknowledge critiques of versions of his chapter presented at the University of Michigan, the École de Hautes Études en Sciences Sociales, and the University of Trondheim. Related papers were presented at the University of Campinas and at the University of California, San Diego. His research has benefited from the assistance of archivists at the Archives Nationales, Section Outre-Mer, in Aix-en-Provence, France, and at the Archives Nationales du Sénégal. Cooper has greatly benefited from the friendship and critical insight of Babacar Fall, whose own contributions to the study of forced labor in French Africa have been of major importance.

Thomas Holt's essay has benefited from comments and criticisms on various drafts presented at conferences and faculty seminars, beginning with the international conferences "Slavery and Freedom" at the University of California, San Diego, in the fall of 1991 and "Racism and Race Relations in the Countries of the African Diaspora," hosted by the Centro de Estudos Afro-Asiáticos in Rio de Janeiro in April 1992. Especially stimulating were presentations at faculty seminars hosted by the Committee on Critical Practice at the University of Chicago and by the Atlantic Studies Seminar at Johns Hopkins in the winter of 1992.

Holt is especially grateful to Leora Auslander, Noralee Frankel, Miriam Hansen, and Moishe Postone for reading early drafts. Earlier versions of Holt's essay have been published previously as " 'La Esencia del Contrato': La Articulación de la Raza, el Género, y la Economía Política en la Programa de Emancipación del Gobierno Británico, 1838–1865," Historia Social [Valencia, Spain] 22 (Fall 1995), which was reprinted as " 'A essència do contrato': a articulação de raça, gênero e economia na política de emancipação britânica (1838–1866)," Estudos Afro-Asiáticos [Rio de Janeiro, Brazil] 28 (October 1995). Parts of the essay are also drawn from his previously published book, The Problem of Freedom: Race, Labor, and Politics in Jamaica and Britain, 1832–1938 (Baltimore: Johns Hopkins University Press, 1992).

Rebecca Scott offers particular thanks to colleagues who responded to early drafts presented at Yale University, the Universitat Pompeu Fabra in Barcelona, the Centro de Estudos Afro-Asiáticos in Rio de Janeiro, and the International Congress of Historical Sciences in Montreal in 1996. A preliminary, much-abbreviated version of Scott's essay appeared as "Building, Bridging, and Breaching the Color Line: Rural Collective Action in Louisiana and Cuba, 1865–1912," in Democracy, Revolution, and History, edited by Theda Skocpol, with

George Ross, Tony Smith, and Judith Eisenberg Vichniac (Ithaca, N.Y.: Cornell University Press, 1998), 143–66. Portions also appeared in Spanish in a special issue of the journal *Historia Social* [Valencia, Spain] 22 (Fall 1995): 125–49, and in Portuguese in the journal *Estudos Afro-Asiáticos* [Rio de Janeiro, Brazil] 27 (April 1995): 111–36. Scott would like to thank the many colleagues who provided comments and assistance on these and other related essays, including, most recently, Alejandra Bronfman, Sueann Caulfield, Frederick Cooper, Jeanne Chase, Alejandro de la Fuente, Paul Eiss, Ada Ferrer, Josep Fradera, Orlando García Martínez, Jeffrey Gould, Albert Hirschman, Sarah Hirschman, Thomas Holt, Robin Kelley, Earl Lewis, Kathleen Lopez, Aims McGuinness, Louis A. Pérez Jr., Lawrence Powell, Lara Putnam, Peter Railton, Alice Ritscherle, John Rodrigue, David Sartorius, John Shy, Stanley Stein, Peter Wade, and Michael Zeuske. She would like to thank as well a legion of generous archivists, including, in particular, Carol Matthias of the Allen J. Ellender Archives, Ellender Memorial Library, Nicholls State University, Thibodaux, Louisiana; Peter Drummey of the Massachusetts Historical Society, Boston, Massachusetts; and Orlando García Martínez, director of the Archivo Provincial de Cienfuegos, Cienfuegos, Cuba. She is also very grateful to the dozens of residents of Cienfuegos who have spoken to her about rural life and labor in the late nineteenth and early twentieth centuries. Many are cited by name in her chapter in the reference to oral history interviews.

Beyond Slavery

Introduction

Slavery—"the peculiar institution"—has held a peculiar grip on the imaginations of historians of the Americas. In this "new" world, one imagined to hold unparalleled opportunities for human aspirations and potential, an institution embodying the "old" world's inhumanity produced perhaps its highest level of exploitation. By designating it a peculiar institution, even its nineteenth-century North American defenders conceded some of slavery's anachronistic quality; only die-hards in the United States South defended it as a positive good rather than a necessary, perishing evil. For most subsequent historians, to write about slavery meant confronting an evil that sullied the historic promise of the new American world, but it was a well-bounded evil, one that was located in the past.

The historical and moral locatedness of slavery made it an attractive subject for comparative studies: one could examine seemingly discrete "slave systems," seeking to explain how the social deprivations of slaves varied with particular characteristics of a society, such as religion. Indeed, the enormous interest in comparative slavery, which began with Frank Tannenbaum's *Slave and Citizen* (1946) and reached a peak in the 1960s and 1970s, was hardly re-mote from presentist concerns, particularly with the renewed debate about issues of race that surfaced after World War II and became acute with the civil rights movement of the postwar decades. Tannenbaum's book, as well as Stanley Elkins's *Slavery* (1959) and several others, used comparison to make a point about the contemporary United States: that it excluded the descen-dants of slaves from important dimensions of citizenship in a particularly severe and brutal way as a direct consequence of the nature of its slave sys-tem.[1] Tannenbaum argued that the greater salience of the Catholic Church and the state in Latin America meant that slaves, no matter how severely ex-ploited economically, had a fuller legal and religious persona there because of the direct interest of legal and religious institutions in them. Such com-parison implied alternatives: perhaps institutional reform and a rethinking of values would allow the United States finally to overcome the legacy of its slavery and find ways of extending a broader citizenship to African Americans.

What was missing in these discussions, however, was everything that fell in between the end of slavery and the present day. In the United States, the Civil War and emancipation ran like a river Jordan across the pages of American history. Historians of the later period tended to ask what mistakes, errors of political judgment, or moral failings had prevented the nation from fully inte-grating former slaves into the American political, economic, and social sys-tems. Slavery and the racism it engendered were thought to have planted the seeds of these failures. In sharp contrast with studies of the slave era, those of the later period rarely asked fundamental questions of the new systems into which freedpeople were supposed to be integrated; rather, they debated whether institutions like sharecropping represented coercive distortions of an ideal-typical free labor system. Scholars of Latin America and the Caribbean were somewhat more likely to scrutinize the concept of free labor itself with a critical eye. But in Jamaica, Brazil, or Cuba, no less than in Alabama or South Carolina, the ultimate fate of the freedpeople and their descendants was more likely to find explanation in the legacies of slavery than in the problems of freedom.

Students of African history, in contrast, initially had trouble thinking about slavery itself. Suggesting that such an institution existed among African soci-eties seemed to invoke a comparison that took much of the moral force out of the telling of the history of slavery in the Americas. Later, as Africanists be-came self-confident enough to admit that in Africa, as in the rest of the world, economic growth and state-building could imply exploitation and oppres-sion, they ran up against the fact that the archives were filled with silences.

Having justified colonial conquest in the late nineteenth century on the grounds that Africa's slave-trading, tyrannical regimes were isolating the continent from the benefits of commerce, civilization, and Christianity, colonizing elites had soon discovered that colonial stability and revenues depended on alliances with the very forces they had been attacking. The category of slave became one that official records avoided or defined in a sufficiently narrow way that the problem could be declared to be solved. Yet colonial power, whatever the intentions of those who enforced it, did in fact disrupt the mechanisms by which slaveholders controlled and replenished slave populations. At a still later date, when ethnographers began to look for institutions resembling enslavement and domestic slavery, they often found relevant status distinctions without the institutions of power and labor exploitation once connected to them. Consequently, instead of leaping over the postemancipation period, as occurred in studies of the Americas, historians of Africa implicitly or explicitly declared that the problem of emancipation did not exist.[2]

What lay beyond slavery, on both sides of the Atlantic, thus proved hard to grasp, disappearing in the one case into the uncertainties of freedom and in the other into the study of a rather different form of power and exploitation, colonialism. The question of what free labor meant, in the very different contexts of independent versus colonial regimes, of contestations over who was included and excluded from the realm of citizenship, has proven an elusive one. All too often students of slavery treated its aftermath—freedom—as an undifferentiated, unexamined conceptual foil to bondage. Slave labor could be analyzed in economic, social, and political terms, but free labor was often defined as simply the ending of coercion, not as a structure of labor control that needed to be analyzed in its own way. These conceptual and analytical difficulties may arise in part from the fact that freedom is neither past nor elsewhere; it is the historical terrain we currently inhabit, the system that governs our lives, our livelihoods, and our consciousness.

Over the past two decades, scholars of postemancipation societies have begun to address these problems, reframing the analysis of the emancipation process and adding to the depth and breadth of our understanding of slavery as well as freedom.[3] Yet there remains something ambiguous, even intractable, about "the beyond" as a subject of historical inquiry. What are the appropriate boundaries of the study of postemancipation societies?

The question is temporal, spatial, and conceptual. Temporally we have beginning dates but no clear end. Unlike slavery studies, where the time frame—at least for the Atlantic world—might be from the beginning of the slave trade in the sixteenth century to Brazilian emancipation in 1888, the aftermath of slavery sprawls deep into the twentieth century, with the demise of southern United States sharecropping and of West Indian peasantries in the 1930s, the mass migrations to cities and decolonization in the 1950s and 1960s, or even the establishment of postindustrial economic orders all vying to mark its outer boundaries. Spatially we have studied slavery largely where slave systems were in place. The metropole was primarily important for its policy formulations and ideological constructions. But after slavery, former slave societies were by definition supposed to be integrated into the world of the metropole, and former slaves often did move freely into metropolitan spaces. Might Paris, London, and New York City become equally important loci of inquiry as Mombasa, Kingston, and Charleston? Or had they always been? And if, as has become increasingly clear, the economic and social arrangements that followed slavery fell far short of the ideals of free soil, free labor, and free men—if, indeed, a plethora of systems of labor and social-political arrangements ensued, engendering a diverse array of new struggles—then what is our object of study? The concept of slave societies suggested, and encouraged the study of, a totality: a political economy, its ideological legitimization, and its ecological and cultural consequences, all somehow illuminated through and illuminating in turn a particular set of social relations of labor. We are not accustomed to thinking about "freedom" and "free societies" in quite the same way.

The essays in this volume seek to explore the various dimensions of what lies beyond slavery. They do so in a chronological sense, focusing on the periods after slavery and related forms of coerced labor were abolished in different parts of the Caribbean, the United States, and Africa. They thus range from abolition in the British Caribbean in 1833, to Louisiana after 1864, to Cuba in 1886, to British East Africa in 1897–1907, and, indeed, to 1946, when forced labor was ended in French Africa. The essays offer explorations in an analytic sense as well, not assuming a sharply distinctive category of slavery, but asking questions about the history of the category itself and about its relationship to forced labor and to those categories of labor—indenture, gang labor, sharecropping—that many of the governments that abolished slavery did not want considered in the same breath. These essays explore the relationship of slavery and its abolition to capitalism and to imperialism, examining the tensions among these constructs and their often paradoxical historical relationship. They explore the place of slaves in political mobilizations against colonial rule as well as against slavery, and they examine the implications of race in the formation of political alliances. Most important, they take up a theme of Tannenbaum's 1946 book that has largely become lost in the discussion of his comparison of Anglo and Latin American slave systems: citizenship. The specific and changing meanings of this concept—in relation to political theory focused on the "universal" individual as well as to thinking about people as gendered, racialized, culturally specific beings—may help to move the focus from what ended with slave emancipation to what began.

The Meanings of Freedom and Slavery

Any comparison, particularly one that puts vastly different forms of social organization and ideology into the same framework, must confront the question of whether the central constructs are indeed comparable. Defining slavery and freedom, as noted already, has provoked political as well as conceptual anxieties. In their examination of Africa, Igor Kopytoff and Suzanne Miers have tried to pry apart this common dyad, insisting that both elements are fundamentally "Western" concepts applied to Africa at considerable peril to the understanding of African societies as they actually were and are. They argue that "in the Western conception, the antithesis of 'slavery' is 'freedom,' and 'freedom' means autonomy and a lack of social bonds." However, "[i]n most African societies, 'freedom' lay not in a withdrawal into a meaningless and a dangerous autonomy but in attachment to a kin group, to a patron, to a power—an attachment that occurred within a well-defined hierarchical framework. It was in this direction that the acquired outsider had to move if he was to reduce his initial marginality. Here the antithesis of 'slavery' is not 'freedom' qua autonomy but rather 'belonging.' "[4]

Kopytoff and Miers rightly point to a real tension in the conceptual scheme that twentieth-century Americans or Europeans are likely to bring to the question at hand: an assumption that our perceptions of our own society provide a universal standard, against which slavery can be defined as a lack of something we now take for granted. But in contrasting an essentially "Western" concept of autonomy against an essentially "African" concept of belonging, they miss the fact that such notions are contested in both contexts. Emancipated slaves in the Americas also struggled hard to find a sense of belonging as citizens of formally defined nation-states and as members of communities worked out among former slaves and other subordinated people themselves. Moreover, Africans have struggled to escape oppressive forms of belonging—perhaps to redefine new ones, but certainly to exercise choice in the kinds of networks, affiliations, and bonds of sentiment to which they will belong. Indeed, Kopytoff comes close to implying that African slaves who left the communities into which they had been forcibly incorporated, who sought to break rather than bend bonds of dependence, did not understand African society as well as the Western anthropologist.[5] But this vision of an Africa of coherent groups, of accepted senses of hierarchy, and of collectivist mentalities is as much a Western concept as the ethnocentrism he criticizes.

For North Americans, and perhaps others, the image of a sugar or cotton plantation in the early nineteenth century—with a labor force comprised of black slaves subject to arduous work routines and harsh discipline from white owners and overseers, living in "quarters" sharply demarcated from the housing of those not enslaved—is so powerful that it tends to stand in for the very essence of slavery. These images make it hard to tell a more nuanced and complicated story, wider in space and deeper in time, about a set of practices that can still usefully be labeled slavery. Orlando Patterson and Moses Finley, both concerned with slavery outside its most familiar contexts, have defined it as the forceful removal of a person from his or her social milieu. Patterson calls it natal alienation or social death. This may—and most often does—entail physical removal, taking a person away from familiar space as well as familiar social relations, but it could also take place through a ritualized process that symbolically stripped a person of an entire web of relations, as long as the community as a whole saw this as a definitive alienation. Finley and Patterson see this natal alienation as the basis of the wide variety of fates that slaves, in different historical contexts, suffer: as kinless people, as people without honor, they can be introduced into a new space and into a new social structure in which they will be far more vulnerable than people with local knowledge and local connections. Thus the enslavement process—removal from one context and introduction into a new one—creates beings who can fit a variety of possibilities: young women adding reproductive potential to a kinship group without the distraction of the women's natal kinship groups, young men who can perform military or administrative service to powerful slaveowners, their loyalty assured by the absence of any alternative to the ruler's patronage except abject dishonor, or men and women made to labor in places where others would resist going, under conditions those with better connections would not accept. The idea of slaves as property, Patterson insists, is derivative: it is because of slaves' vulnerability that they can be treated as chattel in systems that recognize such notions.[6]

Patterson's conception of social death, however, remains an abstract one. Although a useful analytical tool, it may not convey an accurate sense of the situations in which slaves actually existed, or of how they might have responded to those situations. He has pinpointed the social and ideological problem that people torn from their roots might experience, but not the actual, messy, contradictory worlds that slaves and slaveowners created as they struggled within these parameters. Much of the history of slave communities, from East Africa to Brazil, has been a history of the carving out of a modicum of social life—among slaves as much as within the dyad of enslavers and enslaved that Patterson stresses.

A definition of slavery is in some sense necessarily timeless, but slavery was experienced in time; in other words, it has in each instance a history. And those histories, in turn, though unfolding in different parts of the world, were not separate, and they certainly were not equal. In western Europe as in Africa, slavery before the fifteenth century was a familiar concept—subject to legal definitions, religious notions, and social conventions—but it took on particular connotations with the extension of long-distance commercial networks and the development of new techniques of plantation production in the Americas from the fifteenth century onward, becoming more intense in the eighteenth and nineteenth centuries.

In Africa before the sixteenth century, many—but hardly all—kings and powerful chiefs used slaves within royal households as servants, soldiers, concubines, and laborers, obtaining them via kidnapping, warfare, and purchase. In smaller-scale communities in Africa, slaves were often brought into existing social units, their marginal status changing over generations if not over a lifetime. But the growth of external slave markets, first to North Africa and the Middle East, then on a larger scale across the Atlantic Ocean, transformed the significance of enslavement. Mechanisms for enslavement and transport developed, and certain groups hitched their fortunes to the movement of slaves in a way that had not been true before. Then, in the nineteenth century, when Europeans began to suppress the trade they had fostered, that infrastructure began increasingly to supply domestic units of agricultural production—for local consumption, for regional trade, and, in some instances, for export into world markets—and so slavery's significance in Africa changed yet again.[7]

Both the regions where most African slaves had gone—Brazil, the Caribbean, and the southern United States—and those parts of Africa that supplied them were by then already caught up as well in another global trend: a moral, ideological, and political argument, originating in the very continent that had spawned the massive enslavement mechanisms and had linked them to an expanding transcontinental economic system. This argument, spread by new humanitarian organizations originating in Great Britain, sharply distinguished slavery from other forms of domination and exploitation. Great Britain, its example enhanced by its visible economic success and by its navy, managed to effect a momentous ideological change across national borders, pressuring other European nations in 1815 into condemning the slave trade as "repugnant to the principles of humanity and universal morality."[8] Indeed, the antislavery movement both reflected and contributed to increasingly universalistic discourses about social and political norms in European states, especially France and Great Britain. These movements worked out a rhetoric for distinguishing what modes of authority and what forms of labor organization could be deemed morally acceptable, and they insisted that these arguments applied to "civilized" states generally—and to their colonies in the West Indies and elsewhere. Some nations would honor these propositions by temporizing and denial—the slave trade to Spain's colony of Cuba lasted into the 1860s, slavery until 1886—but the standard had been set. Most important, the evil that was being acknowledged was a precisely bounded evil, marking slavery apart from other modes of controlling labor and other modes of exercising authority.

In this sense, the category of freedom did indeed arrive in the context of the power of the West, and in a specific manifestation of that power—colonization. Slavery had been contested in Africa before that day, as individuals and collectivities fought or fled slavers as well as the users of slave labor, sometimes trying to replicate such structures with themselves on top, sometimes trying to maintain or create less hierarchical forms of social order. African history is filled with such power struggles—over principles of social organization as much as over power within accepted constructs. How those struggles might have played themselves out without European intervention is unknown and unknowable. What is known is that those struggles took place in a very specific context. The isolation of slavery as a problem in Africa was an offshoot of the ideological processes that made it a problem in the colonies of European conquest in the Americas. In the nineteenth century, this particular representation of the issue was brought, forcibly, to the African continent itself.

This brings us back to the examination of the concept of freedom itself. Orlando Patterson makes an argument that is in some ways the mirror image of his conception of slavery as a social process found in many different forms throughout history. For him, freedom has a more specific historical origin. "Freedom," he argues, "was generated from the experience of slavery," and it was generated in classical Europe.[9] He divides freedom into three notions: personal freedom, or not being coerced, and doing as one pleases within the limits of the desires of others; sovereignal freedom, or the power to act as one pleases, even if that means restricting another's personal freedom; and civil freedom, or "the capacity of adult members of a community to participate in its life and governance."[10] Applying to the "non-western world" in general what Kopytoff claimed was specifically African, Patterson argues that freedom initially made sense only in the sovereignal sense. Since social relations could not be experienced outside of dependency and group membership, not being a slave was experienced as one kind of belonging, while being a slave was experienced as another—vastly inferior—form of belonging within the same social entity, and there were no other alternatives.

Patterson argues that the category of personal freedom took on a new meaning in the context of the agricultural and commercial expansion of ancient Greece, when slaveowning aristocrats sought the support of nonslave elements during a period when the city-state polity was becoming stronger. Beginning with women—who feared enslavement as men feared death—and extending throughout the polis, consciousness of slavery and its alternatives grew wider. The extension of Greek power implied more foreign slaves and a sharper cultural distinction between the barbarian slave and the free Athenian; thus the growth of slavery and the growth of civic as well as personal freedom were two sides of the same historical process.

Our concern here is not with the specifics of Patterson's argument—or even with the likelihood that his claims for the global significance of a specifically Western construct may be overstated—but rather with the simple point that freedom is not a natural state. It is a social construct, a collectively shared set of values reinforced by ritual, philosophical, literary, and everyday discourse. Freedom has a history that contains distinct notions whose conflation in a particular historical tradition is itself as important as the tension among them. That "slave" was a recognizable category in many places and many times—its powerful associations with fear and dishonor vivid in people's immediate imagination even as it was also a concept to be analyzed by statesmen and philosophers—created the potential for many different frameworks for thinking through the boundary of slave/not-slave.

One can acknowledge a specific intellectual history of the framing of freedom as historical and social construct *and* insist that the meanings of freedom must be sought in a whole sequence of particular historical and social contexts. The three essays in this volume thus confront both the specificity of the people involved in the emancipation process and the universal principles invoked in justifying it. Thomas Holt examines the former slave communities of Jamaica, looking at the particular sorts of aspirations Jamaicans had, the connection of gender relations among them to the expectations of the imperial emancipators, and the way in which the nonconformity of the former slaves to imperial notions shaped the subsequent coding of their behavior in racial terms and the defining of them as outside the bounds of "citizen." Rebecca Scott examines the question of mobilization of former slaves and their descendants in Cuba and Louisiana, the one in the context of struggles over imperial rule in one of the last of Europe's American colonies, the other in the context of struggles over what freedom would mean in the post–Civil War United States South. Looking at two different sugar plantation societies, her essay treats race not as a determinant of human interaction but as a construct whose political meaning could shift sharply over time and space, rendering inclusion or exclusion in the polity historically contingent. Frederick Cooper reviews issues of forced labor in the history of French and British colonization in Africa, pointing out how the evocations of "progress" were offered first as a reason to intervene in Africa and later as a rationale for the allegedly temporary use of forced labor to bring about "development." He ends by showing that the twin issues of citizenship and labor could not be pried apart—and, indeed, contributed to the undermining of colonial legitimacy and self-confidence in the 1940s.

In each of these case studies we try to remain sensitive to the conflicting meanings freedom might have, as well as to the tension between freedom as a marker of individual choice and as an index of belonging, and to the tension between freedom to exercise power over others and freedom to reject power over one's self. Most important, we recognize that the importance of Western concepts of freedom—with their conflation of personal, sovereignal, and civic freedoms, all treated as precipitates of the West's own history—lies not simply in the intrinsic intellectual power of these concepts, but in their linkage to a history of European power extended over much of the globe. What made this particular history of general importance was—as among the Greeks—a process in which enslavement and exploitation were central: the rise of plantation economies in the Americas and the enmeshing of Africa in a slave trade on such a scale that it redefined social conventions. The dialectic of slave agriculture and democratic voice may have been born among slaveholders in the Greek polis, but it took on a different meaning in the West Indian colonies and matured among the slaveholding leadership of a postcolonial United States. The connection of enslavement and colonization was to prove just as contradictory in slavery's decline as it had been in democracy's rise.

There are three overlapping dimensions of our analyses that are useful to address by way of introduction to the case studies that follow: first, the links among labor, race, and citizenship; second, the dynamics of collective action by freedpeople themselves and the impact of those actions on citizenship in both theory and practice; and third, the notion of the universality of work and the worker, alongside of which evolved varying notions of the "peculiarity" of the African, ultimately complicating the meaning and practice of freedom in the modern world.

Labor, Race, and Citizenship

A particular shadow hangs over both nineteenth- and twentieth-century discussions of freedom—that of the Haitian Revolution. Its often unacknowledged presence reveals much about the continuing relationship between labor, race, and citizenship. Revolutions in Saint Domingue (Haiti) and France at the end of the eighteenth century helped to give each other their form and meaning and raised sharply and at a startlingly early date the question of just who was to be included under the notion of "rights of man."[11] The Saint Domingue revolution succeeded in overthrowing slavery and creating a new nation, both monumental achievements in the history of opposition to European imperialism and colonialism, the first some decades before many Europeans would admit the time was ripe, and the second accompanied by the first a distinct innovation.

To this day, Haiti is often represented as a kind of black mischief, an entity taking the form of a modern nation-state but without its contents, the site of brutal tyranny and strange religious beliefs, its poverty as much a marker of its alleged primitiveness as of its exploitation by European nations and the United States. Although Haiti's success in establishing the second new nation in the Americas has been celebrated as the triumph of "black Jacobinism" at a time when white Jacobinism was still unstable and certainly untriumphant, it has also been lamented as a radical negation of progress, particularly as embodied in export agriculture and the evolving European-type nation-state.[12] Over the first half-century of its existence, Haiti's dominant image among elites outside the island was that of the inevitable fall into savagery awaiting black peoples left to govern themselves.

Its image among non-elites in the Caribbean was, one should note, very different.[13] Yet in the final decades of the twentieth century, Haitians fleeing the rampages of dictatorial regimes were excluded from the status of refugee— itself part of the international codification of universal human rights—on the grounds, essentially, that Haiti's very backwardness superseded the oppressiveness of its rulers. Their flight was deemed "economic" rather than "political." Over the two centuries of its existence, therefore, Haiti has symbolized not only the exclusions that lie within constructions of the world as a collection of states, but the continuing, complex intersection of labor and race in the very constitution of those constructs.[14]

The Haitian Revolution threw into relief a connection that European powers would try to keep under wraps for the next century and a half: the relationship of slavery and colonialism. For a moment after 1789, the discourse of the rights of man seemingly applied to both: one appeared to be the denial of personal freedom to a class of individuals, the other a denial of civil freedom to a people. Indeed, slaveholders in Saint Domingue (the *gens de couleur* as well as whites) had claimed political rights against the French administration on a quite sound reading of the Declaration of the Rights of Man, only to find that their slaves were claiming another sort of right against them. Debates over these issues moved back and forth between Paris and Saint Domingue. The failure of Napoleon's efforts to reassert authority and reestablish slavery in Saint Domingue pointed to the dangers to imperial power of allowing these two issues to be conflated by their enemies. Spain would later face the same problem in Cuba, where antislavery sentiment and slaves' aspirations for freedom would nourish the evolving anticolonial movement.

Throughout the rest of the nineteenth century, even as European views on slavery evolved, colonial authority came to be invoked as much to superintend emancipation as to sustain slavery. By mid-century, for many leaders of the antislavery movement in Europe, colonization could be construed as a liberating ideology: it promised to free Africans from the tyranny of the slave trade and of their own slaveholding leaders. Rather than the older claims to particularistic power intrinsic to both colonialism and slavery, there emerged new variants on universalistic logics that conferred on other grounds rightful authority over people seen as not worthy of exercising such authority over themselves.

The market economics of Adam Smith, the politics of John Locke, or the rights of man rhetoric of the French Revolution all depended on universalistic modes of reasoning, but they all left open the question of the boundaries of the universe to which they applied. The universality of the language has made principles of the "free" exercise of choice in a labor market or of a "free" voice in a polity into powerful rhetorical devices across geographic and cultural lines—the plight of the slave in Timbuktu could be evoked in comprehensible terms in Paris. But the very rhetoric posed the question of whether power of a more particularistic sort could be legitimately deployed—by men of power and men of reason—so as to bring the unenlightened into the world of market economies, good government, and cultural progress.[15]

It would thus be a mistake to consider Enlightenment reasoning, market economics, or liberal political theory either as a clear set of principles betrayed by the hypocrisy of European colonialism or as a totalizing imposition of European political ideas on the rest of the world in the name of universality. What could not be escaped in Europe and its colonies in the nineteenth century was that such constructs became crucial reference points that could be used to justify colonization or to condemn it. However much nineteenth-century colonizations had in common with those of the conquistadors, they could not be talked about in the same way. Even as French, British, Belgian, and German armies were conquering African kingdoms and villages, Spanish armies in Cuba were fighting the gathering forces set out to end their colonial status—and these forces in turn were transforming the meanings of slavery and race in Cuban ideologies. From Saint Domingue in the 1790s to French West Africa in the 1940s, ideas of rights that could be deemed "European" or "universal" were invoked and transformed by leaders of a variety of popular movements challenging the actions or the legitimacy of repressive states. The question of who was to be included in market economies and political communities was both pried open and obscured time and time again in the nineteenth and twentieth centuries—in the halls of legislatures, in the fields of sugar estates, and in the hills where rebels plotted and planned.

Indeed, by the beginning of the third decade of the nineteenth century, large numbers of slaves in the Americas lived in republican states. In some cases, in fact, slave emancipation was itself directly linked to the establishment of those republics, as in the northern United States and the former Spanish colonies on the mainland. In other cases—most notably the British West Indies—hundreds of thousands of slaves were owned by masters who owed allegiance to a constitutionally limited monarch, who may have embodied "the nation," and to an elected parliament that represented "the people." For a substantial number of slave masters, therefore, the meaning and limits of subjecthood were fundamentally different from what they had been a century before, and for practically all of them the meaning and limits of "the people" and "the nation" were contested and in the process of change.

The critical point here, in any case, is that by the mid-nineteenth century, freedom for most white men on both sides of the Atlantic world involved membership in a body politic. One belonged to a community as a citizen and through one's citizenship; citizens as a collective body constituted and, in theory, governed the society of which they were a part. With this change —and irrespective of how real it may have been in practice—the problems of manumission and emancipation were redefined. To the question of how slaves would become free laborers was added the problem of what their new relation to society as a whole would entail. Would they also be citizens?

We need to pause to examine this word "citizenship," for what Barbara Fields has said about freedom is equally true of citizenship: it is a "moving target." [16] That certain people claimed that citizenship applied to them changed what the concept meant. For Tannenbaum in 1946, citizenship was more than a category of academic inquiry: he used the word to make clear that he shared in the aspirations of ongoing social movements for a more inclusive and just society. But the ambiguities of the idea need to be confronted, for citizenship could also be a category of exclusion. If political trends in Europe were (with many reversals) producing citizens, nineteenth-century conquests were producing colonial subjects. Although emancipation in the British West Indies in the 1830s made citizenship for former slaves a discussible proposition, the colonial status of the islands meant that for former slaves—or, indeed, anyone else—whatever political rights accrued could be taken away, as in fact they were.

Some scholars have argued that the citizenship construct is wedded to colonialism in an even more profound way: that it came to most of the world in the baggage of European colonizers and brought with it a fundamentally Euro-centric notion of an individual in unmediated relationship to the state. So an assertion of the rights of a citizen that might in Europe be a "liberating" move to sweep away the claims of upper classes to represent their subordinates to the state could in the colonies be confining, denying any place in politics to groups intermediary between the state and the individual, or shunting aside notions of community and culture not coterminous with state boundaries. The colonial genealogy of citizenship survived colonialism itself, implying a politics centered on the state and a culture centered on the individual.[17]

A discussion of citizenship now needs to address this argument. Otherwise, one risks endless recapitulations of "neo-abolitionist" arguments that acknowledge the blemishes on the European past without asking to what extent the categories for understanding freedom emerge as well from a complex and painful history. Forms of political organization as much as labor organization in the present are constrained by a history in which the expansion of European power and of European capitalism play central roles. That said, the critique of citizenship emerging from postcolonial theory still has two basic shortcomings: First, its summary of the genealogy of citizenship in Europe often misses the tensions and openings—as well as closures and constraints—that the concept presupposes. Second, the genealogical method is itself inadequate to get at the ways in which the struggles of former slaves and colonized people altered the ancestral meanings of citizenship.[18]

In England, Margaret Somers shows, the concept of citizenship derived not from an individualistic notion of the rights-bearing Englishman who established a direct relationship to his state that was unrestricted and unmarked by his social status, but rather from a legal system that emphasized that only a "jury of one's peers" could convict a person of violating the norms of a community. Even as the state tried to shift the citizenship concept toward a direct relationship with its citizenry, such jealously guarded prerogatives as "jury nullification"—the ability of a jury to refuse to apply a law within its own jurisdiction—kept the idea of community alive within the state-citizen relationship.[19] So rather than seeing "citizenship" as opposed to "community," one can argue that the two could exist in close relation to each other. The citizenship construct abstracted the community construct to a level beyond face-to-face relations, but it retained the sense of belonging and of participation in collective affairs even as it was linked to a state whose formal apparatus could be distant. This ambiguity attaching to citizenship is crucial. From the start—and to the present—citizenship has had cultural content. There has always been a question of what sort of people were "in," what sort "out." But the act of abstraction—as well as the institutions in which people came into relations with each other as citizens—meant that this question did not have an immediate and obvious answer. It could and would be the subject of numerous debates and political mobilizations.[20]

The argument that every citizen existed in individual relationship to the state was used by some political actors to counter exclusions on cultural or physical grounds and to deny the claims of property owners or patriarchs to speak for others. Now, some political theorists claim that the individualism implicit in the citizenship concept is inadequate to express the need of collectivities—defined by race, gender, or another commonality—for representation. Yet the idea of the relationship of an individual to a state, unmediated by any other affiliation, has always been a form of claim-making, not an essence of citizenship, and debates about the relationship of citizenship to other forms of social affinity are long-standing and ongoing within communities of citizens.

The Lockean notion of a political actor, as Uday Mehta has pointed out, had within it an implicit "anthropological minimum," a set of characteristics that were the preconditions for citizenship. These could encompass age, gender, race, property ownership, or literacy. Mehta argues that in some ways the anthropological threshold rose as the British Empire expanded. In France, citizenship after the Revolution was usually defined by the "right of the soil," the notion that anyone born within the borders of the French state was a citizen, whereas the Germanic territories operated on a principle of the "right of blood," a notion of citizenship grown out of kinship—one had to be descended from a German to be German.[21] These concepts are still the framework for debate in France and Germany today, meaning that discussions of assimilation and naturalization rely on different rhetorics between these two neighbors.

The openings (1830s) and closures (1860s) of citizenship rights in the British West Indies, or the fact that the French Empire defined most people in the colonies to be "subjects" while pronouncing some of them (people in specific towns, a few local elites, certain former soldiers of the French army) to be "citizens," were thus not anomalies specific to nineteenth-century colonialism. They were part of a broader question of just what citizenship meant and to whom.

It would be a mistake to assume that in Europe—let alone its empires—citizenship expanded unilineally. Feminist scholars have argued that new exclusions and new distinctions among the rights and obligations of particular categories of citizens have repeatedly appeared as others have fallen.[22] This still leaves the question of whether the rhetoric of citizenship, even if far from determinant, carried with it a special sort of volatility. Citizenship has a particular power precisely because in modern states rulers demand a lot of their subjects, although they do not necessarily remember that states evolved as they did because subjects were themselves demanding. The ruling fictions of republican or democratic forms of government involve the expectation that citizens will act on their own in ways conducive to the operation of the state, even if the mixture of coercion and consent involved is necessarily more complicated than that. In some ways, rulers wanted and still want to believe the rhetoric of citizenship—that people subject to their rule have a sense of belonging and a willingness to accept obligations. A claim made in terms of citizenship ratifies an elite's image of itself even as it potentially constrains that elite's options. This will not explain the ability of a social movement to have its demands met, but it helps to explain why social movements in the twentieth century have so often claimed the rights of citizens, and why that rhetoric could lead to a dialogue in ways that demands for redistribution of income or "social equality," for example, could not. The essays that follow will reveal different examples of the rhetoric of citizenship in use and, in contradistinction to the dismissal of citizenship as an imperial imposition, will argue that the deployment of this concept opened wider the possible meanings that citizenship could entail.

This brings us back to Tannenbaum, with a new emphasis on what was at stake in his use of the term "citizen" in 1946. His central question—Would those liberated from slavery also become citizens?—was scarcely taken up in the wake of the torrent of belated criticism that his invidious comparison of Anglo-Saxon with Iberian slave systems provoked. Much of that criticism focused on how slaves were treated as slaves; the question of the differential routes from slavery to citizenship was thereby reduced to *merely* one of how brutal was the enslavement. To be sure, the possibility for the slave's acceptance as a citizen after slavery was, for Tannenbaum, an outgrowth of, and contingent upon, the recognition of what he called the "moral status" of the slave *while* he or she was a slave. And treatment was an indicator of how that moral personality was conceived. Tannenbaum's argument has, over time, shown critical weaknesses on the question of treatment itself, on the presumed tight linkage between treatment and legal/religious institutions, and on the reading of the preconditions of citizenship back into the conditions of slavery. Nonetheless, Tannenbaum did get the essential problem right. The fate of slaves after slavery had a great deal to do with the political, ideological, and cultural evolution of the metropolitan societies to which they were linked.

In some ways, however, Tannenbaum's polarity can be reversed: those societies that had gone furthest in explicitly linking the political-cultural role of citizen to the fate of the national economy offered, at once, the greatest potential for slaves to become equal citizens and the greatest peril to that status actually being realized. Policymakers in both the republican United States and the constitutional monarchy of Britain had begun to elaborate a political sociology in which the problem of free labor and issues of social order and governance were linked. Yet, by different routes, their ruling elites concluded that free labor and equal citizenship were essential pillars of the social contract from which former slaves could not be excluded. For brief, historic moments, then, in the southern United States and in parts of the British West Indies, men who were former slaves voted and held high elective offices.

In none of these societies were freedwomen included in the implicit emancipation contract. Their exclusion from the active category of citizen was congruent with the exclusion of their white female peers, but it was differently framed, and its implications differed as well. The gendered basis of citizenship reflected both how women were thought to relate to the polity and how a polity of free men was thought to relate to the economy and to social order. Each of the major late-eighteenth-century revolutions that gave birth to republican governments—namely, the American and French Revolutions —sparked important debates about the role of women in a republican society. Each resolved the debate by consigning women to the task of sustaining the domestic, moral basis of the nation-state—its figurative and literal reproduction—while men took on the task of making (and making up) the state.[23] In each instance the making of the home took on unprecedented importance because the conceptual basis for social and political order had fundamentally changed. To the extent that the nation was thought to be governed by its male citizens, the processes by which those citizens were made became crucial both to how well the polity functioned and to how it was held together.

To reinvoke Tannenbaum's pregnant phrase, it was a question of "moral status." By this Tannenbaum meant simply those features of being in the world and before God that made slaves recognizably human. But by the late nineteenth century, the most socially relevant features of humankind had less to do with one's standing before God and much more to do with the supposed qualities of mind and spirit that governed how one functioned in the world.

In this view, a "slavish personality" was not consistent with the character required of a free citizen, but perhaps the slave could learn the ways of free men. The possibility, or at least the price, of "learning" was thought to be different for women—and perhaps altogether problematic for blacks. Central to the ways of free white men, to the formation of the moral personality of the citizen, and to the ligatures that bound a civilized social order together was the mode of labor recruitment and discipline. Thus were the problem of labor and the problem of citizenship linked to conceptions of culture, especially to questions of cultural difference and cultural change.

The political scenarios in the United States and the British West Indies were obviously exceptional, but their brief linkage of—in Orlando Patterson's terminology—a personal with a civic freedom was decisive: citizenship would be at issue in any future emancipation. Thus, although the timing and specifics of the political-ideological scenarios would be different in Cuba, Brazil, and the French West Indies, for example, the question of the former slave as citizen would have to be addressed, even if in the negative. Cubans who counted themselves white, for example, quickly realized that they could not sustain a successful rebellion against Spain without addressing the issue of emancipation and enlisting slaves in their cause. But a more inclusive rebellion meant a socially transformed popular mobilization. Eventually the promise of liberty and equality for all in the new nation became central to the idea of Cuban nationhood itself.[24] Brazilians and French Antilleans were allowed only tentative and incomplete steps back and forth across the line of equal citizenship for all and citizenship for some, postponing the day of reckoning until the twentieth century.

Of course, even in the nineteenth century, the most progressive former slave societies in the Americas would eventually retreat from the full promise of emancipation. In both the British West Indies and the southern United States, the freedpeople's choices on how and toward what ends they would exercise the franchise "disappointed" the assumptions and hopes of the emancipators, even as they excited the violent antagonism of those who opposed emancipation altogether. British Jamaica lost its right to self-government in 1866 and would not fully regain it until 1944. A decade later, in the mid-1870s, the federal government of the United States retreated from the promise implicit in the Fifteenth Amendment, and over the next years it confirmed its intent to turn a blind eye to the disfranchisement of freedmen in the South. The descendants of slaves would not regain an unrestricted right to vote until 1965.

One cannot understand how and why these scenarios played out as they did without recognizing the crucial linkage between ideas and practices of citizenship, race, and labor—in a word, the evolution of a capitalist system and of liberal ideology. An important aspect of this linkage was first proposed by Eric Williams. That the simplified versions of his thesis connecting capitalism and slavery have been vigorously and effectively criticized does not negate the importance of the fundamental connection he pointed to. Most scholars no longer argue that capital formation from the slave trade unleashed the industrial revolution, but the evolving structures of the British domestic economy made the impact of increased global trade—including that in slaves and slave-grown commodities—particularly dynamic. The relationship between production at home and the slave trade abroad was dialectical rather than one-directional. The first experiments in the management and coordination of large labor forces occurred on sugar plantations in the West Indies using slave labor rather than in textile factories in England employing wage laborers. Industrialization, in turn, created a demand for raw materials, notably cotton, to feed the factories and for commodities that workers could purchase with their cash wages, notably sugar. The circuit of labor and capital whose spiraling growth was unleashed in the eighteenth century thus involved the exploitation of colonies and slaves at crucial points.[25]

One can analyze the question of capitalism's role in the destruction of slave regimes—the second half of Williams's thesis—in similar terms. The question of whether colonial societies without slavery could function turned upon the prior question of whether blacks freed from slavery *would* work. The framing of both questions was profoundly constrained by evolving bourgeois social relations and by liberal ideology, but they were genuine questions nonetheless. As the debate over abolishing slavery in the West Indies neared its climax in the early 1830s—the slave trade having been banned to British subjects since 1807—a parliamentary committee asked itself whether "the slaves, if emancipated would maintain themselves, would be industrious and disposed to acquire property by labour." It duly interrogated supposedly knowledgeable witnesses on this subject. Parliament was equally eager to learn whether or not the "danger of convulsions are greater from Freedom withheld than from Freedom granted to the slaves," undoubtedly with that other model of emancipation, Saint Domingue, very much in mind.[26]

For the inquiring parliamentarians, the problem was to find means of effecting a transition from the experience of slavery, which denied self-discipline and degraded work, to the actual conditions of wage labor, where former slaves would have to calculate their interests and accordingly make themselves report to work each morning. Alternative drafts of the emancipation act set out to solve what was construed as a problem of culture, discipline, and incentive. Officials worried that slaves would wander off in search of vacant land on which they could live a life of "savage sloth."[27] Slaves had to learn that free labor meant the "dread of starvation" instead of "the dread of being flogged"; this was what the architects of emancipation meant by the "transition from the brutal to the rational predicament."[28] The implication of this discussion was that black former slaves could, perhaps, effect such a transition, even if the visible hand of the state had to press them to do so.

The transition had to be a directed one, and the metaphor by which officials chose to describe their solution was telling: "apprenticeship." Apprenticeship was, precisely, a metaphor. It applied to adults as much as to young people, to a collectivity as much as to individuals, and it taught former slaves no skill—they knew perfectly well how to cut cane. It applied to them a discipline that was now supposed to be salutary. It was a self-consciously "intermediate" state intended to push slaves to "acquire the habits of free labourers, and prepare themselves for the enjoyment of entire freedom." This was a compromise of free labor ideology, and some abolitionists with more purist views opposed apprenticeship as a restriction on free labor and hence a diminishment of the "influence of wants" on former slaves' behavior. There was hope that the educational metaphor would indeed transform the work culture of former slaves, but also concern that it would not. The colonial secretary, circulating the plan for a directed transition to free labor to his governors, admitted, "I cannot, however, conceal from myself the possibility that these hopes, however reasonable, may be disappointed."[29]

Official rhetoric in 1833 was turning emancipation into a test, a test of the slaves. Would slaves show themselves to be universal men and women, responsive to the rationality of the market? It was, of course, the rationality of the slaves that would be tested, not that of a labor system that depended for its success on denying them access to the resources of nature.

For some abolitionists, the test was beside the point: emancipation represented a human liberation whose success could not be measured in terms of the continuity of sugar exports. But in a colonial system in which government revenues and the supply of cheap sugar to British consumers, as well as profits for planters and a whole chain of merchants, depended on the continuity of sugar production, it was difficult to keep rhetoric on such a lofty plane. The qualified hope that the former slave would prove to be Economic Man risked becoming instead proof of the peculiarity of the African.

What actually happened in the sugar fields, as Holt has shown in the case of Jamaica, cannot be understood in the terms in which British policymakers framed the question. What some called savage sloth was in fact an alternative vision of economic life, based on small plots of land that slaves had been able to use even before emancipation, on cooperation within families and within communities, and on the selective playing off of available possibilities within and outside of markets. Slaves did not flee from the plantations but sought to determine the timing and conditions of their labor; they marketed produce in local markets, but not necessarily the produce officials wanted to see; they built relationships based on affinity as well as exchange. Their activities were not incompatible with a degree of estate-based sugar production, and they led to the development of new export crops, notably the banana. But sugar production fell and sugar's cost in Great Britain in the first four years of free labor rose to 48 percent over that of the last four years of slave labor.[30]

Officials, meanwhile, were trying to keep former slaves from moving into nonplantation areas of the larger islands, not just because of concern that access to land would drive up the supply price of labor, but because dispersal would stand in the way of the state's efforts to build the right sort of society and culture. The colonial secretary, Lord Glenelg, wrote in 1836: "Society, being thus kept together, is more open to civilizing influences, more directly under the control of Government, more full of the activity which is inspired by common wants, and the strength which is derived from the division of labour; and altogether is in a sound state, morally, politically and economically, than if left to pursue its natural course."[31] The last words indicate that the test of free labor was not being passed: it was the state, not a law of nature, that had to steer former slaves toward progress and civilization.

By 1838, apprenticeship had failed; it gave rise to conflict and uncertainty and was brought to an early end. In the 1840s, free trade legislation heightened the competition with slave-grown sugar and underscored Jamaica's economic weakness. And in 1865, government pressure against black smallholders culminated in riots at Morant Bay. That proved to be a symbolic turning point: it was held to confirm that idle blacks were not only economically useless but dangerous. Although abolitionists criticized the governor's brutal repression of the riots, he was able to defend himself by arguing that stern measures were needed to deal with uncivilized blacks.[32] Ultimately, then, the test had been failed—by black Jamaicans. The ideological implications of that alleged failure were strong: the idea that the descendants of Africans were a lazy and disorderly people had gained ascendancy over the expectation that they too might aspire to economic rationality. They came to be constituted as a racial exception to the universal rules of economic behavior.[33]

Meanwhile, Great Britain and France honored the rhetorical power of free labor while seeking practical solutions to real labor problems in their colonies, both postemancipation colonies and areas of new settlement. Both developed mechanisms to transport indentured laborers, who supposedly had accepted contracts to labor for an agreed-upon number of years, over long distances to their sugar colonies. French officials had the chutzpah to call their laborers *libres engagés*; the Portuguese called them *libertos*; British officials invoked the sanctified concept of contract. The British only stopped their Indian recruiting system in 1920, by which time they were under pressure from Indian nationalists, and the French kept sending contract laborers to Réunion until 1933. In all cases, recruited workers were put through various ritual processes to emphasize their exercise of choice and the contractual nature of their service, and in all cases the rituals substituted for serious examination of the mixtures of intimidation and deception, of dire need and false expectations, that led the poor of Asia or Africa into boats headed, like the slave ships, for the West Indies or the sugar islands of the Indian Ocean— or, later, the cocoa islands off Central Africa. Opponents of the system, like its apologists, argued within the rhetoric of free labor ideology, terming this stretching of the notion of contract "a new system of slavery."[34]

In contrast, therefore, to Eric Williams's argument that capitalism undermined and eventually destroyed slavery, these semifree systems developed within and at the very moment that the wage labor–driven capitalist system was maturing on a global scale. If this historical and systemic conjuncture seems somehow anomalous, it was clearly a "necessary anomaly" in situations where labor was not readily available in the right place, at the right price, or sufficiently detached from noncapitalist relations of production.[35] But this view, like Williams's, is overly economistic. The anomaly was powerful enough to cause considerable economic unease among the employers of labor themselves, as the ritualistic invocation of the contract described above makes clear. More important, labor was not merely labor but was embedded in a system of social relations and social order. In any historical context, slaves and other subordinated laborers were likely to be more than passive instruments of someone else's will. But by the mid- and late nineteenth century the social relations of labor had fundamentally changed. The free laborer was now an imaginable possibility—often working in the town or on a farm down the road—and even the norm in many places. Consequently, the apparent contradiction of slavery and semifree labor in an age of freedom was more than an abstract problem. The laborers themselves were all too likely to be aware of the political ambivalence surrounding their situation and might very well act to force the issue. Moreover, in this context, the struggle to become a free laborer could quickly evolve into a struggle to become a free citizen.

Collective Action and the Struggle to Define Citizenship

However refined the theorizing of citizenship by metropolitans in different times and places, the concept of citizenship was not theirs alone to invent. The case studies that follow point to the complicated ways in which collective action could confront the exclusions built up around dominant notions of citizenship. Under certain circumstances, radically inclusive rather than exclusive definitions of citizenship emerged to challenge the more restrictive formulations. It often seems to have taken a war to start a nation down that path. The brief experiment in cross-racial democracy that was Reconstruction in the United States followed upon an immense war, and the remarkable transracial nationalism of Cuba emerged from an anticolonial conflict that spanned thirty years. In each case, emancipation was indissolubly linked to the definition of the nation itself. In the United States, the survival of the Union came to depend upon both a forthright emancipationism and the mobilization of former slaves as soldiers. In Cuba, the creation of a Cuban nation that could win its independence from Spain required transcending the exclusionary elite formulations of nationality and drawing together a fighting force that crossed lines defined as racial.

The trajectory of events in Cuba is of particular interest, given its contrast with that of the United States. In the United States, an inclusive notion of citizenship remained permanently on the books after the ratification of the Fourteenth and Fifteenth Amendments to the Constitution. But within a decade it was clear that citizenship was going to be sharply constrained for the descendants of slaves throughout the southern states, and that it would be radically severed from the notion of a right to vote. In its infamous Cruikshank decision in 1875, the Supreme Court went so far as to reiterate that, the Fifteenth Amendment notwithstanding, the Constitution "has not conferred the right of suffrage upon any one."[36] In Cuba, by contrast, the idea and reality of inclusion were persistent. For its own purposes, the Spanish colonial government had by the 1890s extended the franchise to people of color who could meet certain property requirements, though this franchise operated in the context of a highly dilute colonial citizenship. More important, the ideologists of Cuban independence moved toward an explicitly inclusive formulation of the nation as their multiple insurgencies came to encompass increasing numbers of rebels of African descent.

In her recent work on race and Cuban nationality, Ada Ferrer has demonstrated that as elite Cuban authors grappled with the question of the boundaries of nationality, they rewrote the history of the "black insurgent" as one of loyal and grateful service to the Cuban separatist ideal rather than one of autonomous action. Conservative Cuban nationalists had long cultivated the enduring image of "another Haiti" as the outcome to be avoided at all costs, and they were ill at ease with the idea of armed black insurgency. But the classic demonization and exclusion of black Cubans ran squarely against the necessity of constructing an effective separatist army and of winning freedom from Spain. In the 1880s and the 1890s the ideologists of Cuban separatism converged on a notion of a transracial Cuban nationality, one in which blackness would pose no threat because it no longer mattered.[37]

Ideological invention, however, was only half the story. Within the separatist fighting force, the large-scale mobilization of Cubans from all socioracial groups, often under the leadership of officers categorized as black or mulatto, created a very particular kind of "republic in arms." When the war ended, thousands of Cubans descended from slaves stood indisputably among the forgers of national freedom. Cubans of different racial categories had called one another ciudadano (citizen) during the war. Victory, many assumed, would consolidate this gain.

Cubans of African descent stood also as the backbone, but by no means the sole component, of the rural work force. Decades of large-scale Spanish immigration to the cane fields, combined with the recruitment of sugar workers from the heterogeneous population of Cuban smallholders, had effectively closed off the segregationist alternative. While the plantation owners of Louisiana might claim by the end of the nineteenth century to understand the peculiarities of what they labeled "the Negro worker," a being they relegated to hard labor and political silence, the planters of Cuba had no choice but to scramble to cope with a thoroughly multiracial work force and a highly politicized countryside.

The Cuban Constitution of 1901 formalized universal manhood suffrage, and the discourse of the new nation implied a commitment to racial equality. Rebecca Scott's essay in this volume explores further the ambiguities of that commitment, examining the ways in which the insistence on a transracial national identity both opened up possibilities for participation and placed boundaries on the ways that participation could be claimed and exercised. Several recent authors have pointed to the seeming "silence" on race in Cuban national discourse and highlighted the inhibiting effect of that enforced silence. One should not lose sight, however, of the liberatory *potential* within the early formulations of the ideology of race-blind democracy and transracial citizenship, an ideology whose authors included Cubans of color such as Antonio Maceo, the rebel general from Oriente, and Ricardo Batrell, a foot soldier born to slave parents on a plantation in Matanzas. It is not surprising that even the most resolute black veterans of the anticolonial struggle hesitated to attack that ideology head-on, even as they watched it be manipulated by conservative white political figures. Their reluctance stemmed not just from prudence, but from a lingering hope that some kind of ethic of justice and reciprocity might still be extracted from the notion that "here there are neither blacks nor whites, just Cubans."[38]

For the descendants of slaves in Cuba, moreover, the contrast between blunt exclusion and a qualified inclusion was not just hypothetical. The United States occupied their island for six years in the first decade of the twentieth century, and Cubans could see at first hand the flowering of the white supremacist ideology that had accompanied the closing down of Reconstruction in the United States. The very word "racist" came to be a big gun in the ideological artillery of the Cuban nationalist elite: they used it to label the discriminatory actions of the occupying North Americans and then turned it against Cubans of color who questioned the actual egalitarianism of the newly independent state. This double legacy of pride in the racial inclusiveness of the national project and hostility to any questioning of actual discriminatory practice proved durable indeed. It caught many Cubans of color in a particularly excruciating bind as they tried to reclaim the democratic potential within an ideology that could easily become suffocating.[39]

The idea of race-blind patriotism that proved so durable in Cuba had a fleeting counterpart in the United States, where service in the war to preserve the Union had strengthened the claim to citizenship of former slaves. As in Cuba, the significance of veteran status tended to reinforce the masculine construction of prevailing notions of citizenship and suffrage. But the tradition of armed service, re-created in the militias and Union Leagues of the Reconstruction era, did not in fact preclude the participation of women. A white-line Democratic leader from Louisiana recalled bitterly that the "negro militia" active in his parish in the 1870s had been accompanied by "colored Amazons."[40] And the local paper invoked the image of "the wives and sisters and mothers of those licensed banditti, going about our town armed with cans of coal oil and cane knives."[41] These descriptions contained the usual alarmist hyperbole, but what is interesting for our purposes is the conspicuous role attributed to women in the process of public mobilization. Disbanding this militia—and silencing its female supporters—came to seem a precondition for the definitive reversal of Reconstruction.

The trend toward exclusion in the southern United States was powerful and nearly relentless, but even in the last years before full disfranchisement, groups of former slaves and descendants of slaves actively sought to give fuller meaning to their freedom. The 1887 strike of sugar workers described in Scott's essay below was a remarkable instance of sustained and partially cross-racial mobilization. It was the *repression* of that strike that was marked by a stark racialization of the struggle over wages and hours, not the strike itself. And it was Mary Pugh, a planter's daughter hostile to the strikers, who described it bluntly as a contest over "the question of who is to rule[,] the nigger or the white man?"[42]

For Mary Pugh and her neighbors, it was essential to reduce to nil the claims to citizenship of the descendants of slaves—and to erase the possibility of an alliance of black workers and white. If that required a massacre of largely unarmed strikers, so be it. Once the question of citizenship had been settled in the negative, proper attention could be paid to the peculiarities of "the negro worker," an ideal type on whom planters still relied, and about whom they claimed special expertise.

The Universal Worker and the Peculiarity of the African

The tensions between universalistic conceptions of humanity and discussions of the virtues and failings—as well as the culturally specific ways of acting and being—of particular groups are illustrated in various ways in the three chapters that follow. What is striking is the length of time over which these tensions played out. If it is surprising how open the discussions were in Great Britain and Jamaica in the 1830s over the relationship of economic rationality and race, it is equally surprising how constricting official conceptions of race, culture, and economic rationality were in French West Africa by the 1940s. The point, however, is not simply to tilt against the windmill of assumed "progress" in the history of race and cultural difference in Western thought, but to chart where and why it was that openings occurred and how and why they were shut down. Such questions remain relevant to this day.

It was around the time that British rulers were closing down the economic and political space in which former slaves in Jamaica could move—in the wake of the Morant Bay Rebellion—that the Africans' deficiencies in quite another form became the subject of a new wave of middle-class agitation in England. The dramatic travels of David Livingstone across south-central Africa gave rise to vivid reports of a society decimated by slave raiding, giving a renewed vigor to the British public's engagement with issues of morality. Coming at the time of disillusionment with Africans' descendants in the Americas, the attack on Africans as slavers on their own continent brought out a sharp contrast with European images of benign progress in their own metropoles.

The missionaries' crusade to open Africa to Christianity, commerce, and civilization did not in itself bring about the new wave of colonizing initiatives in Africa, but it did place a long series of trading ventures, conflicts with African kings and traders, and often-grandiose projects for exploiting Africa's resources into a moral context in which a case for systematic intervention into Africa could be made, as Frederick Cooper's essay in this volume demonstrates. The slavery that was coming under attack now was not one whose rise was patently connected to Europe's own empires and to Europeans' profits, but one that appeared as an indicator of other peoples' backwardness. That Europe had only recently weaned itself from slavery quickly passed into the background. By the 1880s a consensus was emerging among conquering powers about the linkage of European colonization with the eradication of slavery from non-European societies, even as the "European" elites who ruled Cuba and Brazil were still taking the final steps to rid their ter-

ritories of such an evil. The consensus was formalized at meetings of colonizing powers between 1884 and 1890 at which they bound each other to eradi-
cate the slave trade. The commerce that a century earlier had been crucial to
Europe's fatal intrusion into African trade now became the marker of Africans' disposition to oppression and lack of self-control, as well as the means
of indicating that modern colonization would be undertaken in the name of
order, of imperial self-restraint, and of progress.

The image of the African (and the Arab) as enslaver and exploiter thus
took its place alongside the image of the African as victim. Once again, a
discourse of hope opened up: Africa could be remade. The African could become a Christian; he could engage in labor and commerce. The problem, as
Cooper explains more fully below, was that colonial governments—as well as
their African subjects—would step into the intimacy of complex relations of
power, and the clarity of the message of Christianity, commerce, and civilization would quickly be clouded. Colonial governments, trying to turn the rapid
movement of conquering armies into routinized power over vast territories,
would be drawn into relationships with the very African elites whose tyranny
had been the focus of the indignation of Livingstone and others. Moreover,
the colonial regimes would soon find that their allies' conceptions of civilization—not to mention labor—were too important to social order to be so
easily replaced. The reformist element of colonization, so evident in the propaganda of empire at home and, indeed, in discussions of policy in the first
years of colonial rule in French and British Africa, would narrow not long after
it confronted reality.

Yet the very constricting of the colonial "civilizing mission" was portrayed
to followers of colonial politics not as a test of European will that had fallen
short, but as a test of Africans, whose failure proved that only a wise ruler
capable of understanding the limits of African capacity could exercise control. The sleight of hand of colonial rule, most explicit in the early 1920s, was
to transform colonial governments from the source of progress modeled on
Europe into guardians of the peculiarity of the African.[43]

What is equally striking, both for its initially radical implications and for
its subsequent conservative readings, was the application of a discourse about
slavery to a discourse about peasants. Like the slave, the peasant did not fall
under the "rational predicament." Having access to land, as well as the possibility of selling a surplus, peasants could secure their subsistence needs and
acquire minimal benefits from exchange without having to conform to the
discipline of a fully developed market. Some peasants might eat a little less
well than others, but even a little land gave protection against losing eco-

nomic security altogether. As Holt shows in relation to Jamaica, even in a postemancipation context this kind of security could be the basis for defending a great variety of ways of life—and could greatly trouble the exploiters of low-cost labor.

The assimilation of the African peasantry to the idea of backwardness was pioneered in South Africa, beginning when the British government applied its emancipation legislation there in the 1830s, taking on a new dimension after the 1860s as diamond mines joined white farmers in demanding labor, and escalating again with the opening of gold mines in the 1880s.[44] The former slaves of white settler-farmers were concentrated in one area (the Western Cape) and constituted a small percentage of the potential labor power of the South African region as a whole. Some missionaries raised early on the same question about neighboring groups as about former slaves in the West Indies and South Africa itself: Would they work under "the same inducements of interest that are operative with other classes"? The answer from the state was a qualified "no"—a dose of colonial authority had to be added.[45] Ironically, many African communities outside the areas most densely settled by whites and their former slaves had participated actively in market relations, bringing a modest prosperity to themselves and a more substantial one to white merchants. The problem of prying labor from such communities was not simply that the Africans did not want to work for wages, but that they had other things to do and other resources to deploy.

The quest for African labor power in South Africa would be a long and violent one, entailing not only the taking of land but the erecting of a state apparatus to channel labor and restrict its options. To be sure, many whites talked about this struggle as if it were being waged against Africans' work habits, an argument akin to the evocations of "savage sloth" in the West Indies. But as Keletso Atkins has forcefully argued, Africans had their own work ethics, their own conceptions of when it made sense to put out energy and when—and for whom—it did not.[46] Even the South African regime reached the limits of its ability to substitute its work ethic for the others. By the early 1900s the South African government was also posing as the guardian of African particularity, this time to insist that Africans keep their ways of life on the increasingly constricted spaces called "Reserves," emerging to do stints as migrant laborers as the area of the Reserves shrank. Migrant labor has been described as a means by which colonial regimes extracted labor without paying for the full costs of its reproduction (that is, bringing up a new generation of workers and keeping alive people who could no longer work actively). But it is not clear that the architects of migrant labor had any choice: labor was available in small units from people who were themselves trying to keep the labor market from absorbing their being and their communities.[47]

The ideological constructs of South Africa—and the variants in colonial regimes farther north—were another sleight of hand, exploiting labor power as they could while attributing the limits of their power to the unchanging peculiarity of African culture. South Africa differed from its neighbors to the north mainly in the extent of its demand for labor, the size of the white population eager to exercise direct supervision over wage workers, and the power of the state—with its large white bureaucracy—capable of supervising the migratory system and stifling the anger to which it gave rise. The South African regime was for a time—a rather long time—able to cite its economic growth as evidence of its progressive nature, thus avoiding the label of backwardness that attached to the slaveholders of the nineteenth century, but it was never able to protect itself from principled critics of the coercion in its labor policy or of the explicit racism of its political and social policies. It was to succumb, nearly two centuries after the Haitian Revolution, to a movement that was at once deeply rooted in South Africa's varied social landscapes and mobilized worldwide and whose language of emancipation echoed the high hopes of slave emancipation. This liberation would also leave in place the question of just how far the remaking of South African society would go beyond the elimination of specifically racist policies and the specifically coercive dimensions of labor control.

That, however, is another story. The last of the stories told in this book shows the idea of the peculiarity of the African beginning to unravel, and it shows that the causes and consequences of that unraveling go to the heart of issues about compulsion and labor and well beyond them at the same time. The final section of Cooper's chapter, focusing on French Africa in the 1940s, looks at the implications of the "test" that people of African descent in the British Caribbean had apparently failed a century earlier. The peculiarity of the African was invoked even at this late date to explain why the stern hand of colonial authority was still necessary to get Africans to do what their own welfare required. Forced labor for public purposes had been justified in the early colonial period as necessary to build the roads and railroads that would bring Africans the incentives (and the constraints) of the free market. The contradictions of such an argument were manifest, as critics pointed out, so coercion was either justified as a temporary measure, a one-shot effort to get Africans habituated to modern economic activities, or it was covered up. From the end of the 1920s, a formal acceptance of free recruitment of labor as incumbent upon any colonial power coexisted with a great variety of actual practices, as had also been the case with antislavery ideology between the declarations of the Congress of Vienna in 1815 and the abolition of slavery in Brazil in 1888, to take two symbolic dates.

During the great war against Nazi tyranny and racism, pragmatism pushed principle aside yet again, and France and Great Britain escalated their use of forced labor. Then, as the Free French made use of Africa as a base for the reconquest of the metropole, these "progressive" forces acknowledged that a future colonialism—defensible in international discourse, as well as helping to rebuild the imperial economy—could not be built on forced labor. But in the short run, the very need for "development"—for the mutual benefit of colonies and metropoles—was said to require an additional five years of forced labor. This was a sad, even pathetic, commentary on the fifty-year history of colonial rule in French Africa—or, indeed, on the century since France had formally emancipated the slaves of its colonies.

It was precisely here that the labor question exploded out of its boundaries into a wider discussion of citizenship and its implications, just as the question of antislavery had expanded within the cross-racial, anticolonial movements in Cuba in the 1870s and 1890s. Whereas Great Britain tried to deflect international criticism of colonial rule by insisting that British imperial policy was intended, now as before, to lead colonies toward self-government, French policy insisted that colonies were not really colonies, but part of a "Greater France" in which colonial subjects became citizens.[48] The former approach could, in theory, be neutralized by endless postponement, while the latter could be neutralized by mechanisms that diluted the voice of colonials in central institutions responsible for Greater France. But the very opening of a debate in which those few colonials allowed into the Paris legislature participated could not be insulated from the question of what political voice was to mean. In April 1946 deputies from Africa brought the issue of forced labor to the legislature in Paris, insisting that it be debated not only publicly, but also in the context of a profound discussion over the postwar constitution. The ability of the African deputies to put the issue in terms central to France's political image of itself—evoking the language of emancipation and citizenship—was part of the story, but so were the actions of unnamed Africans in rural and urban areas of West Africa, who made the existing labor regime untenable unless authorities were willing to resort to a direct, large-scale, and visible escalation of coercion. This combination of universal appeal and localized mobilization echoed antislavery campaigns going back to the 1830s and anticipated the anti-apartheid struggles of the 1960s to the 1990s. In this instance the population of French Africa acquired formal, if diluted, French citizenship and won the removal of a humiliating form of coercion within a matter of months. In 1946 French Africans became, in this double sense, free.

But this kind of freedom was barely achieved before its limits were forced open by social and political movements, as was also the case with the freedoms enjoyed by African Americans or Afro-Jamaicans or Afro-Cubans as of 1946. The "emancipation" of 1946, as the African deputies in France described the legislation they had pushed onto the agenda, left crucial questions on the table. Would forced labor be defined, as slavery so often had been, in a sharply bounded way that excised a precise evil while obscuring the operation of the many-faceted relations of power within the organization of the economy? Would new peculiarities emerge to define Africans now that they had been formally assimilated to the category of universal worker? Would citizenship continue to be narrowly construed, or would the new citizens use even small rifts to pry much wider openings in the structure of power? Such were the questions posed in 1946, as they had been posed numerous times before and will undoubtedly be posed numerous times again.

As the question now
stands a race has been
freed but a society has not
been formed.
—Lord George Harris,
governor of Trinidad, 1848

Thomas C. Holt

The Essence of the Contract

The Articulation of Race, Gender, and Political
Economy in British Emancipation Policy, 1838–1866

Governor Harris's pithy assertion that slavery emancipation necessarily entailed the creation of a new society nicely frames the essential problematic of contemporary studies of postemancipation societies. Yet the novelty of this proposition has scarcely been interrogated, either by Harris's contemporaries or by historians. From the perspective of the twentieth century, emancipation appears as a dramatic historical rupture: beyond slavery lay the transition to a "free" society and the vast social upheavals and transformations that such a transition entailed. From the perspective of earlier generations, however, the freeing of slaves had occasioned no such radical break with the past; indeed, slave manumission had long been an integral part of the very management of slave labor. Why could emancipation not simply be manumission on a larger scale? After all, the newly independent American republics had achieved something of the sort in the late eighteenth and early nine-

teenth centuries. Why should a change in the labor system necessita
new society be formed? What kind of social transformation did Harris
mind?

Exactly a decade earlier, during the last full year of apprenticeship (a ....gually
mandated transition period between slavery and freedom), Lord Glenelg, Britain's colonial secretary, had provided a partial answer to at least the second of
these questions. Glenelg urged the governors of the British West Indian colonies to amend all laws left over from the slavery era. They should take special
note of those laws that made "innumerable distinctions of the most invidious nature in favor of Europeans and their descendants, and to the prejudice
of persons of African birth or origin." Not only should all these be abolished,
Glenelg insisted, but even "disguised references" should be struck from colonial laws. With these instructions, Glenelg, a former liberal Tory who had converted to Whiggery, offered a much more detailed and far-reaching definition
of the meaning of freedom than that which had been suggested just four years
earlier, during discussions of the Abolition Act of 1833. "The great cardinal
principle of the law for the abolition of slavery," Glenelg wrote, "is, that the
apprenticeship of the emancipated slaves is to be immediately succeeded by
personal freedom, in that full and unlimited sense of the term in which it is
used in reference to the other subjects of the British Crown." [1]

To implement this policy Glenelg ordered that the governors and their at-
torneys general should survey colonial laws with regard to access to the elective franchise, schools, churches, the militia, and other publicly supported institutions and report on them to his office. They should note any restraints
on occupations freedpeople were likely to resort to in lieu of plantation labor,
such as peddler, porter, and boatman. They should study the administration
of poor relief, vagrancy laws, the tax system, road maintenance, Crown land
sales, and prison discipline. All these should be reviewed to ensure that they
did not involve any vestiges of racial discrimination. This, Glenelg pointed
out, was "the essence of the contract between Great Britain and the colonies."

Glenelg's tenure as colonial secretary lasted little more than a year longer,
but his doctrine of civil and political equality continued to inform the policies of his successors, more or less, through the following decade. In 1849,
however, Earl Grey, one of Glenelg's successors as colonial secretary, wrote
a private and confidential letter to his cousin, Charles Grey, the governor of
Jamaica, expressing his mounting concern about what a genuine political democracy for former slaves might portend in managing colonial affairs in that
island.

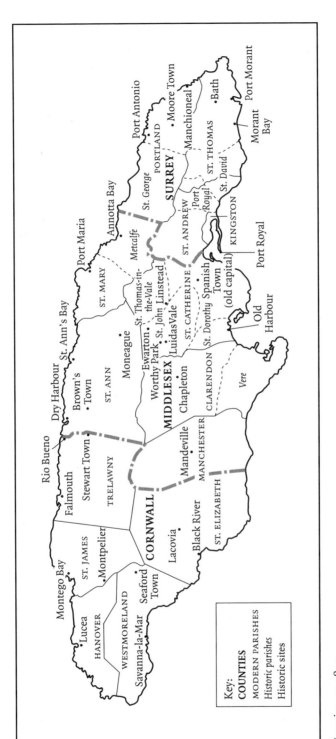

Jamaica, ca. 1895

Key:
COUNTIES
MODERN PARISHES
Historic parishes
Historic sites

SURREY
PORTLAND
ST. THOMAS
ST. DAVID
ST. ANDREW
ST. GEORGE
KINGSTON
ST. CATHERINE
ST. DOROTHY
MIDDLESEX
ST. MARY
ST. ANN
CLARENDON
MANCHESTER
TRELAWNY
CORNWALL
ST. ELIZABETH
ST. JAMES
HANOVER
WESTMORELAND

Port Morant
Port Antonio
Moore Town
Manchioneal
Bath
Morant Bay
Port Royal
Spanish Town (old capital)
Old Harbour
Port Royal
St. David
Port Royal
St. Thomas-in-the-Vale
St. John
Luidas Vale
Linstead
Ewarton
Worthy Park
Metcalfe
Port Maria
Annotta Bay
St. George
Moneague
Vere
Chapleton
Mandeville
Brown's Town
Stewart Town
Dry Harbour
St. Ann's Bay
Rio Bueno
Falmouth
Black River
Lacovia
Seaford Town
Montpelier
Montego Bay
Lucea
Savanna-la-Mar

Looking to the comparative numbers of the black & white inhabitants of Jamaica, & to the absence of any real impediment to the acquisit'n of the elective franchise by the former, it seems impossible to doubt that at no very distant period they must acquire a paramount influence in the legislature [and use their power] with little regard to the interests of the planters or even to justice, & that therefore if the planters were wise they wd. use the authority they now possess, not to break down the power of the Crown but . . . to strengthen it.[2]

Grey's letter signaled the beginning of a dramatic policy shift at the Colonial Office. By mid-century Glenelg's confident embrace of political democracy had given way to mounting anxiety that black political power in Jamaica might actually be used in black people's political and economic interests. From that point forward, colonial officials sought ways to blunt the impact of black political participation, first through changes in Jamaica's governmental structure in 1854, then through what amounted to a poll tax on voters in 1859, and finally by abolishing Jamaican self-government altogether in 1866.

The brief interlude that separates these moments in Jamaican emancipation—an interlude not dissimilar to Reconstruction in the United States thirty years later—helps frame the political problem that emancipation posed for the British in particular and for societies espousing liberal democratic values in general.[3] Glenelg's proposal to make, in Frank Tannenbaum's terms, citizens of ex-slaves poses two questions that further refine those initially raised by Lord Harris's statement. First, why should equality and political participation have been considered "the essence of the contract between Great Britain and the colonies"? And second, why was that policy so quickly abandoned? Answering the second question may be overdetermined by the solution of the first, which is in many respects the more puzzling. Britain's was not the first emancipation, and none hitherto had embraced racial egalitarianism as a necessary moral or political corollary to the renunciation of slavery. Indeed, as Tocqueville observed of the U.S. North, site of the first slavery emancipation in the Americas, it sometimes appeared that those free states were more racist than the southern slave states.[4] What, then, was different about the British experience, or, more precisely perhaps, about the timing of its experience, that made racial equality an essential contractual feature of its emancipation policy? Given a better understanding of what made that policy possible in the first place, we might be better able to explain its rapid retrenchment.[5]

One might be tempted to explain Glenelg's policy as simply an expression of contemporary idealism, which was at its high tide following the abolitionist success. But as we have learned from earlier studies of abolitionism, idealism is not temporally transcendent; rather, it is rooted in a social life that is historically specific.[6] Thus idealism, too, must be accounted for historically. In any event, the idealism of Glenelg's doctrine does not appear to have been rooted in the prior antislavery campaign. Although some individuals may have espoused political democracy for former slaves, nothing in the abolitionist campaign as such or in the debates before Parliament suggested that full political rights for blacks would follow as a consequence of emancipation. British abolitionists would have been more likely to press for enlightened but undemocratic dictation of colonial legislation by the home government (over which they might reasonably have expected to exercise more influence than in the colonies) than to trust the fate of reform to local political processes. Abolitionists raised no noticeable outcry in 1839, for example, when the Colonial Office advanced proposals that envisaged elimination of democratic governance in the colonies altogether, nor did they oppose the Crown colony system where it already existed. Indeed, some colonial bureaucrats argued that contraction, not expansion, of democracy would better serve their efforts to manage efficiently the transition from slavery to free labor.

If not from idealism, then, perhaps egalitarian colonial policy was dictated by political expediency, a ploy of colonial bureaucrats to checkmate planter obstructionism by cultivating a competing power bloc in their midst. Discussions between Glenelg and some Jamaican governors lend some support to this scenario, but those discussions did not result in a consistent or sustained policy.[7] The Colonial Office appears to have sought, by its lights, a moderate and judicious approach to colonial politics, neither liberalizing the franchise appreciably nor acceding to the planters' efforts to restrict it. Property, salary, or tax prerequisites were imposed on prospective voters, but given similar restrictions on the electorate in Britain, even a democratically minded contemporary would not have thought them unreasonable.[8] Indeed, the most vocal complaint at the time was that the Jamaican franchise was too liberal! It is true that given the overwhelming black population majority, such suffrage requirements did augur a potential electoral majority of black peasant freeholders, even as they excluded *most* blacks from the polls. By mid-century that black political potential appeared real enough to British policymakers that they began scurrying for legal ways to curtail or constrain it.[9]

Glenelg and his colleagues could conceive of political and social equality as "the essence" of the emancipation contract with freedpeople, not from idealism, pragmatism, or a fit of absentmindedness, but because that policy articulated with broader ideological developments, namely, with a particular moment in the history of classical liberalism. The question of whether freed slaves would become citizens was a peculiarly nineteenth-century query. Irrespective of how it might have been answered, it could not have even been raised before citizenship became the norm of civil status. The rise of the modern nation-state in the late eighteenth and early nineteenth centuries raised the stakes for any general slave emancipation. Once the nation came to be constituted of "citizens" sharing a nationality rather than "subjects" sharing obedience to a monarchy, not only was the basis for inclusion in or exclusion from the nation necessarily transformed, but the question of citizenship as such was inescapably posed.[10] According to Orlando Patterson, all slave systems invoked some kind of ritual process of incorporation as slaves moved from the "social death" of bondage to the civic life of freedom.[11] But one might surmise that as long as all the inhabitants of a polity were subjects firmly located within a status hierarchy, the incorporation of freed slaves occasioned no threat to existing social order. The Age of Revolution, however, had changed the logic, if not the facts, of the social relations within national polities. Thomas Jefferson, perhaps the most powerful rhetorician of the new democratic ideology, was also among the first to sense its larger import: any move to emancipate the slaves confronted the problem of incorporating them as equals into a free society. Like many others to follow — including the northern states that actually freed their slaves — Jefferson, for all his antislavery precepts, could not abide the prospect of equal citizenship for former slaves.[12]

What was unthinkable in the earlier stages of the Age of Revolution had become more palatable in the years of its culmination. By the time Britain emancipated the slaves in its West Indian possessions, it had experienced a half-century of internal political and economic turmoil that not only had made the difficulties of sustaining social order and political legitimacy a paramount concern but also had refined its thinking on that problem. Stable social orders depended on the character of the citizens constituting the polity, and stability of character depended on the efficacy of the key institutions that made the citizen. Different social sectors and bourgeois class strata therefore found common ground in an ideology of domesticity that defined separate but interdependent spheres for men and women, prescribed the attributes of masculinity and femininity, and made the link between home life and statecraft indispensable to the political and the social as well as to the economic order.[13]

Both the initiation of the Glenelg doctrine and its retrenchment are products of this ideological construction. Classical liberalism had served colonial policymakers as an essential guide in the transition from slavery to free labor. Abolitionism and emancipation were in large part the product of that ideology, achieving their greatest success at precisely the moment it became hegemonic in Britain's public discourse, politics, and bureaucracy, and facing their severest crisis as that ideology underwent significant revision and retrenchment.[14] Much as the transition from slavery to wage labor tested the economic tenets of classical liberal democratic thought, the transition from slave to citizen tested its political tenets. To put the argument in its broadest and bluntest form, bourgeois ideology gave rise to the British experiment with slavery emancipation, only to have that experiment expose the ideology's central contradictions; the dominant response to that exposure was a general retrenchment and reformulation of bourgeois freedom itself. In this sense, then, the debates over the political and economic policies appropriate to newly emancipated societies laid bare issues relevant to other human societies that might otherwise have remained unarticulated.

Politics and Society in Classical Liberal Theory

Classical liberal ideology, as it had evolved by the mid-nineteenth century, posited a model of social order in which basic and functional divisions existed between state and civil society and between public and private life.[15] Human activity was allocated among overlapping but different spheres: the administrative and policing activities of the state; the private (non-state) activities that governed and reproduced economic and social life; the public arena (distinct from both civil society and the state) where democratic, collective rule or norm-making transpired; and, finally, the intimate sphere of the home, the patriarchal and conjugal family, where emotional life was nurtured. A key innovation in this theory of social relations was the idea that civil society constituted a private sphere, independent of the state, animated by autonomous individuals rather than by feudal estates, and that, in principle, these individuals each possessed equal access to and control of their persons, resources, and powers. Theoretically, each person (though in fact, each man) possessed equal standing before the law, was capable of accumulating goods and resources in unlimited quantity, and was free therefore to maximize his gains so as to satisfy innate materialist appetites. Given this premise, all relevant social interactions could be modeled on exchange relations and as such were both self-actuated and self-regulating. In short, individual self-interest, uninhibited by state regulation, was expected to inspire greater effort and productivity, thereby enriching society as a whole. Public virtue would be generated out of private vices.

But the notion that a social order could cohere around human greed was not unproblematic, either logically or as a basis for actual social policy.[16] Theoretically at least, the new order of relations in the marketplace had to be linked to a new moral basis for political relations. The state could not just disappear; it had to be reformulated and repositioned. Thus the political counterpart of the competitive, self-regulating economic marketplace was the public sphere, the marketplace of opinion. It was a sphere that was part of, but distinct from, civil society; within it private, educated, and propertied men exercised influence over both the state (lawmaking) and civil life (the various systems of exchange—economic and social—between individuals). Moreover, political and economic relations were not simply complementary, in the sense that both were conceptualized as exchanges between autonomous subjects; they were in fact functionally linked, because the privatized economic and the intimate household spheres were both crucial realms for fashioning those individual subjects who would enter the public sphere. The economic/civil realm produced men of property; the household produced reflective men capable of civilized discourse and norm-governed interactions.

This process of man/citizen-making is sketched out by Jürgen Habermas, who suggests that it was within "the interiority of the conjugal family" that there developed the subjectivity necessary for men to enter the public sphere as autonomous individuals: "For the experiences about which a public passionately concerned with itself sought agreement and enlightenment through the rational-critical public debate of private persons with one another flowed from the well-spring of a specific subjectivity. The latter had its home, literally, in the sphere of the patriarchal conjugal family."[17] That is, the subjectivity of independent, reflecting men, fashioned in the intimacy of the home, produced the civil "opinions" that were exchanged like goods in this market of critical-rational argument. Out of such exchanges came a collective "public opinion," a concept emerging both in Britain and on the continent in the late eighteenth century, making it, temporally and instrumentally, precursor to the political revolutions in France and America, to the industrial takeoff in Britain, and to the abolitionist movement.[18] In many respects, public opinion was visualized as a regulator in politics, comparable to the role Adam Smith's "invisible hand" played in economic life. The legitimacy and authority of public opinion was dependent, however, on there being a process of open and free exchange (i.e., democracy).

But the unstated precondition for this democratic exchange was harmony in the basic purposes and assumptions of the participants, which in turn could arise only from the compatibility of each subject's relation to the whole. Thus an essential condition for admission to the rule-making public sphere at the outset was that one be an educated man of property (in skills or in land); this would ensure a like commitment to preserving a social order that guaranteed property.[19] Also essential to this liberal discourse was the assumption that such citizens would be the progeny of an intimate sphere, the patriarchal, conjugal family, for it was there that innate desires and ambitions for self-aggrandizement were somehow rendered compatible or, quite literally, domesticated.

In sum, then, the "free" and open exchanges in the public sphere presumed a homogeneity of participants, a mutuality of fundamental interests, and, withal, the discussability of differences.[20] Consequently, political life (and democratic practice) was ultimately dependent on similarities in the citizens' location in and relation to the social order. In short, while a democratic political order was required to protect the autonomous private sphere from encroachment by the state or antagonist feudal estates, systematic exclusions from the decision-making realm (the public sphere) were necessary to protect that same social order from challenges by the dispossessed.[21] Over time, the criteria for admission might be expanded, but the fundamental test or principle remained that the new admittees not threaten the social order.

There was, of course, an apparent contradiction between the self-possession and autonomy implied by economic liberalism and the obviously selective dispossession inherent in the constitution of the political sphere. Every member of a society was not just eligible for but compelled to participate in economic exchanges in the civil sphere, but only educated and propertied men were eligible for admission to the public sphere, which controlled the norm-making functions of the whole society. This contradiction could be accommodated in two ways: by defining, de jure, a system in which there was equality of opportunity for *eventual* inclusion, or by redrawing the boundaries of membership so that some persons or groups were defined, de facto, outside the public sphere by virtue of their deviance from those "natural" or innate human attributes that equipped one to earn eligibility.[22] Historically, of course, boundaries were drawn so as to exclude whole social categories—racial, national, gender, and class—that were deemed "residual" elements of the social order.[23] At the time of emancipation, however, the operative assumption among the relevant elites was that all men were capable of taking advantage of putatively equal opportunities for acquiring the property, education, or skills that would admit them to the public sphere.

This secular faith notwithstanding, the transition from a slave to a free society eventually exposed the contradictions in liberal ideology, which found expression in the colonial bureaucracy's efforts to formulate emancipation policy. The formation of a free society first required the creation of persons with bourgeois values, which in turn implied state intrusions of totalitarian dimensions into the social sphere. But the policies actually pursued—involving reforms in education, taxation, and labor recruitment—employed indirect rather than direct means to achieve these ends, and, consistent with their ideological presumptions, policymakers undervalued the force of culture and class as factors shaping human desire and social relations. Moreover, there was a blatant contradiction between the notion that workers would imitate the bourgeois private sphere and the planters' demand to control the labor of whole families. These contradictions undercut British designs for a liberal democratic society; the policies failed either to remake slaves into a contented proletariat or to turn slaveowners into bourgeois employers. Out of these failures emerged racist reformulations of the founding liberal doctrine, which elided its inherent contradictions. In the process of trying to envision and legislate how, in Governor Harris's trenchant phrases, a society might be formed as well as a race freed, British policymakers thus exposed both the nature and the limits of their vision.

Liberal Democracy and Emancipation in Jamaica

Skepticism about applying liberal democratic theory to the problem of emancipation—or at least about the mode of application—was a muted oppositional theme in Britain's colonial policy deliberations almost from the outset. Almost concurrently with Glenelg's policy declaration of "full equality," a former Jamaican governor and absentee planter, the Marquis of Sligo, pointed out the pitfalls in achieving a full social transformation in that island under such auspices.

> In truth, there is no justice in the general local institutions of Jamaica; because there is no public opinion to which an appeal can be made. Slavery has divided society into two classes; to one it has given power, but to the other it has not extended protection. One of these classes is above public opinion, and the other is below it; neither are, therefore, under its influence; and it is much to be feared, that owing to the want of sympathy between them, to the want of dependence and mutual confidence, to the poorer class being able to provide for the necessities of life without any application to the higher, there never will be in Jamaica, or in any other slave colony, a community of feeling on which public opinion can operate beneficially.[24]

That the aristocratic Sligo offered an analysis of the Jamaican social order replete with the dogma of classical liberalism suggests how hegemonic, even commonplace, such notions had become by the late 1830s. But his doubts about the practical applications of liberal doctrine under Jamaican social conditions expose its general underlying contradictions as well. Sligo recognized that a disinterested public opinion was an essential arbiter among competing interests in a modern society. Such opinion depended, however, on the existence of a public sphere constituted by educated, propertied, private individuals who could engage in what Habermas would describe as a nonantagonistic, rational debate, which was the only avenue to truth and a sound, unbiased public policy. No such public sphere, and thus no "publicity," existed in Jamaica because slavery had produced a society divided into the powerful and the unprotected, the one dominating the public sphere, the other outside it. Neither was reachable by reasoned opinion, and consequently there was no social basis *within* the society for political legitimacy. It was a situation that imperiled any effort at locally authorized reform. Moreover, under Jamaican conditions (i.e., the growth of its independent peasantry) there was not even the moderating effect of economic ties such as one might find in the rural areas of Britain, where one class was dependent on the other for subsistence and thus both were subject to mutual influences. Instead, two hostile classes with antagonistic interests confronted each other across a social void. The irony, of course, is that the fundamental contradiction that Sligo could see so clearly in Jamaica would soon rupture the self-confident façade of liberal discourse in the metropolis as well.

Almost simultaneously with the appearance of Sligo's anonymous pamphlet, Henry Taylor, head of the West Indian division of the Colonial Office, wrote a very similar critique of Jamaican society—one aimed at persuading Glenelg to abandon his racially egalitarian policy and impose Crown colony rule throughout the West Indies. A veteran of the botched efforts to convince planters to ameliorate slave conditions during the 1820s as well as of the failure of the apprenticeship system to achieve a smooth transition from slavery to freedom, Taylor had concluded by 1838 that the West Indian legislative assemblies were "by their constitution and the nature of the societies for which they legislated, absolutely incompetent and unfit to deal with the new state of things." With respect to the self-governing West Indian colonies, there was an "inherent and permanent incongruity of the system [of free labor and political democracy] and the state of society." By "state of society" Taylor meant its division into antagonist sections: a black, mostly ex-slave majority; a brown, mostly freeborn plurality; and a white, planter-dominated minority. Under a democratic system, the black majority should rule but was not enabled by education to do so; the brown plurality could rule but was disqualified by alienation from the two other social sectors from doing so; the white oligarchy should not rule, but undoubtedly would.[25] Since the planters could not be convinced by argument to relent in obstructing the necessary transformation of the social order and creation of a civil society, the home government should exert "at once and conclusively, a power which shall overrule all opposition and set the question at rest."[26] In its political features, Glenelg's doctrine clearly was inappropriate in a society thus constituted, because "to force this social change, and yet to leave the political frame-work of the totally different society the same as it was, would seem even in a mere theoretical view to be in the nature of a political solecism."[27]

The critiques of former Jamaican governor Sligo and Colonial Officer Taylor thus framed the limits of democratic reform in former slave societies. Sligo's analysis in particular couples the two core issues for British emancipation policy: on the one hand, the challenge that the transition from slavery to free labor posed to classical liberalism's well-developed economic theory; on the other, the challenge that transforming a slave hierarchy into a liberal democratic society presented to its more inchoate political doctrine. That these challenges were perceived to be interlinked suggests an answer for the question of why Glenelg's policy was proposed in the first place; the fact that that linkage soon came to be seen as perilous to social order in general helps explain its eventual abandonment. But neither Taylor nor Sligo addressed—indeed, they probably could not see—the general contradiction inherent in seeking the legitimacy of democratic rule in a social order ultimately dependent on economic and social inequalities; rather, the "solecism" they saw was the coupling of these imperatives in former slave societies where the public sphere was as yet undeveloped.

Although these dissents from, or reservations about, Glenelg's doctrine remained suppressed themes that would not emerge full-blown until the end of the following decade, they highlighted a polarity that framed a profound though muted tension in policymaking from the very outset. At every level, officials charged with managing the transition from slavery to free labor and building a democratic society were conscious of the functional linkage between the diverse spheres of social relations. Even as Sligo was writing his pamphlet, Special Magistrate Richard Chamberlaine, a native-born Afro-Jamaican, was explaining classical liberal economic doctrine to the newly freed people of St. Thomas-in-the-East, gathered on 1 August 1838 to celebrate their emancipation and the ending of apprenticeship. Chamberlaine

A formal dinner at Dawkins Caymanis Estate in Jamaica, one of many such events celebrating the end of apprenticeship on 1 August 1838. (Courtesy of National Library of Jamaica)

wanted them to understand the brave new world they were about to enter, especially the "duties and responsibilities of a rational and unfettered freedom" and their special obligation to prove "that black men are as susceptible of the value and responsibility of freedom as any other race of human beings." [28] Interestingly enough, in the course of this explanation, he made explicit the dependence of civil and public arenas on the proper functioning of an intimate sphere.

In order to meet their responsibilities to enslaved blacks elsewhere, Chamberlaine argued, Jamaican freedmen must remain on the plantations, working diligently for their former masters. They would do this not because of slavish deference, however, nor simply because the survival of the sugar estates required it. Rather, Chamberlaine was confident that their labor would be motivated by refinements in their tastes and expansion of their desires for material goods. No longer content with the crude subsistence of the slave, "a pot of coco soup and herring tail," they would acquire new needs and desires, discovering in the process the iron law that bound the social world to the economic, and the market in goods to the market in labor:

Your wives and your daughters will require their fine clothes for their chapels, churches, and holidays. You will visit your friends with your coat and your shoes, and you will require your dinners prepared for you with some respect to comfort and cleanliness; your soup will be seasoned with beef and pork; and in order to obtain these, the comforts and necessaries of civilized life, you will have to labour industriously—for the more work you do, the more money you must obtain, and the better will you be enabled to increase and extend your comforts.

This passage suggests that one could not appeal to autonomous individuals for ever-expanding expenditures of labor power solely on the basis of their ostensibly innate desires for self-aggrandizement; labor beyond what was necessary to acquire a subsistence required other incentives than the mere material. It was this circle of dependents, "wives and daughters," that moved men to labor beyond the minimum. At the heart of Chamberlaine's message, therefore, was a veritable word picture of an ideal bourgeois domestic scene:

> Your wives, hitherto accustomed to be partakers in your daily toils, running to the fields with you in the morning, and returning with you down-spirited and dejected at sun set day by day, bringing no alleviations, will be enabled to remain at home, to look after your clothes, and your children's clothes —your household affairs—your stock—your comfortable dinner, so that whilst you are at work in the field, as the day advances, instead of lagging in your work, you are more cheerful, more industrious, because moving in the certainty of finding every thing comfortable when you get home.

One of the boons of freedom, then, would be this newfound prospect of establishing gendered spheres of activity and authority. Freedmen should remain on the plantations, working for wages to support freedwomen and children at home, who in turn would be dependent and subservient. In the refuge of his home the workingman was served, obeyed, and nurtured. By Chamberlaine's reckoning, this domestic hierarchy and dependence was a key incentive for the freedmen's willing acquiescence to the principles of a bourgeois social order, namely, personal accumulation and deference to proper authority.

Furthermore, he argued, freedmen, though reputedly able to satisfy their basic needs by working just two days each week, should work the other four days as well in order to accumulate savings "for the winter of your days, when you will have no master's bounty or humanity to appeal to." And even as they foreswore paternal dependence on the propertied classes, they should affirm that men without masters must still defer to their betters. All were now "as free as the Queen," and no man was more "free than another," but still it was necessary "for the purposes of civilized society, that there should be gradations of rank in all communities." Freedmen must be civil, respectful, and obedient not only to their masters, but to all in authority over them. The claims of deference and authority were thus extended from the domestic fireside to the public sphere.[29]

Chamberlaine's address assumes, much as Habermas suggests, a very specific subjectivity: that wage-earning men were formed and motivated by the privileges, dependency, and emotional sustenance of the domestic hearth. Assumed also, as Fraser argues, is a thoroughly gendered notion of the respective roles of worker and consumer.[30]

Although this vision was a replica of the ongoing creation of European bourgeois society, its special force in the West Indies probably owed a great deal to that region's fearful counterexample, the Haitian nightmare of former slaves succumbing to an African savagery. This was the image that Henry Taylor had invoked in 1833 when he urged the cabinet to implement emancipation gradually through an apprenticeship system designed to prepare slaves for wage labor. It was also a recurring image in governors' correspondence and travelers' diaries. The fear, as historian James Anthony Froude phrased it in the late 1880s, was that "in a few generations they will peel off such civilisation as they have learnt as easily and as willingly as their coats and trousers."[31] What Chamberlaine described, then, was a process that, in both senses of the word, *domesticated* savage instincts.

The image of menacing savagery also lurked behind Colonial Secretary Glenelg's other major policy declaration of the late 1830s. Early in 1836, he forwarded to all the West Indian governors a dispatch addressing the problem anticipated with controlling land settlement by freed people after apprenticeship. He began by noting that during slavery, labor could be compelled to be applied wherever the owner desired. But, upon the end of apprenticeship, the laborer would apply himself only to those tasks that promised personal benefit. Therefore, if the cultivation of sugar and coffee were to continue, "we must make it the immediate and apparent interest of the negro population to employ their labour in raising them." Glenelg was apprehensive about their ability to do this, repeating the now familiar Wakefieldian maxim that given the demographic patterns of former slave colonies such as Jamaica—"where there is land enough to yield an abundant subsistence to the whole population in return for slight labour"—blacks would not work for wages. Eventually, a proper equilibrium between land and labor would be established by the inexorable flywheel of natural forces that govern the social order, that is, population growth, but the colonies could not afford the luxury of waiting.[32]

Should things be left to their natural course, labour would not be attracted to the cultivation of exportable produce, until population began to press upon the means of subsistence, and the land failed (without a more assiduous and economical culture) to supply all its occupants with the necessaries of life. As soon as the natural labouring population should thus arise and the growing necessity of making the most of the land should ensure the proper application of their labour, it might be expected that the present staples would again be brought into cultivation. But the depreciation which would take place in property, and the rude state into which society would fall back in the mean time, make it desirable to adopt measures to check this apparently natural course.[33]

Having conceded that the freedpeople's prospective behavior, by Wakefieldian and Malthusian dicta, was natural, Glenelg went on to prescribe the means by which the government would interdict these natural proclivities: it was essential that the former slaves be prevented from obtaining land. While he was uncertain how to proceed with the land that was already in private hands, he recommended that persons without land titles be excluded from occupying Crown lands and that the price be raised so as to keep those lands "out of the reach of persons without capital." Following a policy successfully employed in Canada and Australia during this period, Glenelg recommended that a minimum price be set for all Crown land, that it be sold only to the highest bidder, and that a 10 percent down payment be required for purchase. Furthermore, he recommended that an investigation be launched immediately into the means by which squatters could be prevented from occupying public land.

Lord Glenelg offered the following arguments to justify these extraordinary steps to constrain the free enterprise of the freedpeople. First, the prosperity of any society depended upon maintaining an appropriate balance between labor supply and demand. If that definition of social utility were accepted, then it followed that government intervention was justified to establish conditions for its realization. "In new countries, where the whole unoccupied territory belongs to the Crown, and settlers are continually flowing in, it is possible, by fixing the price of fresh land so high as to place it above the reach of the poorest class of settlers, to keep the labour market in its most prosperous state from the beginning." With this policy the government not only assured an adequate supply of landless laborers to the estates but also boosted the value of land, which in turn would make "it more profitable to cultivate old land well than to purchase new."[34] But the ultimate goal of these economic maneuvers was moral: to domesticate "natural" desires and behavior, to hold safe the boundary between civilized life and a Hobbesian jungle.

The natural tendency of the population to spread over the surface of the country, each man settling where he may, or roving from place to place in pursuit of virgin soil, is thus impeded. The territory, expanding only with the pressure of population, is commensurate with the actual wants of the entire community. Society, being thus kept together, is more open to civilizing influences, more directly under the control of Government, more full of the activity which is inspired by common wants, and the strength which is derived from the division of labour; and altogether is in a sound state, morally, politically and economically, than if left to pursue its natural course.

Thus Glenelg's policy was intended to prevent situations such as those Henry Taylor had conjured up in his 1833 memorandum—scattered villages of former slaves descending rapidly into "savage sloth"—and to foster domestic scenes like the one Chamberlaine described. Glenelg hastened to add, however, that the government's policy was not intended to favor one class over another. The object of the government was not to force the freedpeople to stay on the plantations by depriving them of alternative employment, "but merely to condense and keep together the population in such a manner that it may always contain a due proportion of labourers." Since "the most profitable produce will always afford the highest wages, and the highest wages will always draw the largest supply of labour," the government should not discourage the cultivation of nonplantation crops. "But some security should if possible be taken, that all the territory which is cultivated at all shall be cultivated well. The minimum price of land, therefore, should be high enough to leave a considerable portion of the population unable to buy it until they have saved some capital out of the wages of their industry, and at the same time low enough to encourage such savings by making the possession of land a reasonable object of ambition to all." Thus men hungry for land would first have to be desirous of capital and anxious to accumulate it. Presumably, such men would also be inclined to protect capital accumulation in general. Indeed, it was possibly this latter effect that glossed over—or perhaps resolved—the other glaring contradiction in liberal policy and thought: that a proletariat motivated by bourgeois values and incentives would remain contentedly proletarian.

Clearly Glenelg was also searching for a way to reconcile, rhetorically at least, draconian state intervention with the requirements of the doctrine of full civil equality, which he would articulate just a few months later. His argument exposed, however, the necessary tension between elaborating policy according to the requirements of a liberal doctrine premised on ostensibly natural and innate human desires in a social order premised on material inequality. Natural or not, such desires had to be channeled if social order were to be preserved; this in turn required embracing the necessity for forceful intervention to fashion and reproduce the subjects that the new social order required. Like Magistrate Chamberlaine, Glenelg also envisioned a social order founded on a collectivity of bourgeois-aspiring men; the role of the state was to foster the conditions and institutions that would produce such men.

The Original "White Man's Burden": Fashioning Ex-slaves into Bourgeois Subjects

Glenelg's dilemma prefigured the policy conflicts of the first decade of emancipation. Over that decade both Conservative and Liberal administrations at the Colonial Office invoked the tenets, or at least the language, of bourgeois political economy. It was clear to all, moreover, that bourgeois freedom could not have an immaculate conception; the state must plant and nurture its seed. Indeed, the Jamaican administration of Lord Elgin (1842–46), a Tory appointee, was perhaps the most exemplary of contemporary liberalism. Elgin arrived on the island convinced that the manner in which Britain shepherded its transformation from a slave to a free society would set an example for the world. There was a close connection "between the course of Policy which ought to be pursued here and the interests of Christian civilization both within the Island and beyond it." [35]

Unhesitatingly, therefore, Elgin took up Glenelg's doctrine that it was Britain's obligation to raise the emancipated slave morally, intellectually, and socially as well as to obliterate racial animosities. Consistent with classical liberal theory, he saw material prosperity and moral progress as mutually interactive and inseparable. Recognizing the fundamental division of Jamaican society along class lines—between planters and their retainers on the one side and freedpeople and their supporters on the other—he argued that the main cause of the island's problems was that its potential working class was not completely deprived of the means of production. Or, as Sligo had put it, "the poorer class [was] able to provide for the necessities of life without any application to the higher." [36] In the fashion of a classic nineteenth-century liberal, however, Elgin contended that the interests of both classes were in fact compatible and mutual. The solution, therefore, was to find "common ground" on which to found "a scheme of policy sufficiently progressive to contribute towards the development of that new order of social relations into which the materials supplied by Emancipation were about to arrange themselves." The role of government was to get the conflicting parties to recognize their mutual interests, and this would assure prosperity. Thus, having acknowledged class, Elgin sought to deny the incompatibility of antagonistic class interests.[37]

Repeating the standard formula of the day, Elgin insisted that "civilization" would stimulate tastes and habits in the black worker that could only be satisfied with a monetary income. Indeed, his very first tour of the island had convinced him that "civilization, the spread of knowledge, habits of greater expense in respect of living, dress and dwellings, will conspire to render a relapse to a former and lower condition distasteful and I trust improbable."[38] It followed that "the improvement of the negro is the first interest of the Planter."[39]

Planters would have to reform, too. They must be "weaned" away from the coercive management and wasteful cultivation techniques characteristic of slavery. With an abundance of cheap land, it would be impossible to coerce labor by means of immigration or similar measures. Elgin was convinced that the adoption of scientific agricultural practices by the planters and industrial education for the blacks would make the mutual dependence of worker and employer self-evident. Innovation and scientific agricultural practices would call, in turn, for higher skills and intelligence from the laborer and "redeem the pursuits of the husbandman from the discredit into which they had fallen as the avocation of slaves, and thus enlist the hearty co-operation" of friends of the blacks.[40]

Laborers resisted innovation because "they are in some quarters keenly alive to the effect which the proposed change of system may have in reducing the value of their labor."[41] Industrial schools would overcome their opposition by creating "a feeling favorable to the subject by presenting it to the Public in its most attractive guise as connected with questions of scientific and practical interest."[42] Such education would provide a practical "illustration of that coincidence between the material interests of one class and the moral interests of another, the recognition of which is an indispensable condition to social progress in these communities."[43]

Elgin's views were not without seconders among the planter class. Recently arrived from England to superintend his Jamaican properties, John Blagrove jotted into his diary an analysis not entirely dissimilar. He began, predictably, with the declaration that immigration was essential to create labor competition and thereby bring costs down. But he also recognized that the impact of immigration would not be evident for generations hence, after natural increase of the population and acculturation had done their work. "Upon this score—combined with religious & temporal instruction, the promotion of marriage, and increased desire of industrious habits—Jamaica I conceive will yet hold up its head. The present prospects are far from flattering however. Still I see no reason to dispair—by the [illegible] assistance & desire of both black & white to conduce to the welfare of one & the other—to lay aside all recollection of Olden Times—& each & all to remember that as Human-beings we are dependent one on the other." Meanwhile, staple production would increase "in proportion [to] the ideas & wants of Jamaica's indigenous 'habitants." Like Elgin, Blagrove was convinced that the moral and religious education of the blacks was vital to the planters' interests.[44]

Meanwhile, the planter-dominated Jamaica Assembly, in which Blagrove sat, not only approved Elgin's enthusiasm for industrial education but did so in language that reflected aspects of the metropolitan view of social order. Schools that coupled labor with moral instruction would be especially useful, the assembly thought, in stimulating the necessary moral regeneration of the workers.

[W]hat has hitherto been defective in the parent ought to be supplied in the tuition of the child; There can be little doubt that these deficiencies in a large and important class of our population are produced in a great degree by an injurious absence of parental guidance and control. At a maturer age these must infallibly result in the want of due appreciation of the restraints of social order; of the advantages of a steady pursuit of domestic happiness and comfort through a course of usefulness; and of a proper understanding of those relative interests in the fair rewards of labour which identify individual with general prosperity.[45]

In this passage, of course, the planters also expressed their skepticism about seeing these citizen-making functions carried out within the freedmen's private households. In time that skepticism would be found among special magistrates and other colonial officials as well, providing common ground for a future agreement to abandon democratic practice.

At this juncture, however, the issue was already moot, because agreement on first principles did not lead to an agreement on an effective educational system. Most of the planters educated their children in England or in private schools on the island and thus were not themselves beneficiaries of the public system; it is also likely that, like planters elsewhere in the Americas, some feared the uncertain effects of education on their labor supply. Consequently, schools remained underfunded and underdeveloped largely because of the planters' resistance to providing adequate funding. Not until six years after emancipation was any significant local public effort made to organize and fund a public education system for the black majority. About £1,000 was appropriated in 1844 to finance public education through grants to existing parochial schools, but the system—if it can be called that—remained underfunded and served only a minority of the island's eligible youth. An 1847 report counted 178 schools with a total enrollment of 14,532, which amounted to about 20 percent of the eligible children in a school-age population estimated to be 75,558.[46]

Public schooling also suffered because the Baptist missionaries, whose schools enrolled the majority of freedpeople's children, strongly resisted industrial schools, seeing them as little more than new instruments of planter coercion. Thus the Baptists declined public financial assistance, as did the Church Missionary Society, the Roman Catholics, and the Jewish congregations. Only the Methodists, Presbyterians, Moravians, and the American Congregationalists accepted state funding.[47] By the mid-1850s, therefore, education was declared to be "at its lowest grasp," with "scarcely half as many children receiving instruction as had done so the year before."[48] By 1858 Jamaica had spent about ten times more on the immigration of indentured laborers (£231,488) than on public schools.[49]

Much like this debate over industrial education, there followed a series of similar conflicts—over state-funded recruitment of indentured labor, allocation of the tax burden between working and owning classes, and developing systems for the administration of justice—in which notions of liberal statecraft floundered on the shoals of real politics.[50] Whatever "mutuality of interests" planters and freedpeople theoretically shared broke down when decisions were required about specific allocations of scarce resources, rights, and powers. The victims of social inequities sought immediate solutions, which those who benefited from the inequities sought to deny.

But British policymakers not only failed to account for class conflict in their model for democratic reform, they also failed to recognize the extent and power of competing, alternative spheres of publicity in Jamaican life.[51] In their churches, villages, and communities, Jamaican freedpeople nurtured an alternative worldview that proved more resistant to "reformation" than colonial officials had originally foreseen. Consequently, the fashioning of bourgeois man proved a more daunting task than first envisioned. But even as these competing social arenas came gradually into view, they were distorted and misread in official circles. By the time Earl Grey's letter warning of the dangers involved in full political equality was written, official discourse was strongly marked by disgust with the Afro-Jamaicans' "lack of moral progress."

Concurrently with the publication of Thomas Carlyle's infamous "Discourses on the Nigger Question" in 1849, there emerged an official rhetoric indicting the freedpeople's work ethic, family life, and sexuality, sometimes even their very humanity, all part of a general condemnation of their capacity to participate in civil society on the same basis as whites. Thus, even while acknowledging that the prevailing low wages offered "no inducement to the more independent class of people to work on estates," many Jamaican officials insisted that blacks were somehow at fault: "The people betake themselves to the mountains, buy an acre of land, and squat on it. Indolence begets its certain inheritances. We know the rest." [52] The "rest," according to Governor Henry Barkly, writing in 1856 in language reminiscent of Henry Taylor's nightmarish prognosis of 1833, was a dangerously isolated peasantry. Many blacks did not even see whites from one year to the next, Barkly wrote, and obeah practices and other African superstitions and religious beliefs were encouraged by their isolation. During that very year, in fact, colored assemblyman John Castello introduced legislation outlawing obeah, which soon became law. [53]

Thus, despite all evidence to the contrary, there arose the stereotype of "Quashee"—lazy, morally degenerate, licentious, and heedless of the future. By the mid-1850s this characterization laced the special magistrates' reports: the peasantry was unaffected by the moral sanctions of the larger society and adhered to an alternative moral system, it was claimed; for them no shame, but rather a kind of celebrity, attached to criminal convicts, who returned to their communities without stigma. "I regret to state," Special Magistrate Alexander Fyfe reported in 1854, "that I see little improvement in the laboring classes. They work for no prospective or moral object, the incentive is entirely present and physical. They are improvident, reckless of life, and almost indifferent to the ties of kindred. They are scarce grateful for charity in sickness, and whilst they will lavish pounds on a funeral, they grudge a shilling for the medicine which might avert it. Disease entails trouble, death is followed by merriment and feasting." Another magistrate, Robert Emery, added: "Their march back to barbarism has been rapid and successful." [54]

When in 1864 a group of black peasant farmers petitioned Jamaican governor Edward John Eyre for land reform and justice in the local courts, he advised them that the solutions to their problems were moral reformation, piety, and propriety. They must improve in "social habits and in domestic comfort, as well as in material prosperity." They required larger houses so that they could "distribute their families in separate sleeping rooms at night." They must attend more "to their ordinary daily dress, rather than sacrifice that to grand displays on Sundays." The remedy for the larceny of their crops depended upon their own moral choices: they must "improve in civilization," and they must educate their children in religion, industry, and respectability, "both by example and precept." [55]

Though his Victorian platitudes were less than helpful to distressed Afro-Jamaicans, Governor Eyre's address received a favorable reception at the Colonial Office. Indeed, just a year later Henry Taylor drafted a comparable reply to a similar petition, revealing in the process amazing callousness and an obtuse disregard of Jamaican realities. Taylor's response, styled the "Queen's Advice," amounted to a short lecture on classical economics. He advised the land-hungry petitioners that

the prosperity of the Labouring Classes, as well as of all other Classes, depends, in Jamaica, and in other Countries, upon their working for Wages, not uncertainly, or capriciously, but steadily and continuously, at the times when their labour is wanted, and for so long as it is wanted; and if they would use this industry, and thereby render the Plantations productive, they would enable the Planters to pay them higher Wages for the same hours of work than are received by the best Field Labourers in this country; and as the cost of the necessaries of life is much less in Jamaica than it is here, they would be enabled, by adding prudence to industry, to lay by an ample provision for seasons of drought and dearth; and they may be assured, that it is from their own industry and prudence, in availing themselves of the means of prospering that are before them, and not from any such schemes as have been suggested to them, that they must look for an improvement in their condition; and that her Majesty will regard with interest and satisfaction their advancement through their own merits and efforts.[56]

Such determined unresponsiveness by colonial officials at all levels fed a popular discontent that exploded later that year in a bloody rebellion at Morant Bay. Shortly afterward, the British Parliament abolished self-government in Jamaica, acting in response to arguments that Afro-Jamaicans were, as Earl Grey put it to the House of Lords during the debate, "unfit to exercise political power."

It is striking, however, that the Afro-Jamaicans' "unfitness" was coupled with—indeed, was seen to be rooted in—the failure of their households and conjugal arrangements. In the debate, Grey's proposal to strip Jamaicans of political rights was immediately followed by Lord Lyttelton's complaint that "of all the deplorable features exhibited by the Jamaica [parliamentary] papers the most distressing was that describing the demoralized state of the people, especially as regards those in the matrimonial state." Until that was remedied, "no mere political arrangement could confer the least benefit upon the people of Jamaica."[57] It was almost as if a thirty-year discussion had been brought full circle. The earlier debates over the wisdom of slavery emancipation had posited optimism about the "Negro's character," or, more precisely, about the mutability of that character, as grounds for the emancipation experiment. Thirty years later—as the simultaneity of Grey's and Lyttelton's pronouncements confirmed—Britain's Afro-Jamaican subjects were still answerable to a moral and political order that Britons defined. On this occasion, however, they were found falling short of that standard. Their public deficiencies grew out of their private failings, which made them legitimate objects of British hegemony for the foreseeable future.

Thus the Morant Bay Rebellion was taken as an explicit demonstration of the failure of British emancipation policy and as evidence of the former slaves' incapacity for responsible citizenship. The moral contract of emancipation as Glenelg had conceived it would be altered. But it would not be Britain's particular articulation of liberal democracy that was doomed faulty; rather, it was the supposed deficiencies of its beneficiaries. Consequently, the perceived failure of West Indian emancipation resonated with and helped sustain the rise of a virulent official racism, which in turn helped give shape and focus to the racial thought of the larger public. In the rhetorical iconography of the late nineteenth century, people of color were invariably stigmatized as underworked and oversexed, their material interests or drives unaroused while their libidos were out of control. A common theme running through racist thought was that "the natives" had no inner controls and thus required external controllers.[58] Wayward children of the human family, they became fit subjects for a "beneficent despotism." Projected to the world stage, beneficent despotism became "the white man's burden," both justification for and the putative substance of his imperialist adventures.

Conclusion

There is an obvious resonance between the racial justifications for the retreat from the more optimistic hopes of the British emancipation experiment and the subsequent discursive justifications of imperialism; not least of these is that "Quashee" bears a striking resemblance to those characteristics later cataloged under "the peculiarity of the African." Of course, as Frederick Cooper points out below, there was a curious amnesia among twentieth-century European imperialists about that earlier experiment and its implications. Their amnesia should not distract us, however, from grasping both the radical import of nineteenth-century slavery emancipation and the wide-ranging consequences of its flaws. Not only in the British West Indies, but also, as Rebecca Scott shows below, in the United States and Cuba, the abolition of slavery opened space for discussions about a radical transformation of society that entailed much more than the mere manumission of slave laborers. In each case slave emancipation involved potential revisions of the social contract that bound the society together, revisions that embraced— however briefly or ambivalently—aspects of Glenelg's racially egalitarian doctrine. In two of those cases, of course, the broader revisions were incident to revolutionary military conflict; civil wars summoned up visions of a very different civil society. But, as suggested above, the mutual implications of emancipation and the larger social transformations were also rooted in extensive ideological transformations during the nineteenth century.

Recent work in the United States, for example, suggests not only that an ideological revolution was under way in public thought and policy relating to the connections between labor, gender, and domesticity during the emancipation and immediate postemancipation eras, but that it was often specifically linked to the problems and aftermath of slavery emancipation.[59] Other studies go further in linking ideologies and social structures relating to gender roles and identities directly to postemancipation politics and access to the public sphere.[60] In sum, all of these works suggest the centrality of ideologies about gender, households, and domesticity to constituting Anglo-American social orders more generally and political order in particular.

The experience of Jamaican freedpeople suggests, however, even more profound contradictions in the ongoing nineteenth-century efforts to reconstruct the social order. Emblematic of many of those contradictions was the treadmill, a device originally designed for British prisons but introduced into the West Indies during the apprenticeship period to "discipline" refractory workers in lieu of the now banned whip. The treadmill consisted of wooden steps around a hollow cylinder on which a prisoner was made to step as the mechanism turned. The effect was to make the prisoner "work." It was, of course, work disembodied of any material object or product and managed by the state rather than a private employer. The prisoners committed to "the workhouses" were apprentices who refused to work on the plantations under the conditions prescribed by the apprenticeship system established by the Abolition Act of

"Dancing the treadmill" in Jamaica, 1837. (Courtesy of National Library of Jamaica)

1833. The treadmill was intended, therefore, not simply to punish the workers but to reform them.

Most discussions of emancipation policy—in Britain as elsewhere—picture these workers as male. It is evident, however, that most of the inmates portrayed in the treadmill illustration seen here are female. This is consistent with contemporary discussions and official reports, which invariably portray women as the most rebellious and refractory workers.[61] The fact is that in Jamaica, as in many other slave societies, women constituted the core of the field labor force, especially on sugar plantations. Consequently, in striking contrast to the emancipators' discursive construction of the slave worker as male, slave women were necessarily the principal targets of any effort to instill work discipline in free laborers.

The reality portrayed in the treadmill scene, therefore, not only contrasts sharply with the rhetoric of domestic reformation that pervaded classical liberal ideology and emancipation policy, it underscores one of the fundamental contradictions between the two. The plantations were dependent not simply on proletarian labor but on a female proletariat. The bourgeois domestic scene that Special Magistrate Chamberlaine described, with the dutiful wife preparing supper as the male head of the household made his way home, was at odds with that reality—and, indeed, at odds as well with the state's efforts to achieve a more coercive reformation in the workhouses. Jamaican freedpeople, like those in many other former slave societies, attempted to work a very different social transformation, building on alternative conceptions of gender roles and identities, of family and community.[62] In their view, what lay beyond slavery was a world different not only from bondage but also from the "freedom" sketched in liberal democratic ideologies. Their eventual fate was thus a double tragedy: not only was that alternative worldview denied the political and social space necessary for its realization, but this failure provided the opening for a vicious racism that compromised the efforts of future generations as well.

Rebecca J. Scott

Fault Lines, Color Lines, and Party Lines

Race, Labor, and Collective Action
in Louisiana and Cuba, 1862–1912

The debate over the meaning and implications of emancipation repeatedly brought into question the relationship between race and citizenship and profoundly affected liberal and republican ideology within the Atlantic world.[1] These ideological battles had their on-the-ground counterparts in daily struggles over the character of work and the exercise of political voice. At times such struggles were individual or familial, at times community wide. Some were defined by what were seen as racial groupings; others crossed or redefined prior racial lines. Through their initiatives former slaves and other rural dwellers sought to construct their own versions of the meaning of work and citizenship. At a minimum, they attempted to defend themselves against the imposition of renewed constraints on their freedom.

To the end of the nineteenth century and beyond, sugar plantation workers and their descendants were particularly conspicuous in such conflicts. The

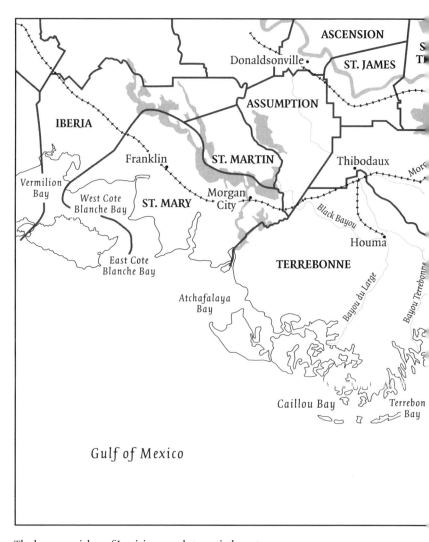

The bayou parishes of Louisiana, early twentieth century

smallholding peasants who rebelled at Morant Bay in Jamaica in 1865 had thwarted planters' attempts to retain former slaves on sugar estates, and they paid a high price. Former slaves in Louisiana who did remain on plantations defied their employers in individual and collective actions. The strike of 1887 mobilized thousands of Louisiana cane workers in a remarkable post-Reconstruction challenge to the landed elite. Cubans of African descent who had grown up within the world of cane played a major role in the cross-racial alliance that underlay Cuba's War for Independence in 1895–98. A comparative analysis of postemancipation sugar regions offers an opportunity to explore the complicated links between the organization of production and the possi-

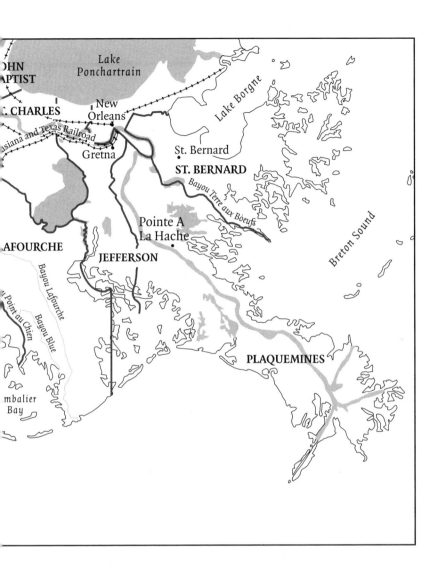

bilities for collective action. It also highlights the very different constructions of race in postemancipation societies, as well as the effect of race as idea and symbol on the practice of politics.

In this essay, the focus is narrowed to Louisiana and Cuba. Both regions saw the end of slavery in the second half of the nineteenth century; both produced sugar for the North American market; both drew on capital from the northern United States and experimented with advanced technology. Each held a large wage labor force dedicated for much of the year to the planting, weeding, harvesting, and processing of cane. Yet their histories in the twentieth century diverged radically. Louisiana sugar workers ended up in a

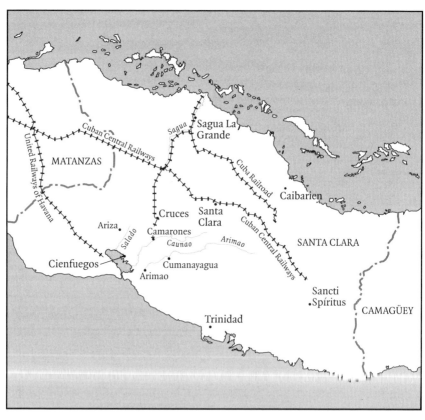

The province of Santa Clara (Las Villas), Cuba, early twentieth century

racially segregated wage labor force that was, after a very long struggle, nearly silenced in the political realm. Cuban sugar workers, despite opposition, went on to become a pivotal group in their nation's history, frequently acting as a mobilized workforce under multiracial leadership.

Within these divergent histories, however, there were in each region dramatic instances of both cross-racial collaboration and racist repression. The meaning of race in public life was bitterly contested both in the elite domain, in which questions of inclusion and exclusion were debated, and in daily life, in which the possibilities of different alliances were tested. Workers categorized as white and black participated in the massive strike of 1887 in Louisiana, but those killed in the massacre that repressed it were all described as black. The Cuban insurgent army of 1895–98 represented perhaps the most democratic interracial fighting force to emerge from a slave society in the Americas, but fourteen years after the end of the war its successor in the

Cuban Republic carried out a murderous assault on black men accused of supporting an "independent party of color."

The purpose of this essay is not to establish a categorical contrast between Louisiana and Cuba in terms of racism and antiracism, or silence and activism, but rather to trace shifting alliances and divisions. There are points of intersection and divergence between patterns of livelihood and resistance in the cane fields of central Cuba and in the bayou country of Louisiana, and a comparative approach can raise new questions and highlight relationships that a national or regional narrative might otherwise obscure.[2] The eventual goal is to explain how certain patterns of production emerged in the aftermath of slavery, how they opened up or constrained the possibilities for collective action, and how those collective actions in turn shaped class relations into the twentieth century.

Louisiana

Slavery ended in southern Louisiana not by law or decree but in multiple wartime scenes of military, bureaucratic, and individual confusion. The sugar parishes came under federal authority following the fall of the Confederate city of New Orleans in the spring of 1862, as Union forces moved up the Mississippi River and down its bayous. Federal authority, however, was ambivalent and divided, both on the question of freedom for those who were enslaved and on the question of the appropriate mix of staple and subsistence agriculture. Slaves themselves pushed into the openings created by these divisions, refusing to work for their former masters, seeking space in which to plant food crops, and, in some instances, enlisting in the Union army to accelerate the general move toward freedom.[3] John J. Moore, a former slave from the parish of St. Mary, described his own trajectory succinctly: "I got my freedom before the surrender by running away. The Union soldiers told me all the time that I was entitled to my freedom, and I had it already. All that I had to do was take my musket to secure it."[4]

The declaration by General Nathaniel P. Banks in January 1864 that laws and provisions of the state constitution pertaining to slavery were "inoperative and void" finally made it clear that there would be no going backward. But the government-supervised labor systems left it unclear just how much forward movement there would be, and in what direction. The Union occupiers tended to derive their regulations from a combination of ideological first principles and practical expediency, with an eye to what could actually be enforced. They did not generally consult the freedpeople on their views of the meaning of freedom. Contention erupted not only over the level and form of payment of wages, but also over access to provision grounds, permissible garden crops, physical mobility, Saturday work, and, perhaps most bitterly, the character and behavior of overseers.[5]

A classic postemancipation struggle quickly emerged: planters and agents of the state sought to enforce wage labor contracts for staple production; many families and a few allies outside the plantation sought to defend the priority of freedpeople's access to land for the production of subsistence and market crops, and their right not to be "driven" by overseers. As long as the war continued, ironically, the extreme vulnerability of both freedpeople and the Union occupiers left room for some compromise, and the presence of armed African American soldiers in the Union forces provided potential alliances for plantation workers. Though the federal government put a priority on the production of sugar, starvation would serve no one's interests; garden plots and even collectively cultivated plantations were often the only practical alternative. On several estates, "labor companies" leased and operated plantations as semiformal partnerships among the freedpeople.[6]

With the end of the war, however, the room for negotiation narrowed. Freedmen's Bureau agents placed a premium on formal, annual contracts. This attempt to control laborers for a full year reflected both the long-standing desire of planters to assure labor at harvest time and the preoccupation of bureau agents with the orderly situating of former slaves in a new productive structure.

Freedpeople often delayed signing contracts, hoping to extract better terms. Agents of the Freedmen's Bureau noted that the freedpeople were quick to distinguish between employers who settled fairly at the end of the season and those who did not. The assistant inspector of freedmen in the parish of Lafourche observed optimistically in early 1866 that "[t]he planters begin to see that they must give justice or they cannot secure labor." If such was the precondition for attracting workers, it is perhaps not surprising that in neighboring Terrebonne Parish the scarcity of laborers was "much complained of." An innovation was reported from the parish of St. Landry: "[M]ost all Overseers or managers of Plantations have been chosen from among the laborers." There the "best of feeling" was said to exist "between the planters and the laborers."[7] Elsewhere, the experiments in collective cultivation of estates by former slaves were dismantled as former owners returned or new ones arrived, and wage labor was imposed on those who had hoped to be able to rent or acquire land. In April 1866, for example, Orange Grove Plantation in Terrebonne Parish appeared in the records as leased for three years to "William James (colored)" and occupied by a group of freedmen working as partners. Three months later an inspection report from the Freedmen's Bureau gave the name of a new lessee and listed the residents as working for rations, quarters, clothing, fuel, and wages.[8]

As the possibility of shared cultivation receded, some freedpeople formed wage labor gangs under the direction of an individual worker. Thus in the papers of the DeClouet plantation, field hands were listed by name, but work was at times recorded in the form "Richard and his gang cleaned the big corn cribs."[9] On balance, the situation in the late 1860s was unstable and uncertain, with relief that peace had arrived, but a great deal of bitterness that it often did not bring justice.

During the first years of Reconstruction, the fragile alliance between freedpeople and the Louisiana Republican Party offered the possibility of some formal political voice for plantation workers, both as voters and as elected officials. John J. Moore, the former slave and plantation laborer quoted above, served as a supervisor at the polls in St. Mary Parish during the 1868 elections and later joined the parish Republican Party executive committee. Isaac Sutton, a field hand, also represented St. Mary Parish, and Thomas A. Cage, born a slave in Terrebonne Parish, was elected justice of the peace in the town of Houma in 1870.[10] It was precisely the exercise by freedpeople of mobility, authority, and voice, however, that planters and some of their white neighbors found nearly unbearable. A group of white men who came looking for the activist John J. Moore on the Cleveland plantation were blunt about their views. Moore recalled what they said to the man who was hiding him: "Now, Fred, there is but one way you niggers can live here with us, and that is to let politics die. Leave them alone; you cannot live with us, and live and work and vote against our interests. All that you get and all that you have comes from us and by us; and now if you do not let politics alone you will all get killed here."[11]

Alongside their efforts to recruit and discipline labor, planters acted to undermine the political alliance that protected freedpeople's initiatives. The DeClouet family in the parish of St. Martin, faced with workers who were vigorously exercising the right to go to town to pray and to vote, stepped up their own electoral involvement. Paul DeClouet was appointed deputy sheriff "to maintain peace & order" during the 1868 elections, which would determine the fate of the proposed state constitution guaranteeing political rights for freedpeople. He noted that in one of the boxes he was guarding the result was "22 votes in favor of the blacks," but he was elated to discover that the results in the parish as a whole were "425 votes majority for the whites (against the Constitution). . . . Hurray for us !!" [12] The constitutional referendum appeared in his eyes as a clear contest of white versus black, and the workers he employed were thus his obvious political enemies. For the moment, however, although DeClouet and his allies had won in the parish, they lost in the state. The statewide voting rolls showed 45,189 white and 84,527 black registrants in 1867, and the 1868 elections ratified a state constitution that formally "desegregated the schools, adopted the bill of rights, rejected a literacy test, and prohibited discrimination in public conveyances and places of public accommodation." The fundamental tenets of white supremacy had been repudiated.[13]

Unable to bend former slaves to their will at the ballot box or at hiring time, employers sought to supplement the diminished plantation workforce by recruiting workers from out of state. A growing seasonal movement of African American workers from Virginia, northern Louisiana, and the Carolinas provided a complement to the resident workforce. One can trace through De-Clouet's daybook, for example, his experiment in 1870 with hiring workers from Virginia.[14] In later years this seasonal movement would become steadier, reinforcing the pattern of a workforce composed of former slaves and their descendants, but broadening the range of origins of such workers.

In 1869 Joseph Pennington Tucker took over the management of Laurel Valley Plantation, located in Lafourche Parish outside of Thibodaux. In addition to employing freedpeople under annual contracts, Tucker signed up twenty-three Chinese workers for a year. The plantation changed hands again in the 1870s, and the new owner, Burch A. Wormald, modernized the milling equipment, bringing production up to its prewar levels. Wormald also diversified the labor force, such that by the 1880s the resident working families on Laurel Valley included not only former slaves and their descendants but some Acadians who had relocated to the sugar plantation from the sandy ridges in the swamplands called brulés, where they had lived as subsistence farmers and gatherers of Spanish moss.[15] Beginning in 1870, a few sugar planters also sought out Italian seasonal laborers, some of whom had come to New Orleans in conjunction with the fruit trade.[16] In the sugar parishes as a whole, however, the number of workers in the cane who counted themselves white remained very small.[17]

The Louisiana sugar industry was not in a strong financial position, and planters were unlikely to attract a significant portion of the flow of international immigrants, or to draw large numbers of white workers from other sectors into a field labor force so strongly characterized as black. Wages in sugar in Louisiana were high by southern standards, but not by national ones.[18] The production of sugar in the state had climbed back up from its wartime collapse, doubling between 1866 and 1869 and reaching 73,000 short tons by 1871. But the totals were still very modest compared to prewar levels, falling far short of the 1861 bumper crop of 264,000 short tons. Moreover, the expanding sugar industry in Cuba met a healthy fraction of U.S. demand, despite protective tariffs.[19]

In 1873 the national and worldwide financial crisis challenged even this modest recovery. In the face of low prices and scarce capital, some reformers suggested that the sugar regions should turn away from reliance on wage labor and look to smallholdings, subdividing the land into small leaseholds from which cane farmers would provide cane to a central mill for processing.[20] A few estates followed this path, though they generally offered the tenancies to white farmers, not black.[21] Most of the larger planters sought instead to compress labor costs and continue to work with gang labor.

Planters in St. Mary, St. James, and Terrebonne Parishes began to collaborate in the mid-1870s to try to cap or lower monthly rates of pay. One employer from St. James Parish candidly wrote to the *New Orleans Daily Picayune* that while wages the previous season had been $18 monthly plus rations, he and his neighbors were now paying $13 per month. "Please publish this, so that the change may be made in other districts, as, by being general, it may become permanent at least until better times." [22]

Sugar workers in Terrebonne Parish declined to accept this wage reduction by fiat. Several hundred laborers met in the Zion church outside the town of Houma in January 1874 to form an association, refusing to work for less than $20 a month and seeking to form subassociations that could collaboratively rent lands for them to work on their own. By January 16 the *Daily Picayune* reported that "the negroes have been marching around the parish, preventing the field hands from working." W. H. Keys and Alfred Kennedy, both African American elected officials, were singled out as inciters and supporters of the strike. Kennedy was said to have accompanied fifty men down the bayou to the Minor plantation. Planters were alarmed, spread rumors of murder and mayhem, called on the governor to send in the militia, and had the leaders arrested. Eventually an agreement was reached, but workers did not get the right to rent lands collectively.[23]

In trying to arrange to lease land, workers in Terrebonne were reiterating a demand that had been made unsuccessfully several times before.[24] The sugar workers of Terrebonne seem to have been adopting a strategy of seeking multiple sources of support: garden plots, leasehold land if possible, and reasonable terms of work when they did labor on plantations. In this respect they closely resembled their counterparts from the postemancipation sugar plantations of Jamaica, who often sought some mix of wage labor and independent production.[25] In the 1860s the editorialists of the *New Orleans Tribune*, representing certain sectors of the urban *gens de couleur*, had called for the subdivision of lands among the freedmen. Some delegates to the Louisiana Constitutional Convention of 1868 had proposed breaking up large estates by placing an upper limit on the size of tracts that could be bought at distress sales, as a means of facilitating the purchase of land by freedmen, but their initiatives were defeated.[26]

Freedpeople and their allies did not have sufficient power to force a land reform and had to concentrate their energy on trying to block wage cuts. The *New Orleans Price-Current* observed smugly in September 1874 that the field hands, "having been taught the necessity of thrift and economy, have really saved more from their two thirds, than they formerly did from full pay while the relations between them and their employers, have been more satisfactory than at any time since the war." Planters in St. Mary Parish attempted wage reductions the following year, and wages of $13 a month were common during 1875 and 1876.[27] Nevertheless, competition among employers, combined with resistance by workers, tended to undermine planter-imposed wage caps, and wages recovered slightly in 1877.[28]

Challenges on the estates were matched by contests for power within the region's parishes, and each election brought new struggles over principles and patronage. As conflicts raged at the state and parish levels, "white-line" Democrats and their supporters increasingly resorted to violence against Republican officeholders and their African American allies.[29] After facing attacks from white vigilante groups of various kinds, the state Republican leadership had turned in 1870 to the formation of a state militia composed of black volunteers, some Irish immigrants, and a certain number of white former Confederate soldiers willing to enlist under General James Longstreet, now a Republican and a proponent of regional reconciliation.[30] In 1873 General Longstreet sought to reinforce existing black and white militia and police units in New Orleans with additional white units, a move that was met with scorn and fury in the Democratic and white supremacist press. Longstreet held firm, however, and built the militia to some 3,000 troops.[31]

As the conflict over the state militia grew, a segment of the rural and urban elite moved to extend the vigilante formations known as White Leagues across the state. Picking up steam through 1873 and 1874, the most aggressive proponents of a white-line strategy anathematized not only Republicans but also the "New Departure" Democrats, Unificationists, and assorted reformers who envisioned a somewhat more pluralistic model of elite rule. The organizers of the leagues heaped abuse on white men who would not endorse the "white line." In March 1874 the *New Orleans Bulletin* was founded to extend and escalate the most openly racist formulation of the white supremacist creed.[32]

The exercise of political voice by African Americans was now imperiled both by the immediate threat to state and local Republican rule and by the resurgence of vigilante violence. The boldest and most dangerous step for black activists and other Republicans to take was to constitute local militias in the rural parishes as on-the-ground counterweights to the White League. In the bayou parishes of Lafourche and Terrebonne, more than a hundred men came forward during the spring and summer of 1874 to do just that. Benjamin Lewis, who taught at the Nichols School in Terrebonne Parish, offered his services and was named captain of Company C of the Sixth Regiment Infantry. In July, Benjamin Peney from Houma was mustered in to lead Company D. Captain Lewis was assisted by First Lieutenant Anatole Panale and Second Lieutenant William Robinson of Thibodaux, and Captain Peney by First Lieutenant James Madison and Second Lieutenant Scott Brown. Each unit had additional noncommissioned officers and some fifty or sixty privates.[33]

Among white Democrats in Lafourche Parish, this force was characterized as a "negro militia" and was regarded as an outrage. Its commanding officer, Benjamin Lewis, was described as "of mixed negro and Indian blood, the Indian in him clearly predominating," and he was said to be married to a "bright mulatress" named Madeline. The former chairman of the Democratic Party in Lafourche Parish, H. N. Michlet, viewed the militia as "warriors" able to rally the support of their wives and sisters, whom he described as "colored Amazons." He reported that this company of "negro Militia armed with state arms" had been drilling every Saturday evening on the commons in the town of Thibodaux. The militia seems to have served as a countervailing force to the civil authorities in matters of day-to-day administration of justice. One local official fumed sarcastically, "The mere arrest by a civil officer of a drunken negro in the town of Thibodaux is the tocsin that sounds to arms and summons these Valiant warriors to bold heroic deeds to wit the rescue from the officer of his prisoner and of the provoking of the turbulent mob to the very verge of riot, bloodshed and arson."[34]

This martial mobilization was closely linked to electoral politics. The local militia functioned as a means of self-defense for African American voters and as a player in the tumultuous struggles—both metaphorical and physical— for control of the ballot box. For two years this militia discomfited the local constabulary and defended Republican interests at the polls. After the decisive elections of 1876, as Democratic governor Francis T. Nicholls gained control of the state and local Democrats sought to determine events in each parish as well, an order was issued for Company C to disband. But the circumstances of the militia's disbanding were disputed and irregular, and their weapons apparently were never turned in. Angry Democrats claimed that the militia members, with their guns, scattered across the state.[35] Census records suggest, however, that Captain Benjamin Lewis himself did not go far. In 1880 he was living in the neighboring First Ward of Terrebonne Parish, and he still listed his occupation as schoolteacher.[36]

Although 1876–77 marked the dramatic formal end to Reconstruction, and the end of the bayou country militia led by Captain Benjamin Lewis, some of these streams of activism nonetheless continued through narrowed channels. The earlier militia experience had reverberated beyond the towns of Thibodaux and Houma, out into the plantations. In a bitter denunciation of what was remembered as "Benjamin's militia," a Democratic leader recalled that "[t]he Majority of the armed men [lived] in all directions out in the country."[37] This link between town and country remained strong, and African American activists continued to move back and forth between the plantations and the parish seat over the next decade. Junius Bailey, for example, too young to have served in the militia, was a member of the black Masonic lodge in Thibodaux in the 1880s and also served as schoolteacher on Laurel Valley Plantation several miles outside of town. Apparently quite formal and respectful in his demeanor, he would become a key figure in the local Knights of Labor, seeking to provide collective representation for rural laborers.[38]

With Democrats back in control of power in most of the towns after 1877, the next wave of challenges built on African American numerical strength in the countryside. In 1880 an estimated 500 black workers went on strike for higher wages in St. Charles Parish, moving in a body from estate to estate to stop work. The group must have been an imposing one, with some workers on horseback and many armed with sticks. Workers in St. John the Baptist Parish came out next. One striker was quoted as believing that "the colored people are a nation and must stand together." The strikers gave political form to that "nation" by drafting a constitution to which strikers should adhere. (Unity was by no means automatic, however, and strikers were reported to be whipping fellow freedmen who blocked their action.) An 1881 strike in St. Bernard Parish was reported to include both black and white workers, who had joined forces to press for wage increases.[39]

In 1886 the Knights of Labor began organizing black and white locals among railway workers in Louisiana, opening the way for a more formal cross-racial alliance. The Knights' "anti-monopolist" platform rapidly gained adherents, and candidates affiliated with the order won elections in the town of Morgan City, where the railroad monopoly made an obvious target. The Knights soon moved out into the sugar regions, organizing around the themes of worker unity, cooperativism, and opposition to monopolies. The task of organizing among black and white sugar workers highlighted the strategic value of the Knights' commitment to interracial solidarity, while raising the question of just how far that commitment extended.[40]

Schreiver Local Assembly was organized in Terrebonne Parish in August 1886 with a nucleus of black workers and then transformed itself into the region's first integrated local. The local of Little Caillou similarly had thirty-two charter members categorized as black in July 1887, but eighty members, black and white, male and female, by October. (Given the complexity of racial categories in the lower bayou country around Little Caillou, it is likely that some of these individuals might have been characterized elsewhere as mulatto, or described by one or another local term designating mixed ancestry.) Of the local assemblies enumerated in Terrebonne, Lafourche, and St. Mary Parishes, the one in Thibodaux (Lafourche) was said to include black plantation hands, as did Local 4738 in Franklin (St. Mary). Local 10336 in Houma (Terrebonne) was distinctive in containing plantation hands, mechanics, and washerwomen and was characterized in Knights of Labor records as a black local.[41]

The leaders of the local assemblies in the sugar region included black, mulatto, and white laborers, farmers, and artisans. Junius Bailey, the schoolteacher, also stepped in to draft petitions and formulate demands. Most of the leaders were apparently literate, and their work experiences often reached beyond the plantations, creating important linkages to small farmers, who could provide food during strikes, and to nearby towns, which could provide refuge in case of evictions.[42]

Within and between these local assemblies, sugar workers and their allies had a concrete experience of collaboration across the color line. One need not exaggerate the egalitarianism of the Knights of Labor in order to recognize the importance of an ideology of producer solidarity in changing the way in which individuals were "marked" in each others' eyes.[43] A brief experience of cooperation might well fail to overcome the weight of quotidian racism, but it posed a challenge to the efforts of planters, the Democratic Party, and paramilitary white supremacist organizations to define a single, racialized fault line in Louisiana society.

A view of Thibodaux, Louisiana, from across Bayou Lafourche. Watercolor by Alfred Waud, 1866. (Courtesy of Historic New Orleans Collection)

The impression of a cross-racial movement is somewhat less clear, however, when one turns to the local descriptions of events, where the coding of sugar workers as "colored" seems to have remained strong. The court records housed in the former jail in the parish of Lafourche show that as early as 19 January 1887, seventeen men described as "colored" were apparently trying to halt work on Mary Plantation. Jordan Brannon, Briscoe Wheeler, Johnny Phillips, William Pearson, Peter Young, and James Lagarde were charged with unlawful disturbance and riotous assembly. In that same month, Clay Williams, Adam Elles, and Israel Lucust were charged with trespassing on Upper Ten Plantation, while Numa Gautreaux was charged with trespass on the plantation of Delphin Babin. In the case of Adam Elles, the charge was more specific: he was said to have prevented one Nelson Christian from working on the plantation.[44]

The owner of Mary Plantation, Richard Foret, testified that on 19 January 1887 he had come up from his estate to the town of Raceland to take "the cars" to Thibodaux to do some business. "On my way I met a crowd of colored men going down the bayou on the levee. . . . When I got to the depot Mr Sevin told me the crowd were going down to stop my hands from working . . . as a mat-

ter of fact my hands stopped working at 12 M that day." The clerk from Raceland whom Foret sent down to warn the overseer of the impending arrival of
"strikers" reported that "I told the boys on Mary Plantation to keep on working but they said no the men who had been there had said if they didn't stop
they would come back and run them out of the field." A resident of Mary Plantation, Lewis Anderson, recalled that the crowd of strikers had specified that
they would not work for sixty cents a day, and that "the Foret hands agreed
at once to stop. They didn't make any threats they didn't have time to make
any threats because the others were willing to stop." The testimony of Wiley
Jackson in defense of Peter Young conveys something of the atmosphere on
the levee at Raceland that morning, as folks milled around the waterfront and
waited to see what would happen: "All I know when the crowd went down
Peter Young was on the levee and when they came back Peter Young was there
yet. He didn't go down. I stayed around there, on the levee at the store, sometimes at the depot and down at the little boat." [45]

One has a sense here of the levee as the site of a tense political promenade
with participants, spectators, surrogates, and bystanders involved in a debate
on the question of whether a man or a woman should work in the fields for

sixty cents a day. (Indeed, even that sixty cents sometimes came in the form of a credit slip at the company store.)[46] Although individual workers may have had prior contact with Knights of Labor organizers, their strike actions were not at this point formally attributed to the Knights.

By late October 1887 the sense of improvisation was gone. District Assembly 194 of the Knights of Labor, located in Morgan City, made the formal call for a strike in the major sugar parishes. When planters refused negotiation, the assembly called together workers from the surrounding sugar parishes and formulated a series of demands. These included a daily wage of $1.25 without board or $1 with board, plus sixty cents for nighttime "watch," if required; an end to payments in scrip; and more regular payment of wages due. Leaders appear to have been uncertain as to whether a strike would be necessary. They declared themselves willing to compromise and set a deadline of 29 October for planters in Lafourche, Terrebonne, St. Mary, Iberia, and St. Martin Parishes to respond to their demands. In Lafourche Parish, Junius Bailey, now president of the joint executive board of the Knights of Labor, took a teacherly (or perhaps lawyerly) tone in his communication: "[S]hould this demand be considered exorbitant by the sugar planters, . . . we ask them to submit such information with reason therewith to this board not later than Sunday, Oct. 29 inst. or appoint a special committee to confer with this board on said date."[47]

Planters had no intention of doing any such thing. The threat of a strike at the moment of harvest brought Democratic and Republican members of the elite together, and they formulated a counterplan, committing themselves to ignoring the demands, blacklisting fired workers, and evicting strikers from their plantations. Employers in Lafourche Parish invoked the contractual obligations of the workers and the "depressed condition of the sugar industry" to justify their opposition, referring to the Knights of Labor District Assembly representatives as "a committee of people claiming to represent a secret organization." They asked the sheriff to request that the governor send in the militia. A similar meeting in St. Mary Parish declared that "after the planters have employed laborers during the whole cultivation of the crop, it is flagrantly unjust and illegal to demand extortionate wages to harvest the same."[48]

When the 29 October deadline passed without satisfactory concessions, workers halted labor on plantations in the region. On 1 November 1887 militia forces under Brigadier General William Pierce took the train to the town of Thibodaux with the aim of "restoring peace in the sugar districts from Berwick's Bay to New Orleans, then seriously threatened by the belligerent attitude of strikers."[49] The press estimated the number of participants in the strike at around 10,000, and some accounts specified that around 9,000 of them were "colored"—the other 1,000, by implication, being white.[50] Although the hostile *Daily Picayune* tended to portray the strikers as black, even it denounced "white mischief-makers" for their role in the events.[51] From early in the strike, however, class and racial divisions reappeared within the Knights of Labor, whose members included some professionals and shopkeepers as well as wage workers. Local 6295 in St. Mary Parish and white Local 10499 voted to disregard the strike call.[52]

In the first days of November, planters attempted to oblige strikers to vacate their plantation cabins. At the same time, the strikers attempted to block the importation of strikebreakers, apparently firing birdshot at those who tried to operate mills, and gathering to challenge those who arrived by train. General Pierce was distressed to find "a very large body of negroes lounging around the depot" at Schreiver. In the town of Thibodaux, a large crowd of strikers, described as "black, white, and curious," watched as the militia disembarked.[53] Although the presence of the militia could be used to back up arrests and evictions, it did not prevent symbolic challenges: General Pierce reported that when troops arrived on one plantation, "the negroes hooted and used violent language, the women waving their skirts on poles, and jeering."[54]

Planters were by now divided and uneasy. Some small-scale growers settled quickly; others brought in strikebreakers. The nephew of one planter in Terrebonne recalled of his uncle:

> He gave in to the demands, not because he wished to, but because he had no other option. He would have lost the crop and everything else, including the place, if he had not done so.
>
> Immediately all the neighboring planters denounced him as "disloyal to his class," declaring he should be willing to lose everything in defense of his class interests. But he could not see it.[55]

Similarly, planters in lower Lafourche Parish, where most estates were relatively small, quickly settled with the strikers. The plantation workforce of lower Lafourche included black, white, and mulatto workers, some of whom were resident on plantations, while others occupied small farms in the area.[56] Many of the white field workers who followed the Knights of Labor were apparently located in this zone.[57]

In St. Mary Parish, events unfolded very quickly. Evicted strikers took refuge in Pattersonville, where they found themselves isolated from the union leadership in Morgan City because of the military control of the railroads.[58] A sheriff's posse, including both planters and local residents, was assembled and moved to confront a crowd of "negro strikers." Accounts of the events varied widely, but at least four strikers were killed, and possibly as many as twenty.[59]

A local planter, Donelson Caffery, took a leading role in the repression and obtained support from some members of the Knights of Labor who had opposed the strike from the beginning.[60] Caffery wrote bluntly to his son on 11 November about conditions in St. Mary: "The strike is effectually squelched. It was necessary to apply a strong remedy—and it has been done. The negroes are quiet and have with few exceptions gone to work."[61] The striking workers were thus relegated to the category "negroes," their demands treated as indiscipline requiring a "strong remedy." The recruitment of non-elite whites to the task of repression, moreover, helped to restore the racial dichotomy threatened by the heterogeneous alliances within the Knights of Labor.

Planters in upper Lafourche, which held the largest and most technologically advanced plantations, continued to carry out large-scale evictions, reconfiguring the stage on which struggles would be carried out. Families were evicted from their cabins and their goods piled high on the levee, outside the plantation's boundary.[62] During November the local press reported on the exodus from the plantations to the town of Thibodaux: "Every vacant room in town tonight is filled with families of penniless and ragged negroes. All day long a long stream of black humanity poured in, . . . bringing all their earthly possessions, which never amounted to more than a frontyard full of babies, dogs, and ragged bedclothing."[63]

As in the days of 1874, when Benjamin Lewis led drills on the town commons, black men and women came to Thibodaux from the surrounding countryside. This time, however, they came as evicted strikers, not as supporters of a bold "negro militia" marching on the courthouse lawn. This time a Gatling gun stood on the steps of the courthouse, deployed by the all-white militia under the command of a brigadier general from New Orleans.

With workers' cabins now emptied, there was room for replacement laborers, and mills could begin to grind again. On 20 November General Pierce declared that the major estates were back at work and the militia were no longer needed. Calling on planters to take responsibility for the defense of their own plantations, he withdrew all but one of his units, a crew from Shreveport that had been dismissed but had not yet headed home. Pierce had earlier noted that the Shreveport militia were not in uniform, and that their officer had had difficulty "preventing a collision between his men and the strikers."[64] It was an exceptionally volatile unit to leave behind.

By 21 November the town of Thibodaux was a powder keg. Mary Pugh, the daughter of a planter, wrote to her son that on her way home from church she met "negro men singly or two or three together with guns on their shoulders going down town & negro women on each side telling them to 'fight-yes-fight we'll be there' (you know what big mouths these Thib. negro women have. I wish they all had been shot-off) they are at the bottom of more than half the devilment."[65]

Despite the exhortations to fight the good fight, striking workers found themselves out on a very fragile limb. Displaced from the plantations to the town, they were lodged by kin and sympathizers but remained largely devoid of protection. Unity within the Knights of Labor had seemed to promise some way to resist wage cuts and assert control over the rhythm of work, but the Knights as an organization could do little to back them up now. The planters had arrayed a formidable alliance against them: the militia had provided the state power necessary to carry out evictions; some 300 white residents had organized to close access to and from the town; and Mary Pugh's own sons were among those whites busily molding bullets in preparation for a coming battle.[66]

The struggle over wages on the plantations had been reinterpreted by planters as a racial struggle, enabling them to draw white townspeople into an alliance by invoking the possibility of violence from the evicted strikers. Thus the resumption of work on estates did not settle the question; some further "remedy" was awaited. Mary Pugh wrote in retrospect: "I had seen for three weeks it had to come or else white people could live in this country no longer."[67]

For strikers and their families, boxed into the back streets of Thibodaux, the town was rapidly becoming a trap rather than a rallying place. Early in the morning of 22 November someone—perhaps a striker trying to leave town, perhaps a member of the Peace and Order Committee confused as to who was who, perhaps one of the unruly Shreveport militia—fired a gun and hit one of the pickets blocking exits from the town. The shot wounded two of the white men on duty. Other guards "ran to their assistance and this opened the *Ball*." Mary Pugh's description continued, "[T]hey began then hunting up the [strike] leaders and every one that was found or any suspicious character was shot. Before Allen got back the rifles on St. Charles Street sounded like a battle." Pugh witnessed the capture of one hidden striker:

[T]hey brought them by our side gate. I thought [they] were taking them to jail instead they walked with one over to the lumber yard where they told him to "run for his life" [and] gave the order to fire. All raised their rifles and shot him dead. This was the worst sight I saw but I tell you we have had a horrible three days & Wednesday excelled any thing I ever saw even during the war. I am sick with the horror of it. but I know it had to be else we would all have been murdered before a great while. I think this will settle the question of who is to rule the nigger or the white man? for the next 50 years but it has been *well done* & I hope all trouble is ended. The niggers are as humble as pie today. Very different from last week.[68]

Shooting appears to have gone on for hours. There is no way to estimate accurately the number of deaths. Officially, some eight or nine people were killed; later scholars estimate that at least thirty black men and women were killed, and hundreds injured.[69] Covington Hall, whose uncle lived nearby, recalled that "[n]ewly made graves were reported found in the woods around Thibodaux for weeks afterward," and the body of a dead man appeared in the yard of his uncle's place two miles south of Thibodaux.[70]

Told in this way, with the narrative clarity of hindsight, the story may seem to reflect yet another instance of the relentless rise of white supremacy in the postwar South. And when we realize that unions did not organize again in the cane fields of southern Louisiana until the 1950s, class dominance and racial dominance appear to converge quite precisely. But one can also shift the perspective by a quarter turn and see the violence and white vituperation in a somewhat different light. The drama in the Louisiana sugar regions did not simply draw upon a conflict of interests between those denominated black and those denominated white. The physical and rhetorical violence of planters and their allies also helped to *define* groups in this way, radically simplifying complex social and racial categories.

To create a binary world of black and white required multiple elisions. First, the presence among the strikers of laborers who counted themselves white needed to be downplayed. Second, the complex system of color categorization prevalent in the bayou country had to be compressed into a binary division. Finally, the organizations that represented the strikers, however respectful and educated their representatives, had to be redescribed as "wolves" preying on credulous workers who would be better off without them.

The process of "marking" took many forms, but it was most conspicuous when planters and Democratic politicians responded to the exercise of voice by subordinate groups in the public sphere.[71] In the 1870s, for example, Benjamin Lewis had already been characterized as one of a dangerous group of "black banditti," though he was a respected schoolteacher and elsewhere had been described as having predominantly Indian ancestry. And the leader of the Knights of Labor in Terrebonne Parish, Jim Brown, was seen as simply another "colored" striker, though he was later recalled as a "griffe" of mixed ancestry. When one finds in the 1880 manuscript census records for Lafourche Parish an entry in which the husband is listed as a white sharecropper and the wife as mulatto, one wonders how each of them coped with the growing racialization of public life, and with the repeated calls by white supremacists for a clear division of black from white.[72]

In 1869 J. B. Esnard, a Union veteran from Louisiana who represented St. Mary Parish in the 1868 constitutional convention, had been interrogated in a congressional hearing:

Question: Are you colored?
Answer: I cannot answer that; I do not know exactly whether I am or not.
Question: Do you rank and acknowledge yourself as a colored man?
Answer: I do.
Question: But if you have any colored blood you don't know it?
Answer: No, sir.
Question: It is charged and you don't deny it?
Answer: Yes, sir.[73]

Both Esnard and his persistent interlocutor seem to have realized that affiliations were a matter both of ascription and of choice. When this dialogue took place, Anglophone outsiders were still puzzled by the complexity of racial categories in Louisiana. By the late 1870s and 1880s, however, elite Louisianans of both French and English ancestry who counted themselves white demonstrated that they were bound and determined to suppress that complexity in the political sphere, even if they could not altogether ignore it in the social sphere.

Governor McEnery declared in 1887 that "God Almighty has himself drawn the color line."[74] But the compression of socioracial categories and the eliding of class identity and racial identity in the association of "black" with "strikers" was very much the work of men and women. The repression that occurred in Thibodaux and Pattersonville was more than simply racist violence or class war. It was a selective combination of the two, synthesized in such a way as to assist in the construction of whiteness as privileged and blackness as dangerous. It thus mirrored the white-line political strategy that had triumphed a decade earlier in the world of formal politics.

Covington Hall observed in passing that "during the whole period only one white man, a picket in Thibodaux, was reported as seriously wounded. All dead were colored and unionmen, though many whites were active members of the Knights."[75] The reality of a workforce containing individuals categorized as black, Indian, mulatto, *griffe*, and white, comprising laborers, tenants, "petits habitants," and mechanics, was redefined in the theater of repression as white order versus black disorder.

This construction of a binary and highly politicized color line, of course, was not simply a discursive act or a rhetorical ploy. The refusal to rent sugar lands to former slaves, the reconstruction of gang labor, and the recruitment of African American seasonal workers from Virginia and the Carolinas all combined to create a reality in which wage work in the cane was strongly associated with blackness. The process of building the color line might be seen as a reciprocal one, in which racial ideology shaped class relations and class relations in turn shaped the construction of race and politics.

These white supremacist strategies, with their concomitant creation of stark dichotomies, continued to be played out on individual sugar plantations and in towns through the 1890s, as formal electoral disfranchisement progressed and the remaining African American officeholders were displaced. In Plaquemines Parish, for example, a small Italian workforce had been recruited to the estates. In an early-twentieth-century memoir, Florence Dymond recalled events in 1891 on her father's sugar plantation: "[F]ather and the other Democrats in the Parish of Plaquemine made up their minds that it was time to wipe out the remnants of the carpetbag regime, which still existed there, and to elect a full, white democratic ticket the following year. At that time the parish representative to the legislature was as black as the ace of spades, the sheriff of the parish was a negro, as was the clerk of the court. The judge was white, but a Republican." Mr. Dymond posted guards around the polling places, and a group of armed men, accompanied by Italian workers from the estate, took the ballot boxes to the parish Democratic Committee for counting.[76]

Vote suppression was just one component of a far-reaching denial of citizenship. To both planters and Democratic politicians, workers defined as white were citizens eligible for militia duty and neighbors to be recruited into a sheriff's posse. Workers defined as black, by contrast, were perceived as a threat to social order if they left their place of work and, if armed, were assumed to be potential aggressors. The white-line strategy was more than an electoral maneuver; it was also designed to thwart future mobilization.

Elsewhere in Louisiana, some challenges to the color line persisted. Populists and timber workers in the northern part of the state and dockworkers in New Orleans provided continuing glimpses of the possibilities of cross-racial alliance.[77] But within the sugar regions, the battle was largely over. Workers in the cane, resident or migrant, might still carry out fleeting localized strikes to try to push up wages for a given harvest, taking advantage of the vulnerability of planters as frost approached. But there would be no further organization along the lines of the Knights of Labor, and there could be no political expression of power comparable to Benjamin Lewis's militia.

The structuring of the labor force, and the virtual destruction of the Republican Party in the countryside, further reduced the moments and venues in which workers from different groups would find themselves side by side. Moreover, wage levels also differed by color within the state: daily wages for white workers in 1898 were estimated at eighty-four cents; for "colored" workers they were seventy-three cents.[78] In the sugar sector, wage labor was the norm, and the tenancies that were available generally went to white farmers. On rare occasions they might go to a family denominated mulatto, and on rarer occasions still, to a black family who had accumulated capital, credit, and the confidence of a landowner. But by 1900, in the entire state, only 906 farms whose principal product was sugar were cultivated by "colored" farmers as owners, renters, or share tenants.[79]

Writing to a Chicago newspaper in 1919, after race riots there had been reported in the press, a leading planter of Lafourche Parish provided a succinct summary of his intentions: "Send your negroes back to us, we can work them, we know their ways and they know our ways. We have no prejudice against them as negro laborers and value them as such."[80]

In this blunt appeal one hears the voice of employers who sought to have the last word on the meaning of "free labor," and for whom the absence of prejudice meant only a willingness to employ. Former slaves and their descendants refused this distillation of their existence into the category "negro laborers," but there remained very few public spaces in the bayou country in which they could make their challenges felt.[81]

Cuba

In Cuba, as in Louisiana, a nationwide war accelerated the destruction of slavery. By the time of final emancipation, questions of race and citizenship shared center stage with questions of land and labor. From 1868 on, Cuban rebels had challenged Spanish domination—and in the process forced the issue of emancipation onto the agenda. In response, the Spanish parliament struggled to design an "orderly" transition to free labor even as it worked to suppress the rebellion. The processes of insurgent recruitment provided further openings for slave resistance, thus forcing emancipation forward by undermining the social order on which slavery was based. Whatever the divisions and ambivalences within the anticolonialist movement on questions of race and slavery, that movement provided the venue for multiple experiences of contact and collaboration between those who might be denominated white, black, mulatto, Chinese, mestizo, trigueño, or any of Cuba's complex and overlapping sociracial descriptors.[82]

In the face of these challenges, Spanish policymakers improvised and compromised on the organization of labor, while attempting to manipulate the issue of race through invocations of the danger of "race war." Like later white supremacists in Louisiana, colonial officials in Cuba tried to modify reality to substantiate this discourse, at times selectively arresting Afro-Cuban conspirators and allowing white Cubans to go free in order to reinforce an image of the conflict as "racial." Anticolonial agitation was portrayed by the Spanish authorities as evidence of the danger that the island could become "another Haiti." On the other side, white nationalist leaders could point to the Cuban separatist movement as the pioneer in abolition and demand political loyalty, deference, and "gratitude" from Afro-Cubans.[83]

To observe simply that Spanish and Cuban elites were manipulative and reformers opportunistic will not get us very far, however. The unfolding of events on the ground depended also on the precise intertwining of race and labor in the production process, and on the dynamics of specific kinds of collective action. It is thus at the level of particular events in specific locales that the situation of former slaves in Cuba is most usefully juxtaposed with that of their counterparts in Louisiana.

To make the comparison with southern Louisiana feasible, one can move from the national level—where Cuba loomed as the world's largest producer of cane sugar, exporting three to four times as much as Louisiana's total crop —down to a specific sugar region. Because of its importance to sugar production and to national politics, the central province of Santa Clara (Las Villas) provides an excellent case study. Within the province were found the old "valley of the sugar mills" of Trinidad, in decline by the latter part of the nineteenth century; the eastern frontier areas of Sancti-Spíritus, in transition between cattle and sugar; the northern port region of Caibarién, with much shipping and tobacco as well as sugar; and the burgeoning sugar zones of Sagua la Grande and Cienfuegos. Over 72,000 slaves lived in Santa Clara province in 1862, more than 44,000 of them on sugar estates. The majority of the province's sugar mills were steam powered, and their combined output was second only to that of the province of Matanzas.[84]

A large nonslaveholding class of rural dwellers of all racial denominations worked as small-scale farmers, subsistence cultivators, and part-time wage laborers, and central Cuba had for years seen considerable cross-racial interaction in daily life and in marketplaces. Explicit political collaboration became particularly visible as nationalist agitation accelerated. Cuba's first major anticolonial conflict had begun in 1868 as an elite separatist conspiracy, but it quickly became more radical and staked out an explicitly abolitionist position. By the 1870s the insurgent forces, though riven by divisions, had incorporated significant numbers of people of color, including slaves. Spain responded with the Moret Law, declaring children born after 1868, and adult slaves reaching the age of sixty, to be *libertos*, or freedpeople. But this partial measure did not eliminate the insurgency's potential appeal to people of color.

In Santa Clara the presence of "enemies" in the hills contributed to the undermining of control on the plantations. On 7 November 1877 the administrator of the Santa Rosalía estate in Cienfuegos reported that two armed men, one white and one black, had suddenly appeared where the work gang of the neighboring Soledad estate was laboring, asked some questions, and told the gang that they did not need to work there any longer. The two men then moved off, firing a shot as they departed. Witnesses could not identify the white man, but the black man was said to be named Luís, a resident of Santa Rosalía, where he worked as a *montero* (on horseback), keeping track of cattle. The administrator thought he remembered that Luís had been arrested earlier for having gone to buy goods for the enemy and for helping them to steal cattle. He urged the estate's owner, Manuel Blanco, to take steps to prevent Luís from "going around on his own account" and warned that Luís could cause real trouble some day. The administrator suspected that the white man was a neighbor and wanted to take steps against him as well.[85]

The boundary between slave plantations and neighboring farms was porous, and some Afro-Cubans in the plantation workforce exercised considerable freedom of movement. During the late 1870s the administrator of Santa Rosalía complained of slaves who had fled the plantation but had the audacity to return to their huts to sleep. Runaways were also suspected of providing cattle from the estate to the enemy. With the new possibility of active collaboration with insurgents, familiar slave grievances—over food and punishment, for example—took on greater significance. The net effect for the estates in the region was clearly disconcerting.[86]

Owners and administrators had little choice but to adapt to these forms of disruption, though they periodically turned to the forces of order for assistance. Edwin Atkins, later owner of the Soledad estate, recalled that a lieutenant of the Civil Guard had been called in to investigate complaints of cattle stealing. "This lieutenant, with two or three of his men, went into the woods looking for negroes, and later returned to breakfast. When asked whether he had found them, he said he had and that they would give no more trouble, as he had hanged them all on trees."[87]

The first separatist insurgencies were suppressed by 1880, but the breakdown of slavery was now irreversible. The Spanish parliament tried to accommodate the needs of planters in its design of gradual abolition, providing an intermediate period of "apprenticeship" during which former slaves were to work for their former masters for token wages. Many *patrocinados* (apprentices) promptly found ways to obtain their full freedom through self-purchase, legal challenge, or flight. Those who remained on plantations were increasingly unwilling to submit to the authority of overseers and administrators. In 1885 a manager on the Santa Rosalía estate wrote in fury to the owner that a black woman on the estate, thwarted in her attempt to "magnetize" him, had created a scandal by giving him a public kick. His response was to quit, fuming that he had not taken the job in order to be kicked by black women, particularly of her class. It is hard to know which aspect of the incident is more notable, the boldness of the woman or the apparent incapacity of the manager to do anything about it.[88]

Abolition was finally completed in 1886, as the Spanish parliament freed the last remaining apprentices. The larger plantations in central Cuba quickly made the shift to wage labor and expanded the system of decentralized contract cane farming known as the *colonato*. In contrast to Louisiana, where the immediate postemancipation period was one of relative continuity in the organization of field work and slow recovery in output, Cuba's central mills reorganized production on their own land and drew in cane from new suppliers linked by rail lines. By 1890 the Central Constancia in Cienfuegos had the largest capacity of any sugar mill in the world, grinding a staggering 64,000 *arrobas* of cane (1.6 million pounds) every twenty-four hours.[89] Landowners with access to local or North American capital acquired equipment and additional cane land, while smaller-scale cane farmers borrowed locally to finance plantings whose harvest they would provide to the large mills.[90]

Again in contrast to Louisiana, the rural workforce in sugar in Santa Clara was thoroughly multiethnic, drawing from nearly every sociocial group. Former slaves formed a nucleus of key workers on many estates, but they labored alongside numerous immigrants from Spain and the Canary Islands as well as Cubans who counted themselves white.[91] The modest Santa Rosalía Plantation stumbled along in the 1890s, employing dozens of Spaniards along with a somewhat larger number of former slaves. Neighboring Soledad Plantation, whose growth was sustained with infusions of capital by E. Atkins and Company of Boston, employed former slaves, Chinese contract laborers, local smallholders, and hundreds of Spaniards. By 1895 Edwin Atkins could boast that "[t]here are living upon the property during the season of active operations, some 1,200 people." [92]

The underlying problems that had given rise to the earlier insurgencies were not solved by this burst of economic modernization, however. Cubans were still largely disfranchised and faced the hardships of seasonal labor and a militarized colonial state. What looked like a success story in the progress of production figures felt much shakier for former slaves and others living on the land in Santa Clara province. It was true that increasing demand for labor meant that more jobs were to be had, but new arrivals from Spain often got to them first. Moreover, the entire structure depended on expanding cane production into lands that might otherwise be planted in food crops—and on keeping wages low enough to yield profits under the terms of trade in the North American market. This made it difficult for former slaves to find land for subsistence or for wage earners to amass a surplus. When the Foster-Cánovas Treaty expired in 1894 and Spain restored high tariff barriers, the effects were dramatic. The cost of living shot up, laborers lost their jobs, and groups of men on the outskirts of some plantations formed "bands" to try to survive on new terms. [93]

What looked at first like clusters of bandits soon began to take shape as an explicit oppositional movement. By February 1895 émigré separatists had joined forces with nationalist leaders on the island to forge a cross-racial and potentially powerful insurgent alliance. A new rebellion exploded in the eastern province of Oriente and was echoed in Matanzas. Within months the final War for Independence was well under way, and in late 1895 rebel troops mounted an invasion westward to try to reach the central sugar regions. Already local bands in the area around Cienfuegos were harassing both planters and the Spanish forces.

As rebel generals Antonio Maceo and Máximo Gómez arrived in the province of Santa Clara from the hills of Oriente, Maceo is said to have looked out onto the open cane lands and remarked, "Our ship has entered onto the high seas." The dramatic battle of Mal Tiempo, near the town of Cruces in Cienfuegos, provided an impressive demonstration of the capacity of the insurgent armies from eastern Cuba to defeat the Spanish forces. The rank and file of the invading eastern forces, a majority of whom were defined as black or mulatto, were strongly identified with the dynamic figure of Maceo, son of a family of free people of color from Oriente. The irruption of this force into Santa Clara was dramatic, as local rebels linked up with the insurgents from the east.[94]

Those who joined up included individuals categorized as white, mulatto, Chinese, and black. The multiracial world of the sugar plantations and the small farming sector was to a large extent mirrored in the insurgent force. Moreover, the conspicuous presence in the insurgent leadership of respected Afro-Cubans—including Juan Gualberto Gómez, José González Planas, Quintín Bandera, and Antonio Maceo—alongside white leaders like José Martí and Máximo Gómez had made credible the portrayal of the movement as a transracial revindication of Cuban freedoms. But the realities of military authority and decision making could either break down or reinforce prior lines of racial differentiation, depending on the circumstances. In the adjacent province of Matanzas, color lines continued to be sharply etched within the insurgent forces. Some Afro-Cubans, particularly those of African birth, were relegated to the role of "assistant" and denied the right to bear arms. Units composed largely of Afro-Cubans serving under Afro-Cuban officers suffered systematic discrimination from units under white leadership—though they challenged that discrimination using the language of the nationalist movement itself. The result seems to have been a legacy of sacrifice compounded by bitterness.[95]

The picture in the province of Santa Clara was somewhat less clear. While many of the foot soldiers were men of color, most of the rebel high command was composed of individuals who were identified as white Creoles of proximate or distant Spanish descent. José de Jesús Monteagudo, for example, appears to have presented himself and his closest officers as white, as did José Miguel Gómez. The Cienfuegos Brigade, on the other hand, was led by a succession of white commanders but also held several notable Afro-Cuban officers. Brigadier General José González Planas was himself categorized as black, and the officers in his Remedios Brigade seem to have included men of Spanish, African, and Chinese ancestry. Moreover, throughout the war smaller bands under local leadership, often black or mulatto, controlled large sections of the countryside. The result was the development both of Afro-Cuban leadership at the local level and of extensive cross-racial forces led by white officers.[96]

The evolution of the insurgency around Edwin Atkins's Soledad Plantation provides a glimpse of the local dynamics of mobilization.[97] From the beginning of the uprising, the plantation management identified a former slave and cartman, Claudio Sarría, as a key troublemaker. At first Sarría, who like other former slaves on Soledad had taken the surname of the previous owner of the plantation, was portrayed simply as a vengeful individual with a gang of bandits. But by late December 1895, J. N. S. Williams, a manager at Soledad, linked him to a larger network of families of color living on a *sitio*, where they probably grew food crops.[98] By January 1896 there was no denying that Claudio Sarría and his followers were part of a larger structure. Williams reported a "uniting of [the] small parties into one large party" of rebels, a cross-racial group comprising some 300 men.[99] In early February the rebel high command ordered Higinio Esquerra, a white farmer, to gather the scattered local bands formally included in the Fourth Corps and bring them together as an infantry under the command of General Quintín Bandera.[100]

A surviving insurgent enlistment record dated November 1896 from an infantry regiment of the Cienfuegos Brigade, Second Division of the Fourth Corps, conveys something of the internal structure of the local "bands," configured by this point as military units. Claudio Sarría, age twenty-five, married, gave his date of enlistment as August 1895 and was, in November 1896, captain of Company 3 of the First Battalion. There were five men named Sarría in the company: Claudio, José, Lorenzo, Rufino, and Anastasio, as well as three more in Company 2: Felipe, Félix, and Ambrosio. They were accompanied by others with familiar surnames of local planters like Stuart, Tartabull, Ponvert, Acea, and Moré, likely to have been former slaves. Dozens of others had names that provide no clue about race or status, such as Mendoza, Díaz, López, and González.[101]

Company 3 also included former slaves from the neighboring Santa Rosalía Plantation, among them Ciriaco Quesada, age thirty-four, who gave his date of enlistment as August 1895. He had thus been in rebellion for four months before the troops of Maceo and Gómez arrived from the east. His *liberto* neighbor Cayetano Quesada was a foot soldier in Company 2, having enlisted in October 1895 at the age of sixteen or seventeen.[102] Other residents of Santa Rosalía bore the brunt of the policies of the Spanish general Valeriano Weyler, who forced rural people into camps to isolate them from the insurgency. Oral tradition among some of the descendants of Cayetano Quesada holds that many family members ended up in a local camp. One *liberto* named Ramos Quesada stayed on the plantation and tried to protect the livestock—and presumably kept a foothold on the land for possible postwar settlement.[103]

The westward invasion had opened up the rebellion across the island, demonstrating the ability of the insurgents to carry the struggle deep into the sugar regions and to recruit across socioracial lines. By 1897 the effects of the war on exposed areas of the countryside were devastating almost beyond imagining. In September 1897 the mayor of the sugar municipality of Cruces, north of Cienfuegos, sent a terse two-page report to the Spanish military detailing the destruction of his region by fires, which he attributed to the insurgents. He listed the seven major sugar mills that had been destroyed, enumerating the workforces thus displaced. The mayor's rough estimates would place the lost jobs at harvest in Cruces alone at close to 7,000. Moreover, he reported that all of the smaller farms of the region had "disappeared," leaving no house standing except the *bateyes* of the sugar mills.[104]

The Spanish-organized counterinsurgent guerrillas were an additional trial for rural dwellers. Foraging for food and operating with impunity because of their service to the Spanish military, the guerrilla forces seem to have been recruited among Spanish immigrants, renegade insurgents, and impoverished Cubans of all racial groups. Their behavior left scores to be settled after the war.[105]

Direct attacks combined with impoverishment to force many noncombatants to choose between incorporation into the insurgent army as combatants or cultivators, "concentration" in one of the Spanish camps established for the purpose, or retreat to some fortified spot.[106] The increasing ravages of the war made life very difficult for those who remained on sugar plantations, whatever their loyalty to the idea of Cuba Libre. Some estates continued grinding behind the protection of Spanish fortifications, but insecurity was general.[107]

By early 1898 Cubans had fought and harassed the Spanish forces to a standstill, though they could not yet expel them. The rebel general Máximo Gómez expected the insurgent campaign of the summer to be decisive. Instead, the stalemate was abruptly broken in April 1898 by the intervention of U.S. military forces. In North American eyes, the long Cuban struggle was compressed into a brief "Spanish-American War" in which "America" emerged victorious. On 1 January 1899 the United States took over direct administration of the island through a military government.[108]

With the U.S. occupation of Cuba in 1899, the histories of Louisiana and Cuba intersect in a new way. No longer simply a competing sugar producer, Cuba became another setting in which evolving North American racial ideologies would be expressed and contested. Many among the occupying forces brought with them a rigorous set of racial distinctions and invidious stereotypes, precisely those that had emerged from the postemancipation and post-Reconstruction contest over the meanings of race in the United States. Cuba had never lacked expressions of racism, and some Cuban liberals were among the most vocal proponents of all-white immigration. But the growing preoccupation among many North Americans with whiteness, racial separation, and the degenerative powers of "mongrelization" was a relatively novel element in a rural Cuban society that had long recognized multiple color categories. While for some purposes the dominant racial ideology in Cuba had employed a white/black dichotomy, racial categories were more often portrayed as a kind of continuum, including *blanco* (white), *trigueño* (wheat-colored), *mestizo* (mixed), *pardo* or *mulato* (mulatto), and *negro* or *moreno* (black), each defined both phenotypically and contextually.[109] Such categorization did not preclude racism, of course, but it made strict segregation an implausible project.

North American policymakers were particularly concerned that the "better sort" should regain predominance after the tumult of war, and some doubted the wisdom of allowing Cubans of color to vote in the promised elections. The struggle for independence, however, had created a strong claim to Cuban citizenship that crossed racial lines. It was difficult to challenge publicly the patriotic conviction that all veterans, literate or illiterate, black or white, should participate in the construction of the emergent republic. Full participation could in fact be stalled by continued North American occupation, but it could not be openly and categorically denied without risking a new conflagration.

In the first months after the signing of the Treaty of Paris, however, economic recovery took priority. Demobilized soldiers and impoverished civilians were unemployed and hungry; they needed some combination of land and work quite urgently. Large-scale planters in the Cienfuegos region of Santa Clara, some of them North American, regrouped their holdings and recommenced production. The first postwar harvest at Soledad began one week after the occupation, under the American flag. Immediate tasks of protection were accomplished by private armed guards; larger issues of policy could be discussed with the U.S. forces as among friends.[110]

Throughout the spring and summer of 1899, individuals and families tried to find a place for themselves in the new postwar world. A strong oral tradition holds that former slaves from Santa Rosalía, many of them named Quesada, returned from the wartime camps to the estate but found themselves denied the right to resettle. The correspondence of the plantation administrator tends to corroborate this picture, with repeated references to expulsions, particularly of women. Some of the refugees went to El Palmar, a new multiracial settlement behind the adjacent Soledad Plantation, located on lands owned by a Galician shopkeeper. Cayetano Quesada and Ciriaco Quesada, both veterans of the rebel Liberation Army, settled nearby in San Antón, a longstanding community situated between Santa Rosalía and Soledad. Still others went to Arimao, a riverfront town a short ride to the east, near which there was open land suitable for small-scale cultivation.[111]

Patterns of informal access to land are almost by definition difficult to trace in the documentary record. If one takes literally the goal of exploring the "on the ground" experience of emancipation, however, and walks the back roads around Soledad and Santa Rosalía, the picture becomes somewhat clearer. In the settlement of San Antón, most of whose land came to be owned by the Soledad Sugar Company, several houses occupy plots of land that begin where the canefields end. From the company's point of view, these families were squatters without title. The children of Cayetano Quesada, however, have a different perspective. Their father was born free to a slave mother on Santa Rosalía Plantation and was about seventeen years old when he enlisted in the rebel army in 1895 to fight against Spain. The land on which they live in San Antón belonged to Cayetano Quesada, his daughter believes, "por herencia" ("by inheritance"). Adjacent to it is the *potrero* (stock farm) where Cayetano's longtime friend Ciriaco Quesada raised horses and cattle. One of their closest neighbors was the family of Zacarías González, a white veteran of that same Liberation Army, with whom Cayetano and Ciriaco Quesada used to reminisce about the war. In San Antón, on a jIb of land between two sugar plantations, there had apparently emerged a small settlement whose characteristics as a neighborhood mirrored the cross-racial alliances formed during the war itself.[112]

Still other former slaves with the surnames Quesada, Sarría, or Iznaga left the countryside for the town of Cienfuegos, to work on the docks or in laundry or domestic service. In town the shift away from Spanish authority had brought with it some subtle changes in access to public space. Edwin Atkins noted in passing in January 1899 that "I notice negroes come into the Plaza now, which was never allowed before." When Máximo Gómez made a visit to Cienfuegos in February, the insurgent force of the region, with people of color in the great majority, assembled for a procession, numbering some 800 men under arms. Each display of sentiment in favor of rapid independence, particularly when expressed by those whom the North Americans classed as "negro," reinforced estate owners' fear of the consequences of the withdrawal of U.S. forces.[113]

The U.S. presence could thwart independence at the national level, but it could not prevent continuing challenges on the ground. At Santa Rosalía, the administrator was startled in August 1899 by the assertiveness of Ciriaco Quesada, who returned from the war to claim a mule left on the property three years before. When the administrator, Constantino Pérez, brushed off Ciriaco Quesada's request, the tenacious veteran sought help from the mayor of the nearest town, Arimao. To Pérez's great surprise, a member of the Rural Guard turned up first thing the next morning to press Ciriaco Quesada's claim. Pérez deferred, grumbling about this disrespectful proceeding.[114] As in many a rural society, in postwar Cuba a mule might make the difference between dependence and relative autonomy, either for Ciriaco Quesada himself or for Gregoria Quesada, in whose name he made the claim.[115]

Those who settled on small plots of land generally worked for wages as well. The relative shortage of healthy laborers after the war gave workers a certain edge. Some members of a family might combine food-crop cultivation with day labor in the cane; others offered their labor elsewhere for months at a time. In the province of Santa Clara, railwaymen and longshoremen were among the most militant in demanding higher wages and equity of pay levels between Cuban and foreign employees.[116] Dockworkers in Cienfuegos struck successfully in 1899 and obtained a fifty-cent wage increase. On 19 February 1900 the lightermen struck again; rebuffed by the owners of boats and by merchants, they were joined by a "sympathetic strike of stevedores, wharfmen, freight handlers on railroad, cartmen and etc.," paralyzing business. Leaders of at least two of the three unions were listed as mulattos, and one of them was apparently a former slave of the Jova family.[117]

Because wharves and railroads were completely intertwined with the sugar estates, such strikes threatened the functioning of the plantations. Owners tried multiple strategies in dealing with them. Edwin Atkins identified himself to one leader of the lightermen as "Don Eduardo," whom the former slave had known since boyhood, and obtained a brief return to work by promising to intercede. In Atkins's later published narrative, this was an amicable exchange between a powerful North American and a deferential Cuban of color. But at the time, to both Atkins and to the occupying U.S. military forces, these union leaders were a force to be reckoned with: "Antonio Gomez Sosa, President of the lightermen's association, is head of the combined associations of labor involved in the strike, and is credited with being the leader. Gomez Sosa was a major in the Cuban army and has considerable influence among the laborers."[118]

Atkins himself did not stop with paternalistic appeals. He bluntly telegraphed the U.S. governor his recommendation that the activities of the labor association be suspended. In the end, the strike was settled through negotiations initiated by the mayor. The dockworkers obtained their demand of payment in U.S. currency, and on 24–25 February 1900 the residents of Cienfuegos peacefully celebrated the fifth anniversary of the outbreak of the Cuban War for Independence.[119]

Over the ensuing two years, as the formal principles of the emerging Cuban republic were debated, the U.S. occupiers succeeded in imposing the infamous basis for renewed intervention—the Platt Amendment—but found themselves obliged to back down on the question of limiting the franchise. The Cuban Constituent Assembly not only rejected out of hand any racial distinctions in the definition of voting rights, it went on to eschew property and literacy restrictions as well. Again, the cross-racial alliances within the independence struggle had left a powerful legacy. Even conservative representatives, capable elsewhere of racial prejudice, backed away from etching those prejudices into the constitution of 1901, directly or indirectly.[120]

On 20 May 1902 the transfer of sovereignty from the United States to the Cuban government, under the direction of an elder statesman, Tomás Estrada Palma, was completed. But on the eve of the next sugar harvest, new and more extensive strikes broke out, first in Havana and then in Cienfuegos. The strike began with urban cigar workers but became nearly general in Havana, where it was met with police violence; anarchists and other labor organizers picked up the cause in Cienfuegos. From the city of Cienfuegos it extended directly into the plantations, and workers were said to be marching from estate to estate under a red flag.[121]

The U.S. consul at Cienfuegos reported that work had stopped in the municipalities of Lajas and Cruces, including the plantations Caracas, San Agustín, San Francisco, Andreita, Dos Hermanas, and others. The managers of Hormiguero Plantation claimed that they "have been threatened by colored men to stop work and laborers have quit work through fear." The backdrop to the 1902 strike was the formation of a new and important institutional alliance. As in the dockworkers' strike, veterans of color were active, and Evaristo Landa, a mulatto officer from the War for Independence, was a major leader. But they built on multiple foundations, including traditional mutual-aid associations and newer political groupings.[122]

One meeting of strikers was convened in the old Centro Africano, an African cultural center dating back to colonial times. Such buildings had been constructed in part through a degree of paternalism on the part of former slaveowners like Emilio Terry, whose benefactions helped build the center in Cruces, and in part through the efforts of their members, most of whom were born in Africa. They had been meeting places and a focus for cultural expression, bridging between town and country. In the new republic, some were turned to the explicit interests of working-class organization.[123]

Participants in the new struggle included Spanish anarchists, who contributed not only organizational and oratorical experience but also a blunt ideology that eschewed national divisions and called for "the emancipation of all slaves, the disappearance of all privileges." In 1902 they were active in the formation of a Gremio de Braceros (Workers' Guild) in Cruces, and a Gremio General de Braceros in Lajas, laying the groundwork for the strike that would follow. To Cuban activists, the argumentative style and sectarianism of anarchists from Spain could be wearying, but through their newspapers and public meetings they helped to galvanize support and ensure communication among those engaged in the struggle.[124]

At the national level, the strike was settled through the mediation of major Cuban political figures. In the province of Santa Clara, the civil governor sent in the Rural Guard and ordered the arrest of members of the workers' commission. But agitation on the plantations did not cease; meetings were held, pamphlets circulated, and new strikes broke out at the Caracas and Santíssima Trinidad mills. The wealthy Cienfuegos merchant Nicolás Castaño hastily tried to organize a Planters' Circle that could present a united front to the strikers and lobby for a reorganization and strengthening of the Rural Guard.[125]

The workers' strike exposed a new fault line that cut across the Cuban nationalist coalition. To sustain his political power, the civil governor, José Miguel Gómez, a Liberal veteran of populist leanings, needed both the support of the veterans' organizations and the consent of the property-owning classes. The coalescence of black, mulatto, and white working-class veterans around the new workers' organizations, and their willingness to go on strike, imperiled his strategy and put his political machine at risk. Moreover, continuing strikes on U.S.-owned plantations could provoke a renewed intervention by the United States. The U.S. minister in Havana was blunt in his draft dispatch to the U.S. secretary of state: "A strike in the cane fields would mean the greatest possible danger to life and property in this island, a danger with which this Government could not cope with its available forces." [126]

Repression soon took on an ominously extralegal form. On 7 December 1902 two young workers "disappeared" in the area of Cruces; their bodies were not found until eight months later. The Rural Guard clearly seemed to be responsible. One of the dead men was a young Creole activist and former tobacco worker; the other was a veteran who had worked as a guard on one of the estates.[127]

The events of 1902 offered two portents. First, they made it clear that in the multiethnic world of the sugar fields, large-scale mobilization could and would cross the lines that under other circumstances might divide Cubans of different ethnic and color categories. Second, they revealed that even populist leaders like the charismatic José Miguel Gómez — indeed, perhaps *especially* populist leaders like Goméz — could respond with calculated violence and repression to collective actions that were not under the control of his political machine. But the violence was not, for the time being, "racially" coded.

At the national level, President Tomás Estrada Palma weathered the initial crises but failed to consolidate effective power and legitimacy. In 1906 party politics in the young republic were fractured by his manipulation of the power of incumbency. By purging provincial and municipal offices of those believed to be in sympathy with the Liberal Party, thus assuring his own reelection, Estrada Palma provoked a rebellion that he was quite unable to contain. By this point, it was clear that the old separatist coalition had fractured definitively. Its elite civilian wing apparently formed the nucleus of the Conservative Party, and its socially and racially mixed military wing the basis of the Liberals, though individual affiliations shifted and veterans appeared on the rosters of both groups.[128]

Reluctantly, the United States intervened a second time, blocking an occupation of Havana by Liberal insurgents. Charles Magoon took the reins of power in Havana as provisional governor, and a U.S. "Army of Cuban Pacification" moved into the zones of greatest economic and strategic value. One of its tasks was to try to build the durable local structures of power, favorable to planters and to foreign capital, that the United States had failed to ensure at the time of its departure in 1902. The province of Santa Clara was a major focus of U.S. intelligence efforts, both because of the large U.S. economic investment in its sugar regions and because of its centrality to the growing partisan conflicts. (José Miguel Gómez had been governor of the province and was expected to make another strong bid for the presidency.)

U.S. military and political authorities struggled to understand the continuing social and political conflicts in the countryside and to place groups of Cubans in analytic categories that they could comprehend. The Military Information Division, for example, divided its time between careful reconnaissance of the land, in preparation for possible armed operations, and often inept efforts to find out what occupied the hearts and minds of individual rural Cubans, invoking matters of race, occupation, character, and antecedents in an effort to anticipate lines of future conflict. But the picture of alliances and fault lines in Santa Clara was in many ways beyond the interpretive powers of the intelligence officers assigned to monitor it. Their reports provide rich evidence of mobilization and resistance, but that evidence was continually squeezed into analytic categories of their own making.[129]

One of the features that stood out in the political panorama of the countryside was the strong persistence of mixed groups of what the North Americans categorized as "the negro element" and "the lower class of whites." These groups had their roots in the multiracial rural communities and work crews and in the fighting units of 1895–98, modified and channeled by later mobilization under Liberal Party auspices in 1906. The leadership of these bands included men characterized by the North Americans as white, mulatto, and black. Some of the smaller bands continued to operate in the countryside; others existed only as groups of currently peaceful residents who were seen as the potential followers of one or another individual in times of trouble.

On the Hormiguero estate in the heart of the Cienfuegos sugar region, the local intelligence officer reported in February 1907 on rumors of an uprising to coincide with the anniversary of the outbreak of the 1895 War for Independence; he also noted that there was a "band" of ten men, "most of them negroes," operating "without a leader" in the countryside and committing acts of theft.[130] Challenges also spilled over into the towns, as Cuban veterans and U.S. soldiers vied for symbolic ascendancy in public spaces. In July 1907, in the town of Palmira, a member of the Collado family of prominent white veterans was at the center of one such incident:

> [A] crowd of twenty-five or thirty men, some colored and some white, apparently led by Justo Collado, were galloping about town on horseback. Collado was slightly under the influence of liquor as were a number of the others. As the party passed near the Plaza a Marine started to cross the street and Collado, who speaks English, shouted at him "Get out of the way you ******." . . . This led to hot words between them and Collado rode out in front of the crowd with a great show of bravado and attempted to ride his horse over the Marine.

Collado confronted the marine again the same evening, just as a "negro was attempting to ride down the Marine at the same time." Though he was puzzled by the event, the intelligence officer seemed to understand something of the expressive content of this drama of men on horseback challenging a foreign soldier on foot. He judged that Collado was attempting to establish himself as a leader and to "incite an anti-american feeling." [131]

During the same week, "African negroes" made their bid for a place on the streets of Palmira. Forbidden from holding their "native dances with tom-

toms" in the street, twenty-five or thirty members of a group named after Santa Bárbara appeared in costume and began dancing. Ordered to leave by the mayor, they fought back with sticks, and five were jailed. "This caused wild excitement in the town and large crowds gathered. It is worth noting that the members of this society are mostly of the Gomez political party, and they contend that the Alcalde is persecuting them for that reason. Both parties claim that the affair has some political significance, and it can not be doubted that some bitter feeling has been aroused." [132]

A few weeks later the intelligence officer reported that the people of nearby Cruces, one site of the 1902 sugar strikes, were "unfriendly toward the Americans." [133] A volatile mix of nationalist, cultural, and partisan interests were inspiring multiple acts of hostility to an occupying force that frequently located its headquarters on the property of American-owned sugar estates. Moreover, public spaces were visibly and vocally occupied by successive gatherings of black dancers, assorted Liberals, and patriots of all groups.

Though labor disputes, party conflicts, and nationalist resistance could explain much of the turmoil, explicit considerations of "race" were increasingly invoked both within the old coalitions and by new organizers. Beginning in 1906 and 1907, local officers began reporting word of "negro meetings" and pamphlets addressed to the "colored race." In Palmira there were unconfirmed rumors of "an anti-american movement by the negro element." Some of these reports were closely linked to the political initiatives of Evaristo Estenoz, a black veteran in Havana who was attempting to build an "Independent Association of Color." But much of the agitation arose locally, from Afro-Cuban veterans who saw themselves increasingly marginalized both by the Cuban white elite and by the U.S. occupiers.[134]

Estenoz and other urban activists made the question of public office a major focus of their organizing efforts. This issue resonated to some extent even in the smaller towns, where the post of chief of police, for example, might be contested between a black and a white veteran.[135] Whatever the merits in a particular instance, Afro-Cuban veterans were well aware of a pattern of prejudice. No bitter, fully developed white supremacist ideology comparable to the one that accompanied repression and disfranchisement in Louisiana could be pinpointed. But a quiet, anxious policy and project of selective exclusion on the part of the more conservative members of the elite and their U.S. allies was unmistakable.

These policies of exclusion had particularly serious implications in a society in which public office often represented the only avenue for advancement. The collective goal of Cuban independence was in perpetual tension with a more individualized scramble for positions and security. The Liberal Party was open to Afro-Cubans, particularly veterans, but only within the structure of clientelism presided over by José Miguel Gómez. While the Liberal revolt of 1906 had replicated some of the cross-racial alliances that had marked the wars for independence, its ideal of anticorruption paled in comparison with the goals of earlier struggles. At worst, it could be charged with seeking a mere changing of the guard.

Exclusion took on its most ominous form with the successive reorganizations of military force. During the first occupation the United States had supervised the demobilization of the insurgent army and the formation of a Rural Guard. Initially the Rural Guard built upon local units of the Cuban Ejército Libertador—hence, perhaps, the willingness of a mayor and a Rural Guardsman in Arimao in 1899 to back up the former slave and veteran Ciriaco Quesada's challenge to the Santa Rosalía estate in the matter of a mule. Over time, however, the procedures for enlistment tended to operate against Afro-Cubans, through both criteria of education and requirements for recommendation by "respectable" local figures. By 1900 the Rural Guard had quite clearly become a nexus for the flow of money and patronage from the U.S. military government into the countryside.[136]

This Rural Guard had nonetheless proved inadequate to the task of defending the Estrada Palma government against Liberal attacks. Thus one of the first items of business of the second intervention government was the establishment of a permanent army that was larger and less dispersed—and even less a reflection of the multiracial insurgent army of the end of the nineteenth century. The armed forces increasingly emerged as a partisan and politicized force, wedded to the defense of property and, with time, to the promotion of the incumbent party.[137]

While the occupation government was constructing a potentially repressive force that could serve a role parallel to that of the lily-white militia of the 1880s in Louisiana, however, the working class of the province of Santa Clara was rapidly growing and diversifying. Increasingly, the structure of the field labor force on sugar plantations tended to subordinate rather than elevate racial distinctions: former slaves, long-free Cubans, and immigrants from Spain worked side by side as wage laborers. It was becoming less and less likely that the line between workers and the forces of order could be construed as a color line. At the same time, the rural smallholding population, which provided some seasonal workers to the plantations, included many descendants of slaves and of free persons of color, as well as Cubans who categorized themselves as white. Moreover, the *campesinos* living in settlements like San Antón and El Palmar in Cienfuegos had long since left behind the residential segregation of the slave barracks.

One household in the settlement of El Palmar, located alongside Soledad Plantation, may serve as an example of some of the complexity of occupational and residential patterns. Manuel Lago Tacón, born in Spain, migrated to Cuba to find work and became the second carpenter on Soledad Plantation in the 1890s. At a dance in the town of Arimao he met Bárbara Pérez, born a slave on Santa Teresa Plantation. After emancipation she had moved to Arimao, where she worked as a laundress and apparently smuggled ammunition to the Cuban nationalist insurgency. She and Manuel Lago began to keep company, and he built a house for them in El Palmar, on land belonging to a Spanish shopkeeper. Their neighbors included families with the surnames Iznaga and Quesada, descended from slaves on the Vega Vieja and Santa Rosalía plantations. One of the earliest memories of their son, Tomás Pérez y Pérez, was of the sight of U.S. soldiers stationed on Soledad from 1906 to 1909, and of hearing about a sergeant who waylaid and tried to rape one of the black laundresses on the path from El Palmar to Soledad. When the first carpenter at Soledad died, Manuel Lago expected to be promoted to the job, only to find himself displaced by an even more recent Spanish immigrant, the brother of the deceased. Lago left in anger, abandoning Bárbara Pérez and the children. She continued to take in laundry and trained as a midwife with the doctor at Soledad. Tomás Pérez recalled that jobs in the mill at Soledad were usually closed to men of color, who were expected to work in the fields. But he himself worked in numerous positions at Soledad, including jobs as stevedore, cane farmer, and supervisor of a multiracial crew at the lime kiln. In retrospect, he attributed his access to these jobs to his reputation as a hard worker—and to the fact that some people knew him not only as a man of color, but also as the son of a Spaniard.[138]

In effect, color distinctions mapped onto distinctions of wealth and opportunity, but they did so imperfectly, leaving certain boundaries indistinct. The census revealed sharp racial differences in the degree of access to productive resources, and "colored" renters and owners controlled only a small fraction of the island's land. But the daily working experience of most of those who labored in cane was not one of segregation, even though they might notice— or suffer from—various invidious distinctions based on skin color and ancestry. When the members of the Workers' Guild of Cruces called for an alliance of all those who sweated to earn a paltry wage, without distinction of nationality, they were expressing an anarchist first principle, but it was one that could evoke a certain resonance in the Cuban cane fields.[139]

Tomás Pérez y Pérez, born in 1902 in El Palmar, a small, multiracial settlement in Cienfuegos, Cuba, worked for most of his life on Soledad Plantation. (Photograph by Paul Eiss)

Lines of division were thus crosscutting rather than mutually reinforcing. Despite continuing racial discrimination in the years following emancipation, the field workforce as a whole had become progressively less segregated. And the continued activism in the cane fields and on the waterfront ensured that workers from different socioracial groups would find themselves not only working side by side but pursuing shared goals. Proximity alone would not guarantee alliance, but each successful alliance made further alliances more likely.

Cutting in the other direction, however, planters continued to express a racially coded set of anxieties about any Afro-Cuban assertions of rights. Their anxieties found echoes in the occupying forces, who frequently viewed black veterans as "bad men" likely to "cause trouble." And the construction of a largely white permanent army tended to increase the probability that conflicts of various kinds would taken on racial overtones.

These divisions were thrown into stark relief in 1912. The Partido Independiente de Color, banned by the central government, tried the classic tactic of an armed protest in pursuit of recognition. The consequences, however, were fatal for the rebels in a way that was historically unprecedented. In Oriente, in eastern Cuba, the movement escaped the reformist intentions of its leaders, becoming something of a peasant *jacquerie*. The army was called out, ostensibly to defend property. Constitutional guarantees were suspended, and noncombatants were ordered out of the area. Under the command of the Santa

Clara veteran José de Jesús Monteagudo, the Cuban army engaged in pitiless repression. In scenes reminiscent of rural Louisiana, patrols roamed the back roads of Oriente with machetes, attacking and often hanging the black men whom they encountered. The drama transfixed the local press as far away as Cienfuegos in Santa Clara, where daily bulletins on the rebellion the newspapers labeled the "Movimiento Racista" included reports by military officers and interviews with rebels. Rebel leaders denied that their movement was racial, citing the presence of whites among their supporters, and quickly asked for negotiations, which were refused.[140]

The army suppressed the protest through what amounted to a campaign of assassination. One observer reported that the army "was cutting off heads, pretty much without discrimination, of all negroes found outside the town limits." [141] The estimates of the number of victims of the repression are entirely conjectural but range into the thousands.[142] As in Louisiana, in this moment of repression the forces of order in Oriente imposed a categorical white/black dichotomy and selected victims according to that division. It was this pattern of white alarm and army repression that made this a "race war," rather than any pattern of killing of whites by blacks in the rebellion itself.

In the central province of Santa Clara, however, the picture was somewhat different. The uprising took the form of scattered attacks involving the theft of a saddle here, the cutting of a telegraph line there. Local officials deployed the Rural Guard to pursue rebels characterized as "cabecillas racistas" ("racist chieftains"), following the logic of the Cuban government under which those who asserted a racial identity were perforce "racist." The very idea of an "independent party of color" was, officials claimed, a violation of the nonracial ideals of Cuban patriotism. The movement in and around Cienfuegos never really took off, however. Moreover, the repression seems to a certain extent to have been bounded by networks of clientelism and reciprocity. Unlike Evaristo Estenoz in Oriente, the local *independentista* Simón Armenteros got out alive—and was escorted to jail with some propriety.[143]

The events of 1912—particularly the vicious repression in Oriente—sent a terrible chill through the rural population of color and became a largely unmentionable episode in Cuban history. A few voices defended the victims of the repression, but prudent organizations of *gente de color* hastened to declare their allegiance to the government. A narrowed set of boundaries had been imposed on the discussion of questions of race and social justice. Those who were categorized as Afro-Cubans could still participate in public life, but only on the condition that they deal very cautiously with the issue of discrimination. Universal manhood suffrage remained the rule, and electoral politics continued to be shaped by the very important black electorate, but new limits had been drawn around the permissible forms of assertion for Afro-Cubans.

The net effect, however, was not to silence the rural laborers of Santa Clara. Their organization continued, based on a strong foundation of black, white, mulatto, and Chinese workers. There were at times powerful tensions between Spanish and Cuban workers, but unions continued to build on the basis of racial inclusiveness. A burgeoning sugar industry would get nowhere without an expanding workforce, and such a workforce could not, under the circumstances, be an entirely segregated one. Moreover, the ideology of "patriotism" that had been used to delegitimate the rebels of 1912 carried as a corollary the principle of citizenship and formal equality for those Afro-Cubans who refrained from challenging the concept of a transracial Cuban identity. Even as the repression raged in the east, the local press of Cienfuegos expressed its support for workers in Havana who went on strike against a North American company that refused to employ Afro-Cubans.[144]

Inclusive, multiracial organization continued to be the hallmark of the workers' movement. A 1912 Workers' Congress in Cruces was chaired by a woman, Emilia Rodriguez, and one of the most effective orators was a black man, Gregorio Campos. In 1915 workers from the major estates in the Cienfuegos district who signed a manifesto calling for an eight-hour day and a 25 percent increase in wages were immediately arrested. The arrests diminished the influence of anarchists in the region, and the movement failed to produce a work stoppage. But in 1917 the island was swept by strikes that closed down one central mill after another.[145]

Traumatic though the repression of 1912 had been, it had not succeeded in confining the role of former slaves and their descendants to that of "negro laborer," to use the phrase of the Louisiana planter. Nor had employers managed to contain the initiatives of sugar workers as a group. Continued access to subsistence land, even though constrained, gave workers some bargaining power as individuals; the tenacious organizing of veterans, anarchists, and other activists provided the framework for assertions as a group.

Conclusion

Each of these stories suggests the complexity of the relationship between livelihood, race, and collective action. In Louisiana the fragile solidarity briefly displayed in the strikes of the 1880s showed glimpses of what might have been, but it was quickly buried in the triumph of the white-line strategy and of white supremacist ideology. In Cuba a pattern of uneasy but effective cross-racial alliances was interrupted by a ferocious repressive episode in 1912, but it continued to hold force in a growing labor movement.

Clearly the paths taken out of slavery conditioned a different set of outcomes in the two cases. The evolving structure of the rural labor force in Cuba, with a multiethnic corps of sugar workers embedded within a multiethnic peasantry, helped to open up possibilities that were effectively foreclosed in Louisiana. At the same time, the history and precepts of Cuban nationalism provided a matrix within which to envision cross-racial cooperation—even as they could be used by the elite to block independent Afro-Cuban mobilization.

In Louisiana the construction and politicization of a single color line was encouraged by a specific strategy adopted by a segment of the Democratic Party and its allies throughout the South. That strategy was opposed by a short-lived Unificationism and by a cross-racial Republicanism, but within a decade after the end of the Civil War the most extreme forms of white-supremacist ideology were well on the way to carrying the day. Even after "re-demption" from federal rule was achieved, planters could draw on the de-monology of Reconstruction by invoking the image of large groups of black workers challenging their white employers. But that the groups of strikers should have been composed primarily of workers defined as black was itself the direct result of a specific path taken out of slavery: the large-scale re-imposition of gang labor on former slaves.

In those few areas in southern Louisiana where the rural workforce comprised several socioracial groups in significant numbers, the picture was somewhat different. In Terrebonne Parish and in lower Lafourche Parish, where estates with a multiracial workforce coexisted with a network of small farms, some of them operated by people of color, cross-racial alliances fared slightly better, Republicans sometimes lasted longer, and repression was less severe.[146] But the sharp distinctions of citizenship imposed throughout the state under Democratic rule helped to reinforce the color line during strikes, for only whites were now eligible for militia service.

In Cuba broad rights to formal citizenship coexisted with various forms of discrimination, and racism coexisted with antiracism.[147] In light of the Louisiana experience, it is perhaps the explicit antiracism in Cuba that stands out, for it went far beyond the strategic alliance-building of even the most forthright Louisiana white reformers. In asserting a social base for his trans-racial ideal of nationality, José Martí had argued that divisions between black and white Cubans would be overcome "where all that is just and difficult begins, among the humble folk."[148] This assertion can be seen as a romantic—and somewhat patronizing—populist gesture. But there was good evidence to support such an optimistic picture of potential working-class unity. In the formation of the nation, "race" had been provisionally subordinated to *cubanidad* ("Cuban-ness") both at the level of ideology and in the field of battle. If this ideology did not bring with it effective equality, it nonetheless meant that Cubans were encouraged to view each other as participants in a larger struggle in pursuit of a single goal. No group was marked as irremediably "other"; each group could try to hold the others to a presumed standard of democracy and equality.

After the war, the ideology of a shared identity suffered as the shared goal of national independence receded. At the same time, many politicians sought to interpret the legacy of Martí and Maceo as one that explicitly repudiated any open discussion of the differences in the experiences of Cubans of largely Spanish ancestry and those descended from Africans. Individuals and small groups of intellectuals tried to break through the silence, and candidates for office at times tried to convey a degree of solidarity with Afro-Cuban voters, but the invoking of shared grievances of black Cubans tended to be portrayed in mainstream political discourse as in and of itself a "racist" act that was inherently divisive. As Alejandro de la Fuente has argued, those who regarded racial unity as a fait accompli that precluded discussion tended to override those who regarded it as a yet-to-be-accomplished goal.[149]

This set of constraints had mixed consequences. It tended to thwart Afro-Cuban mobilization of various kinds, and to stifle challenges to the folk stereotyping and elite exclusions that reinforced prejudice. But at the same time, the taboo on talk of race, in conjunction with the very great diversity of the workforce and of the corps of veterans, meant that the color line was not explicitly politicized from the other direction, either. No party undertook to build its strength on an ideology of white supremacy, or on a clear repudiation of all black leadership.[150]

The very effective politicization of the color line in Louisiana may be seen in this light to be a more contingent phenomenon, rather than a direct sequel to slavery or a concomitant of the transition to free labor. The construction of events in the Louisiana "sugar bowl" from the 1860s through the 1890s as racially encoded encounters of civilization and barbarism was an act of interpretation, not an automatic reflex. A newspaper editorial from St. Mary Parish, written in support of the White League, made the metaphor explicit, declaring that civilization was the birthright of the white race, "and it is ours, and ours alone."[151] The editors of the *Caucasian*, published in Alexandria in 1874, called for the formation of a "white man's party" to make the next election a "fair, square fight, Caucasian versus African."[152] These publicists were not simply reflecting existing lines of cleavage. They were attempting to give specific political content to a particular, binary construction of race and racial identity.

The very complexity of these two stories from postemancipation cane regions should make their most virulent incidents look more contingent, less inevitable, and therefore, in a sense, even more troubling. Division and conflict between poor whites and former slaves appear not as necessary legacies of slavery, but rather as the result of the changing circumstances in which these groups were constituted and encountered each other, and of specific political decisions and initiatives taken by leaders.

A substrate of tension, stereotypes, and prejudice may well be the universal legacy of systems of slavery defined as racial. But the question of the meaning of race in public life was opened rather than closed during the process of transition to free labor. Ideologies of antiracism like those proposed by Antonio Maceo and José Martí did not describe the world as it really was in the ranks of the insurgency; they described the world as they hoped that it might become through a joint struggle for national independence. A cane farmer in eastern Cuba observed later that he did not fear the insurgents, many of them black, who rode onto Santa Teresa Plantation, because they drank beer together: "I knew that nothing could happen to me as I was like them." He seems to have been expressing at a popular level the sense of shared sociability and identity on which Martí and Maceo had hoped to build a sense of transracial nationality.[153]

By contrast, the insistence of planters in Louisiana that they would rent no land to former slaves and would continue to operate with centralized gang labor set the stage for separation. And the many ideologists who claimed civilization to be the birthright of the white race, and the white race only, provided a powerful image that marked African Americans as deficient and excluded. On a few occasions the shared interests of workers on Louisiana sugar plantations made room for cross-racial alliances. But with ideology, state power, and brute force all arrayed against them, Louisiana sugar workers lost, after decades of struggle, the space for action that Cuban sugar workers managed to keep open well into the twentieth century.

Frederick Cooper

Conditions Analogous to Slavery

Imperialism and Free Labor Ideology in Africa

From the vantage point of the 1990s, slavery and colonialism appear as two forms of oppression, both based on the conceit that certain categories of people were available to meet the needs of those with more power, more wealth, and more ability to shape what kinds of practices a public would accept as "normal." In some ways, the rhetoric of international movements against colonialism in the 1940s or 1950s (or, more recently, of the international anti-apartheid movement) read like a reenactment of the antislavery campaigns of the nineteenth century, in which the evils of white oppression of blacks were sharply demarcated from socially appropriate practices and combated in the name of principle and humanity. Such movements inspire questions of why evil is bounded in particular ways: Why was slavery distinguished from other forms of labor exploitation, or colonialism from other forms of political and social domination? What made it possible for such movements to cross borders, to make an evil practiced in a particular place appear as an outrage elsewhere? What connected mobilization among the oppressed to mobilization by interested outsiders?

One cannot assume that "slavery" or "colonialism" constitute self-evident targets for political mobilization, or that the two oppressions are seen as parallel in different contexts.[1] Contesting the boundaries of the normal and the unacceptable, within and across different regimes of power and discourse, are at the heart of social mobilization. This chapter is a study of such boundaries—about ways in which political discourse is contained and ways in which such discourse explodes its boundaries.

In the 1890s the idea that slavery and colonialism were analogous would have made little sense in concerned circles in Europe. Indeed, heirs to the antislavery tradition were arguing that vigorous intervention into Africa by civilized powers was the only way to stop Africans from enslaving one another. Later the antislavery lobby, particularly in England, remained true to its heritage by continuing to criticize European governments for failing to live up to their stated objectives of ending African slavery and refraining from coercive labor recruitment themselves. The critique focused specifically on violations of free labor ideology, generally avoiding other dimensions of colonial rule. It treated Africans as potential victims in need of protection from excesses of exploitative zeal or lapses in the implementation of moral principle by Europeans, who were now portrayed as the source of both potential good and potential evil.

Within this framework, the most highly publicized instances of Europeans exploiting Africans in slavelike conditions (not coincidentally, the deeds of weaker colonizing powers) were identified, investigated, and, at least on the surface, stopped. In the 1920s the League of Nations, and later the International Labour Organization, took over the campaign against slavery and its analogues from missionaries and humanitarian lobbies. But like all ideological constructs, the notion of free labor led its proponents to blind spots as well as insights into the uses and abuses of power in a colonial situation: they defined slavery or coercion in a narrow way, giving an aura of normality to other colonial practices.

There is a certain pathos to this effort by well-meaning people to make colonialism a little bit better for Africans. The neo-abolitionist effort was doomed to be forgotten by history as the story of colonialism's final years rightly came to focus on Africans as actors in their own liberation. Even the final episode within the framework of free labor ideology—the decision of France to abolish forced labor in 1946—reveals African political mobilization succeeding where influential and knowledgeable French critics of empire, and

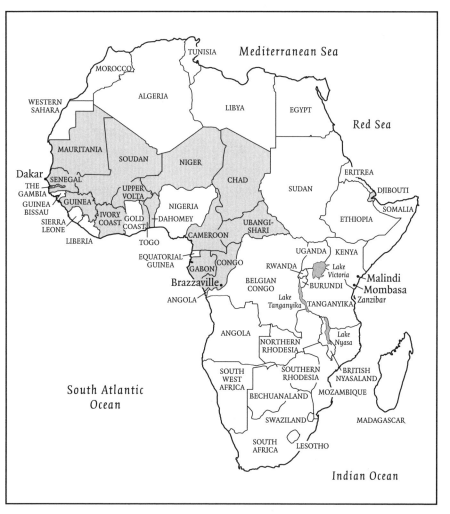

French colonial Africa

conscientious critics of labor policy within the colonial establishment, had failed.

Yet focusing on the limits of attempts to reform imperialism from within does not get to the bottom of the story. A narrowly framed reformist discourse could be seized by others and widened into something whose implications could not be so easily confined. From the first days, colonization was challenged from its interstices as much as head on, from weak points in imperial institutions and ideologies that were gradually pried open. In many parts of Africa, slaves forced colonial authorities to be better emancipators than they wanted to be, sometimes taking advantage of the weakening of slaveowners' authority to flee a plantation region or to redefine terms of access to land, sometimes pushing officials to undertake a more systematic emancipation instead of the disorderly one that seemed to be unfolding. At the same time, efforts by former slaves to free themselves from obligations to owners did not mean that they were becoming the "free laborers" of the colonial imagination, dependent on wage labor for their livelihoods. Instead, they often found niches in urban labor markets that could offset dependence on local landowners, used increased possibilities for safely moving about to return to homelands or to migrate to places where land was more readily available, and otherwise diversified their strategies for combining subsistence with irregular cash earnings.

Whatever future colonial officials had in mind for Africans, the people about whom policy was being made had their own ideas. They forced colonial officials to redefine their sense of what was normal or politically acceptable within a European overseas empire. The terms of the contest over normalcy would change once again—in regard to labor, to education, to political participation. This chapter will show the dialectic relationship of one of the most recent struggles over what free labor would mean to struggles over who should be making decisions about state policy, a dialogue that moved back and forth between the cocoa farms of the Ivory Coast and the legislative halls of Paris in the years after World War II. This debate is an important instance of a discursive framework breaking open, as the categories into which officials hoped to contain controversy were seized and turned around by other political actors, who put more profound issues onto the table. The debate in France and French Africa over forced labor from 1944 to 1946—plus strike movements in 1946–48—shifted the focus of discussion over labor policy from the peculiarity of the African to the universality of wage labor. Once that issue was raised, French officials themselves had to wonder what sense colonial rule made when colonized people were not clearly demarcated as distinct and subordinate.

In these terms, the breaking out of the free labor framework in the 1940s into a wider debate over labor, social distinction, and political participation raises important questions about what would come next. What new frameworks replaced the old, and what were their insights and blind spots?[2] French officials now tried to bring to bear in Africa the knowledge they had acquired in containing the demands of workers in the metropole. They were immediately challenged within the very framework through which they sought to reestablish control—by assertions from a labor movement that if officials expected Africans to work like Europeans they should be paid like Europeans.

Yet the idea of the African as "industrial man" left as many problems obscured — the specificity of the social conditions out of which workers emerged, the family arrangements they might seek to make, the part the wage labor would play in the life cycle — as they seemed to clarify. What kinds of social policies would be imaginable and inconceivable in "modern" Africa and who should set those policies? The question of what lay beyond colonial labor policies weighed just as heavily on African labor movements and African governments in the 1960s as the question of what lay beyond slavery lay on former slaves, former slaveowners, and state officials in the British West Indies in 1838 or in the French Antilles in 1848.

The concern of this chapter is the framework for understanding labor that exploded in the late 1940s, which itself grew out of the uneasy "beyond" that the emancipations of the previous century had left.[3] The critiques of slave labor that had emerged in late-eighteenth- and early-nineteenth-century Great Britain — and less consistently in France and other European states — were in many ways remarkable in their scope, endurance, and significance. The powerful universalism of free labor ideology — linked to the realities of European military and economic power — has confronted Africans and their descendants with a compelling set of images: the idea of a self-motivated, self-disciplined worker, making choices in a labor market and thereby determining the welfare of his or her family. It has been hard for laborers to be cultural relativists, to insist that punctuality, diligence, and obedience were peculiar European folkways. The power to label in international debates has by and large gone the other way, and it has been the work habits of the African that have been labeled peculiar, while market-discipline has been discussed as an acultural, universal norm.[4] In the farms and plantations of Africa or the West Indies, however, the struggle has not been altogether one-sided: imperialist projects have foundered over the inability of the powerful to make the weak into disciplined wage laborers.

The first part of this chapter shows that the imagery of freeing Africans from various forms of bondage — to outsiders and to each other — became in the late nineteenth century an important way in which European nations made their various colonizing ventures into a coherent and moral project. Free labor became a vital concept distinguishing the progressive colonizer of the early twentieth century from the freebooters, bandits, kidnappers, and buyers of human flesh who had for past centuries represented Europe overseas. This schema depended on a particular reading of earlier emancipations. Freeing labor, it seemed, would not itself lead to the kind of progress liberal political theorists in Europe had in mind, and the progressive imperialism of the late nineteenth century was premised on an interventionist state and missionary enterprise that would forcefully undertake the remaking of African society.

The second part of the chapter looks at some emancipations effected by British and French colonizers in Africa. As before, officials encountered a complex reality that the dichotomy of free and coerced labor did not illuminate. This section explores as well the issue of marriage and slavery, and the ways in which a patriarchal view of marriage was solidified in colonial discourse — through an unequal but mutually reinforcing dialogue of African male elders and British district officials — at the same time that slavery was being pushed out of the discourse. Included here is a case study of an early emancipation, the British attempt around 1900 to make good on the implications of the missionary crusade against slavery and the slave trade in East Africa by turning coastal slaveowners into capitalist landlords and slaves into wage laborers — an attempt that ran up against the ability of former slaves and slaveowners to redefine their mutual relationship in still different ways.

The third part of the chapter opens up the question of the colonial regimes' own practices. Policies based on the assumption of African peculiarity — indifference to the incentives of the market — stood in tension with free labor ideology. The latter made the use of force in recruiting labor illegitimate, but the former made it necessary. Colonial regimes tried to finesse this tension in a variety of ways, above all by claiming that forced labor would be used only temporarily and in pursuit of the long-term goals of teaching Africans the value of work and building an infrastructure that would bring in goods that Africans would want to buy. Between 1926 and 1930 the League of Nations and the International Labour Organization reached an understanding that forced labor, whether used for private gain or public purpose, created "conditions analogous to slavery." That understanding left unresolved the question of how and for how long a transition could be effected, while presuming that it was African notions of work that would have to give way to a European conception of labor as a contract between two parties, as something performed over a defined period of time, as a relationship distinct from the ties of kinship and community in which people might be living. The heart of this section is a study of a late emancipation, the end of forced labor in the French colonies in 1946. Here one finds the language of free labor deployed against the French government, which itself was caught amidst uncertainties as to whether the impossibility of obtaining wage labor might condemn French Africa to stagnation.

What distinguished the 1946 emancipation from others was the participation of African actors, not just as menacing rebels whose distant voices could be evoked by white moderates against the pro-slavery die-hards, but as political activists in French institutions. By then the question of free labor was becoming caught up with questions about the entire political and ideological fabric of colonial rule itself. The labor question, among others, was being reframed. The new frame, like the old, would bound the problem in its own particular way.

A Moral Imperialism?: Colonial Progress and African Slavery

The pessimistic twist on free labor ideology in the mid-nineteenth century—that blacks needed the stern supervision of a civilized state before they could embark on the "natural course" of market rationality—was crucial in enabling European powers to acquire a sense of themselves as progressive imperialists in the course of the conquest of Africa. Just as the advance of capitalism and free labor in Europe in the eighteenth and early nineteenth centuries went along with an expansion of slave production in the colonies, the advance of citizens' participation in European state politics in the nineteenth century went along with the imposition of outside power over the continent of Africa. In both cases the ideological contradictions eventually proved impossible to overcome, but for a considerable time colonization could plausibly be talked about within Europe as an element of progress.

In Africa the decline of the overseas slave trade—which finally became decisive in the 1850s—did not by itself turn the continent into a garden of peaceful commerce. In parts of the continent, in fact, the domestic use of slaves in agriculture expanded as slave export prices declined and worldwide commerce in tropical products, led by Europe, expanded. The old slave trade routes fed the slave system, and, particularly in east-central Africa, the slave supply system become more vigorous and highly ramified in response to coastal demands for slave labor. In some contexts slaves provided additional labor to family and kinship units, and the power extended over them was rationalized in patriarchal terms, but in such areas as Zanzibar, coastal Kenya, Dahomey, and much of the western Sudan, slaves either worked in large units under their owners' supervision or were placed in separate villages whose surplus was appropriated. Where state power was limited and political boundaries contested, maintaining discipline over increased numbers of slaves required their gradual movement through a gradation of statuses, so that new slaves had to be continuously brought in.[5]

The continued slave trade, with its violence and brutality, was a sore point in antislavery circles, and it attracted the attention of a wider public as well. The violence of the slave trade became a central theme of the burgeoning literature by explorers. John Speke saw the connection of coastal slavery and hinterland violence in east-central Africa: "To catch slaves is the first thought of every chief in the interior; hence fights and slavery impoverish the land, and that is the reason both why Africa does not improve, and why we find men of all tribes and tongues on the coast."[6]

That was also the region David Livingstone explored, and his reports in the 1860s helped to publicize the image of an Africa ruined by slavery and the slave trade. His arguments appealed to the European merchant as well as to the friends of the native. He portrayed the slave trade as "an insurmountable barrier to all moral and commercial progress," destroying the order necessary for the normal operation of trade, ruining incentives to engage in agriculture or wage labor, pressing people into accepting demeaning forms of protection.[7]

French abolitionism—after the abortive abolition of the Revolution and the reinstatement of slavery by Napoleon—had lacked the consistency and popular appeal of the British version. Its moment came in 1848, in the midst of another revolutionary episode in France, when slavery in French colonies was at last abolished and the idea of the French state as the agent of human progress—to overseas lands as much as to metropolitan France—took root, pressed on by agitation among slaves themselves in the French Antilles.[8] In the ups and downs of monarchist and republican politics in France after that date, both Catholic and Republican propagandists saw the tyranny and backwardness of Africa as a place to mark France's emancipatory destiny. In the 1880s Cardinal Lavigerie led what was in some ways a Catholic equivalent to Livingstone's crusade, while from the 1870s an important element in France's Republican leadership was both abolitionist and imperialist.[9]

But most important, France's tiny colonial outposts in Senegal, spreading outward from trading posts, brought out from an early date the contradictions of the emancipation of 1848, which applied to anyone on French soil, and the reality of a fragile colonization movement whose profits and security depended on not asking too many questions about trading partners and political allies. Local officials often tried to avoid the problem by emphasizing the narrow borders of the colonies—and France's obligation to respect the customs of its African neighbors—but even a formalistic and legalistic antislavery policy could open the door to further action. Indeed, missionaries and the occasional zealous official encouraged prosecution of slave traders and publicized violations of the 1848 act in Paris, where policymakers were less preoccupied with the nuances of African alliances than officials on the spot. And slaves themselves were important in prying open a narrow law, for they learned that fleeing to a French outpost could possibly get them freedom papers, or at least a place to hide. Runaways became frequent causes of friction between African states and the French, repeatedly making slavery into an issue that had to be confronted. Within trading posts like St. Louis, African merchants used their control over housing and their important economic and political connections to build up networks of clients and dependents who could serve them.[10]

By the 1880s and 1890s an argument similar to Livingstone's about the debilitating effects of the slave trade and slavery was being worked out by explorers and others who were bringing West Africa to the attention of a French public. Captain Louis-Gustave Binger was sympathetic to the Muslim slaveowners of Sudanic Africa and to their treatment of domestic slaves, but the slave trade, to him, was entirely "lamentable." Traders raided villages, massacred adult men, and herded women and children into caravans. African rulers were "true tyrants, oppressing the people or selling them." In areas subject to slave raids, "the black not under supervision works little or not at all," and trade led not to progress but to the widening of the regions being despoiled. Binger concluded, "War and its consequences—polygamy and slavery—will only begin to decline when Europe effectively exercises its influence on these people, and to exercise it, means of penetration are necessary"—government, missionaries, traders, and railways.[11]

To be sure, European visions of different parts of Africa were changing and contradictory—the noble savage and the simple, natural life as well as the brutal slaver and the hapless slave. Not all accounts portrayed Africans as lazy. Some observed extensive trade relations, but rarely did one see Europeans acknowledge that African governments were developing a capacity to direct civil society and that African economies were capable of innovation and growth. Even outside of the slave trade areas, the stereotypes of isolation and idleness—particularly male idleness—were rampant; the myth that women did all agricultural labor was the counterpoint to the belief that African men spent their time fighting.[12]

The idea of Africa as a slave-ridden continent, oppressed by its own tyrants and kept off the path to civilization, Christianity, and commerce, was crucial to missionary propaganda from the 1860s on, the rallying cry of antislavery meetings for the rest of the century, and a major component of the knowledge of Africa available to the reading publics of Europe. Such ideological innovation was not in itself the cause of the new wave of conquest, but it did allow the advocates of imperial advance to identify their interests with a larger purpose. The turn to state intervention in trade and production overseas was

consistent with the increasing social interventions of regimes in Europe itself
—state efforts to transform the "residuum" of capitalist development into
"respectable" working classes. The old Europe had profited from and stimu-
lated African violence; the new Europe preferred that economic expansion
be predictable and orderly and that social structures be capable of extending
and reproducing themselves.[13] Such thinking can be traced not only in the
metropole—in the missionary campaign against African slavery—but in the
field, where African violence and its disruptive effects on orderly commerce
were part of complicated debates over exactly where and how European governments should intervene to protect commercial property and ensure commercial progress.[14] The African chief or king—like the West Indian planter of
the 1830s (see Introduction)—stood beside the slaveholder and slavetrader in
imposing the "brutal predicament" on Africa and preventing the rise of the
"rational" one.

What is striking about this moral vision is how international it was, in a
much fuller sense than the British-dominated drive against the slave trade
after 1807. In the midst of their deadly serious rivalries, the imperial powers
met at Berlin in 1884–85 to set out the rules of the game, and they insisted
that colonizing powers act against the African slave trade. At another international conclave in Brussels in 1889–90, they formally resolved that a conquering power undertake the systematic suppression of traffic in slaves, arms, and
liquor. In constructing themselves as civilizing powers, the imperialists constructed Africans as slavers, as disorderly, as incapable of self-control. They
would hold each other to creating the structures for an orderly and rational
utilization of African resources and labor power. Lord Salisbury called the
conference the first in history that met "for the purpose of promoting a matter
of pure humanity and goodwill."[15]

Of concern here are the consequences of such an ideological construction
as European rule was extended over Africa. It implied that colonial regimes
had to come to grips with the complexities of slavery in Africa itself. But they
would soon face the limits of their own tools for understanding and intervening in African society.

The Ambiguities of Coerced Labor

Although more than a few colonial leaders explicitly argued that progress required that European economic models—including private property in land
and wage labor—be imposed on African colonies, the immediate reality they

discovered was that their revenues depended on the exports of crops grown by slaves and peasants. Their fragile political hold sometimes rested on alliances with African leaders who had an interest in slavery, even if the slave trade on which domestic slavery depended for its reproduction did, as missionaries and explorers had rightly argued, create a climate of violence inimical to the colonial peace and to long-distance commerce. Most regimes moved promptly against the slave trade in its most virulent forms but wavered about slavery in its agricultural and domestic forms.

They were not allowed to temporize in peace: the antislavery lobbies made tolerance of slavery in Africa their prime target. "Slavery under the British flag" was a stain on the colonial project, and a French governor-general in 1901 had to remind his subordinates caught between the legacy of 1848 and de facto cover-ups of slavery, "Let us not forget that it is in the name of Liberty and to combat such barbaric customs that European powers have come to the territories of Africa." [16] More important, the conquest disrupted the mechanisms of control and reproduction of African slaveowners, and slaves in many parts of Africa quickly began to take matters under their own control.[17] Even before colonization had advanced very far, slaves deserted their masters for mission stations and European outposts. As European armies moved inward, considerable numbers of slaves became part of their entourages. Some served French troops; some were taken into the French army itself, as part of the African troops known as the *tirailleurs sénégalais*. Others became concubines of French or African soldiers; still others were distributed to African allies of the French. The French — in another rhetorical flourish — called the settlements of former slaves and miscellaneous detached people that they hoped to exploit for military and other manpower "villages de liberté." Freeing the slaves of their enemies, the French set in motion a process in which the slaves of their friends often freed themselves. Behind the advancing lines, slaves took advantage of the possibility of returning home or of seeking a new place to live, or perhaps of shedding debilitating relations of subordination with an owner in order to become the clients of a new patron, such as one of the Muslim leaders who were taking in followers and organizing cultivation in the increasingly prosperous peanut belt of Senegal. In certain places, most strikingly the Sudanese area of Banamba in 1905, the exodus from the slaveowners' farms took place en masse, in such a compelling fashion that the fragile colonial regime could not stop it, but could only try to coordinate it. The French conquest of the western Sudan was, in John Lonsdale's phrase, "almost a creeping slave revolt, but scarcely an emancipation." [18]

However limited the conquerors' goals, their presence threw awry the re-lations of power and dependence in slaveholding societies. The possibility of survival outside of slavery not only encouraged flight but changed relations of production for those who stayed. Flight and disobedience caused tension, worried slaveowners, contributed to antislavery propaganda back home, and undermined the usefulness of slave production to export-minded regimes. The mass exodus in the Sudan in 1905 was instrumental in forcing the French governor-general, William Ponty, to make clear to administrators that slavery was officially over and that former slaves were free to move about. What this meant in practice varied greatly, for the actual possibilities open to former slaves depended very much on the material and social conditions that shaped alternatives. But throughout a vast region, relations of dependence were being redefined even where they were not being broken.

When the British conquered northern Nigeria, where a strong Islamic state presided over a complex agricultural and trading society, and where many slaves toiled on large estates while others passed, over generations, into a de-pendent peasant population, the situation was equally contradictory. British propaganda before the conquest had accused the rulers of having "degener-ated at the present day into . . . unlimited massacre, pillage and slave raiding," but the new rulers feared that, once freed, former slaves would "lead a life of vagrancy." The British were determined to preserve elite property, productive capacity, and power even while formally ending slavery. Their hand was forced by the exodus of slaves from the more recently conquered parts of the state, as well as from core areas. Land deserted in the era of slave raids was reoccupied, and slave revolts occurred. In the first few years of the new century, the gov-ernment had to act to resolve a situation that was politically and ideologically untenable. It tried to reconcile its conflicting goals with a policy of abolishing the "legal status of slavery"—refusing to recognize in court any claim based on the slave status of an individual—while hoping that control of land, pa-tronage, and taxation would maintain the stability of a hierarchical society.[19] In southeastern Nigeria, where political power was more decentralized, colo-nial officials were still "preoccupied with maintaining their alliance with in-digenous ruling classes"; they tried to couple legal abolition with minimal so-cial change. Slaves resorted to flight and other means to try to bring about a more substantive change in their status. Former slaveowners kept trying to maintain the most vulnerable people in a state of dependency, and former slaves kept trying to gain more secure access to resources and more autonomy from their former masters. These conflicts persisted for decades, with vary-ing consequences, perhaps denying to former slaves and slaveowners alike the security that might have helped bring about new and more dynamic forms of agricultural production.[20]

Both French and British rulers tried early on to declare the problems surrounding emancipation to be solved. They did so by defining slavery narrowly and legalistically and insisting that courts no longer recognized such a status. Slavery was generally considered a male problem; the ambiguities of the dependence of women, unless their mode of acquisition was too blatantly violent, were assimilated into the category of marriage.[21] Other relations of subordination were assimilated into tenancy or debt. Colonial archives became filled with evasions and euphemisms—French documents changed what was once called an "esclave" into a "captif," then a "non-libre," then a "serviteur." Indeed, the administration's efforts to define slavery out of existence have made it hard for scholars to study French policy, let alone African practices, from the archives.[22]

But these problems do not undermine the fact that the colonial conquest did bring an end to large-scale, long-distance versions of the slave trade and limited even the more localized forms of slave trading. The colonial system made it possible for slaves to flee a harsh master, to transfer their dependence to other groups or individuals, to redefine relations of dependence, or to take their chances finding jobs in colonial cities, colonial armies, colonial railways, or colonial schools and mission stations. By the end of the first decade of the new century, the British and the French—and, at least on paper, the Portuguese, Belgians, and Germans as well—had ended the legal status of slavery in most of Africa, and the practices of enslavement, of the reproduction of slave populations, and of the large-scale economic exploitation of slaves were in rapid decline.[23]

The contradictions of this period can be seen clearly through a case study of Zanzibar and the coast of Kenya, a region colonized by Great Britain in the 1890s and noted for the intensity of its agriculture and the importance of slaves to it. Parts of that region, particularly in Zanzibar and the coast near Malindi, were characterized by large plantations (growing cloves on Zanzibar and grain and coconuts on the mainland), while others, both rural and urban, featured smaller holdings. In both areas slaves, who came from distant parts of Central Africa, were converted to Islam and were socially defined as inferior members of an extended community. The limits of repression and paternalism were continuously tested, however, and runaway communities were dotted along the coast. The British presence changed relations of power, enabling both an exodus from the plantations and a redefinition of relations of dependence on remaining ones. That was precisely where the idea of free labor—as preached by purists among missionaries or compromisers among officials—failed to come to grips with the complexity of an African social system.

Colonial Conquest, Emancipation, and Work Discipline: A Case Study

In Zanzibar and the East African coast, officials attempted systematically to repeat what they had tried to do in the West Indies: abolish slavery while maintaining a landowning class—Arab and African—that would remain tied to export agriculture and would now employ wage labor.[24] Critics—notably missionaries—denounced any intermediate form of supervised labor as a violation of the tenets of free labor ideology, much as their ideological predecessors had denounced apprenticeship in the 1830s.

Even missionaries were concerned that if slaves were freed but not subjected to close control they "would tend to produce a demoralized and dangerous class of people, such as would be sure in the future to embarrass the good government and to mar the prosperity of the country." An official worried that "if a large number of slaves are liberated at one time, they are apt to break loose, loot shops and shambas [farms] and commit all sorts of excesses."[25]

Officials did not question that slaveowners should retain their property rights in land and productive trees held under Islamic law. Nor did they question the need for a managerial class to superintend production: the option of allowing former slaves to cultivate on their own, as peasants, was not seriously considered. Under the Zanzibar emancipation decree of 1897, slaveowners were paid compensation money to ease their transition from slave to wage labor. The decree attempted, however, to make a compromise between the radical implications of the British view of slavery—that labor be "free"—and the conservative implications of the officials' view of class—that order and production required a class of landowners and managers. Slaves freed under the 1897 decree lost the plots of land that had been the basis of their subsistence and could be declared vagrant unless they agreed to a contract with a landowner. Officials used the intimidating atmosphere of the courts where freedom papers were granted to impose model contracts: former slaves would work three days per week (versus the customary five of slave days), all year, in exchange for a subsistence plot and a place to build a home.

Former slaves often agreed to the contracts, but they did not necessarily do the three days labor. Taking advantage of the new possibilities for mobility among plantations, for finding vacant nonclove land, or for casual labor in towns, former slaves were often able to reach understandings with landlords that gave them access to land in exchange for vague responsibilities to do some work and be part of the landowner's "people." Landowners desperate for some kind of sway over former slaves, as much as former slaves themselves, subverted British notions of contractually specific obligations and regular work. British officials lacked the power and the will to undertake massive evictions and vagrancy prosecutions, and this inability reinforced the tendency of landowners to act within more familiar norms, cultivating long-term ties of dependency rather than contractual obligations. British hopes that labor discipline would be maintained in Africa by the "sanction of the sack" became increasingly irrelevant. Within a few years of emancipation an official was lamenting, typically, "Steady, regular work is just what your slave or free slave dislikes very much." [26]

Zanzibar's clove output was saved by an allocation of time quite different from the regularity of wage labor discipline that British officials had tried to instill. Short-term migrants from nonclove areas of the islands (who had been marginalized by the slave economy) began to pick cloves, working for only a few weeks each year. Long-term migrants from German Africa—where the end of the slave trade, ivory trade, and porterage had undermined young men's access to cash—began to come for periods of two to three years, weeding the plantations. Former slaves filled in the crevices. So clove production actually rose, even as officials lamented the *way* the work was done.

On the mainland coast, officials in Kenya hesitated, worried about a slaveowner-led rebellion and by the results of the Zanzibar experiment. By 1907, however, the slaves had already gone a long way to free themselves, taking advantage of the British presence to undermine the subtle relations of dependency of a slave society. People could now leave plantations without fear for their lives: railway construction and other colonial projects had created alternative loci of employment. The slow but steady exodus of slave labor meant a readjustment of labor conditions for those who stayed: slaves devoted more time and space to their own cultivation and less to their owners' fields.

Kenya's abolition decree of 1907 allowed slaveowners to claim compensation for slaves whose services they lost and effectively ratified the freedom slaves had already claimed, while legitimating the efforts of landowners to get the slaves of other landowners to squat on their land. A labor system tied to the land was giving way to competition between landowners for increasingly mobile workers, and squatters paid only a modest rent or provided vaguely specified labor services. People who lived in the hinterland behind the more fertile coastal belt—members of nine distinct political and communal groups later collectively known as Mijikenda (nine villages)—began to join former slaves as squatters on coastal estates. Near Mombasa, both former slaves and Mijikenda established a symbiosis between urban and rural activities, seeking casual labor, mainly on the docks, that would provide cash for a day's work but would not compromise participation in agriculture.

In both Zanzibar and coastal Kenya the colonial government recognized the titles to land and trees held under Islamic law, so planters retained ownership of land even if they could not translate this into tight control over labor. The compromises worked out day by day in the fields, however, made it risky for landowners to invest in their property or for squatters to improve it by their labor. Economic stagnation became the price of the uneasy social standoff. In theory, title registration permitted the transfer of land to white settlers—the Kenya government was hoping this would happen—but this possibility failed as well, partly because of excessive speculation, partly because of competition in plantation crops from elsewhere in the British Empire, and partly because European planters were unable to recruit labor within the region, despite considerable help from colonial officials. Coastal people would seek to become squatters or would work for indigenous landowners, who made no demands about length of service, while European planters insisted on a commitment of time that would have jeopardized what was most important to the workers: acquiring long-term, reasonably secure access to land.

What collapsed on the old plantations of coastal Kenya (and, to a lesser extent, on Zanzibar) was not so much agriculture as the British fantasy of agricultural wage labor. Regional exchange—between different parts of the coast and between Mombasa and the rural areas around it—became more intense and more varied. Exports decreased, but coconut products and grain continued to be sent forth. In most cases, landowners could only extract a modest rent and a share of the harvest of coconut trees on their plantations; they could not control the production process. For a time, "big men" in the coastal hinterland took advantage of the weakening of coastal landlords to improve their position in regional grain and coconut markets, but they too had trouble keeping their subjects from squatting on coastal land or going to Mombasa.[27]

Officials periodically expressed displeasure at the squatters. The government feared that the presence of squatters would compromise the system of individual land tenure and discourage new purchasers of land, particularly Europeans. Even squatters who were reviving grain production on former plantation lands were accused by the governor of leading a "useless and degenerate existence."[28] In the government blueprint, the coastal zone was for private ownership and wage labor agriculture; African migrants belonged in their hinterland homeland—now labeled a "reserve"—and should only come forth when they had a definite arrangement to work. A government attempt in 1914 to evict squatters from a fertile region north of Malindi resulted in a rebellion and a famine that officials were obliged to relieve. Shortly thereafter, squatters returned to the area where their huts had been burned and fields destroyed, and this time officials gave up. The renewed presence of squatters— welcomed by the hapless Arab landlords of the area—led to a modest revival of grain exports.[29]

The urban labor market of Mombasa developed relatively smoothly in the era of emancipation and expansion, but the rural labor market did not. In the days of slavery, urban slaveowners frequently had their slaves seek day labor, with much of the earnings being turned over to the owner. In the postemancipation era, the hiring process continued—involving former slaves from surrounding areas as well as from the city—with the owner cut out of the picture. The labor market of Mombasa adjusted well because employers willingly accepted labor power in the unit in which coastal Africans wanted to provide it: by the day. Casual workers in the port could earn in ten days of hard work as much as unskilled contract workers—who had no say over when they worked—could earn in a month. Former slaves and Mijikenda found that periods of urban casual labor in the city complemented squatting and cultivating in rural areas.[30]

Given the fluctuating nature of shipping, employers found that day labor served their interests, too: they could adjust their wage bill to actual needs. Officials felt uneasy, however, fearing a population that was unattached to employers, spatially mobile, and resistant to time discipline. In official discourse, the category of casual worker slipped into the category of idler or criminal. But it would only be in the late 1940s that a serious attempt would be made to change the system of casual labor.

In coastal East Africa, the record of officials' intentions about the transformation of slave labor is clear enough: success for them would have meant turning slaves into a landless proletariat, mediated perhaps by contracts and labor tenancy, but certainly extinguishing all rights of access to land and implying landlord control over the labor process itself. Yet it is not clear—in this or many other cases—whether capitalists and officials in the early colonial era had much choice over the kind of labor force they could get: African labor power was hard to detach from the soil and bring forth in small units. Even in Mombasa, where the labor regime worked smoothly enough, officials worried about lack of control. The ideal labor system was a cultural construct of officials, not just a series of cost-minimizing strategies, and members of the colonial elite of Kenya were constrained by their inability to establish the time discipline of European capitalism. When they did not get their way, officials—like their predecessors in the West Indies—blamed it on the slaves: "A human being accustomed to slavery, when freed, seems to have lost all incentive to work," commented the East Africa Commission in 1925, in its post mortem on the coastal region.[31]

It was only after the fact that British colonial officials in Africa—most notably Frederick Lugard—began to make a virtue of their failures. As ruler of northern Nigeria, Lugard had viewed the landowning indigenous elite as worthy intermediaries whose authority should be respected; he had insisted that the key to a prosperous agrarian future was to reinforce their ownership of land, abolish the legal status of slavery, and slowly convert the slaves into proletarians producing under the direct supervision of the indigenous landowners. Lugard's writings from 1906, as his effort got under way, reveal the progressive ideology that underlay even a cautious approach to ending slavery:

> It is not unfrequently urged (especially by those who are new to Africa) that Slavery is an institution well suited to the African, according conditions under which he is, as a rule, happy, and that its supercession is a mistake. . . . [T]hinking men . . . condemn the system of slavery. . . . In the first place, slavery cannot be maintained without a supply of slaves, acquired under all the horrors of slave-raids, and transported with great loss of life from their original habitation; this results, not only in much human suffering, but also in a decrease of the population, and consequently in a decrease of the productive capacity of the country; secondly, no people can ever progress if personal initiative and personal responsibility is denied to them. . . . That existing slaves may be happy in their lot is no argument to the mind of any one who aims at the progress of the race in a remoter future.[32]

Lugard's last phrase says much about his intent: the point of emancipation was not to make slaves better off. The argument that progress needed to be brought to people who did not necessarily want it could also apply to unenslaved peasants in many parts of Africa: their access to land meant that they could choose to participate in market-based progress or to remain aloof. Neither slaves nor peasants faced the "rational predicament" of choosing between wage labor and starvation (to use again the British term of the 1830s), even if the former were no longer under the "brutal predicament" of slavery. In northern Nigeria, Kenya, and elsewhere, peasants and former slaves alike might have to be pushed by old authority patterns and new colonial constraints into producing for someone other than themselves.

In slave-using regions the actual consequences of abolition proved to be much messier than the ideal of slow, elite-directed transition. The capitalists-to-be often preferred to use their authority and the backing of colonial forces to extort tribute from peasants and slaves alike. In northern Nigeria this led to more conflict than the British government was willing to put up with, and elsewhere it led to tense standoffs, with no clear evolution toward new forms of land tenancy and labor mobilization. The British reconciled themselves to the increasing importance of various forms of tenancy and smallholder production, out of which the colonial state, local elites, and merchants would squeeze a surplus by various means.[33] Lugard later espoused the virtues of "indirect rule" and a conservationist approach to African society: he had the genius to define failure as success.[34]

The sequence within British thinking is important here, and it contains echoes of the 1830s: an interventionist episode, followed by a confrontation with the complexity of the local situation and a realization that change could not be directed as desired, followed by an argument that the peculiarity of the former slave (and in this case of the former master as well) frustrated the application of universal principles of social and economic progress to the case at hand.[35] In the West Indies in the 1840s, the explanation for peculiarity was a racial one; in the 1920s, a cultural one. The form of the explanation was similar in both cases. In colonial Africa the arguments that Africans were "natural" peasants, adapted to agriculture and village life and rootless and vulnerable if removed from it, did not apply just to former slaves, although—as in coastal East Africa—the former slaves were sometimes seen as an extreme form of African antipathy to steady labor. In the 1920s, in any case, influential British thinkers were prepared to give African resistance to change a grudging stamp of approval; conserving human variety and allowing change to take place within the bounds of African culture became a raison d'être for a colonial regime. The French policy of "association" entailed a similar move: it too was a retreat from a more activist policy of intervention masquerading as a respectful attitude toward African cultures.[36]

"Traditional" Africa was as much a fiction as the notion that Africa was putty for social engineers.[37] In practice, colonial rulers came to live with the unevenness of their accomplishment: accepting and trying to manipulate peoples who for one reason or another had begun to market increased volumes of export crops; profiting from the fact that areas of stagnation or deep poverty could be sources of irregular but cheap labor; and attempting to balance stability and exploitation in zones of foreign investment. In Great Britain and France, ambitious plans for fostering economic expansion that surfaced within the bureaucracy were shelved in the 1920s, amid fears of disruption and concern that investments would not pay off.[38] The myth of African backwardness and tradition concealed the fact that the leading colonial powers had neither transformed nor exploited Africa as their earlier promises had implied.

Marriage, Tradition, and the Social Meanings of Emancipation

Slaves, laboring in relatively large units under supervision, were fundamental to agricultural production in more places than Zanzibar, coastal Kenya, and northern Nigeria. Much of the Sahelian region of West Africa and coastal zones such as Dahomey are notable in this regard, and in many other regions less differentiated systems, less fully integrated into global and regional trading mechanisms, had the potential of tilting in such a direction. Such was the volatility of enslavement—operating across distance and cultural boundaries, capable of concentrating human beings and using them in diverse ways without their consent. But saying this does not get to the bottom of the problem of emancipation in newly colonized Africa. The issue is not one of typicality, let alone one of trying to characterize certain forms of slavery as "African" while others can be termed, for example, "Islamic," a move by which Igor Kopytoff, in a phrase, deprives Africa of one-third of its population and consigns the other two-thirds to an essentialized conception of culture.[39] Africa, it must be recalled, has long been a diverse and cosmopolitan continent.

The detachment of people from their natal territory and social relationships made them vulnerable, in their new, unsought homes, to a variety of forms of exploitation and opened the question of the basis on which they would come to terms with the new social structure and new cultural forms.[40] The dynamics of affiliation and marginality in formerly slave-absorbing societies, in the context of imposed power and the efforts of former slaves themselves to deflect, redefine, or deny forms of "belonging," remains a complex issue.

An interesting place to examine this problem is in Central Africa, particularly among matrilineal societies. Matrilineal descent posed particular problems in an era of uncertainty and change such as the nineteenth century. A man who acquired wealth and military success could not pass it on to his son; his sisters' sons were his heirs. Such a system did not necessarily convey power to women—although in some conditions it created possibilities for female initiative and collective action—but it posed a particular dilemma when kinship groups were not in a stable relationship to each other and ambitious men wanted to build kinship groups and succession patterns they themselves could control. Where slaves were available—and the matrilineal belt of Central Africa was caught up as both victim and beneficiary of the slave trade—a man might solve the problem by buying or capturing a female slave and marrying her. Since she had become a kinless person, her matrilineage would have no claim over the children. The man could thus expand his own kinship group, whereas marrying nonslaves would expand the kinship groups of his wives.[41]

Such a process contributed to the rapid growth of chiefly power within this region. These marital strategies were, of course, countered by other men who did likewise, and the relative decentralization of the slave-trading process and the slave-trading routes made for a great deal of conflict and insecurity.[42] Power relations between the sexes were affected as men became less concerned with what their wives produced on their farms and more focused on warfare and the market, while the insecurity in the region made women, particularly desirable objects of slaving, vulnerable and hence more dependent on warrior males than before. In patrilineal societies the consequences of a local marriage and a slave marriage were not so starkly different, but the latter nevertheless extended the possibilities of building a large kinship group beyond the boundaries of interlineage relationships.

Emancipation thus posed a problem of power and gender relations. In one area of British Nyasaland (now Malawi), Elias Mandala has shown, the end of slaving and the growth of trade in crops that women could control did for a time empower women—until the cash-crop economy was eroded later in the colonial period.[43] More generally, the local male potentate lost his ability to obtain slave wives, his ability to function independent of his own and his wives' matrilineages, and his dynastic control—as well as opportunities for conquest, enslavement, and trade that were directly thwarted by the Pax Britannica.

The British conquerors worried that too much "freeing" would diminish rather than enhance the possibilities of cash-crop production and would jeopardize a social order that depended on patriarchal authority. Thus they did not actively engage in freeing slaves but directed their efforts toward stopping the trade and those cases of maltreatment that they could not avoid; they were generally happy to define one of the most important forms of enslavement into the category of "marriage" rather than "slavery." There was, nonetheless, considerable confusion over who was and who was not a slave and over what kinds of authority could be exercised over women and by whom. In and out of marriage, "customary legal institutions" were being used to try to "maintain the relations of subservience between slaves and their former masters."[44]

The growth of wage labor migration in the Rhodesias and Nyasaland complicated the issue. Although wage labor was never generalized across the region, enough of it developed (from plantations in southern Nyasaland to mines in Southern Rhodesia or as far away as South Africa, and later to mines in Northern Rhodesia) that young men sometimes saw an opportunity to have access to economic resources independent of their fathers and to use them to marry. Worse still for the insecure patriarchs, young women might see alternatives in new towns themselves, depriving their fathers of bridewealth and of the labor—their own, that of daughters' husbands, and that of future generations—that was essential for a family to do as well as the colonial system allowed.

But male authority was not so easily eroded. Martin Chanock shows how these threats led to a rallying around the banner of "customary legal institutions." These, he points out, were part of a defensive power struggle, an attempt to take an ambiguous past and turn it into a mechanism of control by male elders against uppity young men and wayward young women. The custom of deference to elders and the rigidity of marital roles within gender norms were not inventions out of whole cloth but represented a transformation of a conflicted recent past into ancient custom. British officials— themselves concerned with the overt and subtle social changes they had unleashed—were eager to find precise rules and a clear sense of local authority. They were willing to be told by male elders what "custom" meant—as long as it did not constitute a "barbaric" practice—and they were willing to incorporate those notions into a semibureaucratized court system that codified such claims to marital authority.[45]

Just as in the struggles over labor in coastal Kenya or Zanzibar, colonial officials plunged into a more complex social world than their categories could analyze. They came to accept as African, as immutable, and as traditional certain new notions of social relations that were the product of struggles and of a history that they did not want to know.

The marriage question had important implications for the labor question. When the copper mines of British Northern Rhodesia came into production in the 1920s, the neotraditionalist ideology that the British administrators had by then accepted left them with a profound ambivalence: they wanted Africans to labor for European capital, but they saw order and social stability depending on the preservation of a structure of family relations rooted in the village and in the authority of male elders. Young men themselves might prefer short periods of wage labor so that they could combine it with the security of village land and inclusion in its social arrangements, while older men and younger as well as older women tried to bend the combinations of material and social resources in different directions. European employers were caught between their desire to maximize labor recruitment and their hopes to avoid paying the full social costs of labor in a situation of considerable uncertainty. But the lens through which this complex and shifting set of economic possibilities was examined in official circles was shaped by the provincial administration's preoccupation with a system of authority.

Those officials could conceive of Africans working, but not of Africans *being* workers. Indeed, the preferred word for somebody who had left the village, left the authority of male elders, and left the rule of customary marriage was "detribalized African." Discussions of labor issues up to the 1940s remained trapped in this conceptual limitation, and crucial to maintaining such a construct was the idea that women would remain in villages and that regulations —labor contracts and customary courts—should keep things that way. The mine town or the city might be the site of labor, but not of the reproduction of a labor force.[46]

So in many parts of Africa the revolution that followed emancipation was neither intended nor noisy but entailed, rather, a basic transformation in power and gender relations, treated in official discourse as if it were the maintenance of tradition. Such a set of categories was no better than the concept of free labor in producing an understanding of the dynamics of Africa under colonial rule.

Forced Labor and Colonial Morality

The moral construction of the new colonialism at the end of the nineteenth century implied not only a duty to save Africans from each other, but an obligation on colonial powers to examine each other's practices. The impossibility of the first duty, however, made the second a particularly sensitive issue: given the African's peculiar resistance to steady work, trying to expand production opened the possibility not only that dubious methods of procuring labor would be practiced, but that justifications would be found for them. The former possibility was certainly realized, and not just in the early years of colonization, but it was not so easy for a durable case to be made for any form of coerced labor. The internationalization of imperialism in the 1880s—the articulation of a common facade of reformist ideology combined with continued rivalries among nations—was a crucial factor in this regard: European states kept a watchful eye on each other, and making examples of the weaker members of the colonizing community served notice about the kind of colonialism that was acceptable in polite company.

The Rules of the Game

The key test of their seriousness came in King Leopold's Congo. Leopold II of Belgium, one of the architects of the international agreements under which the European powers had carved up Africa, granted concession companies the right to collect rubber. They did so by terror, brutalizing people who failed to meet quotas. In the 1890s missionaries and traders mounted an international campaign against such practices, and in 1908 Leopold was finally forced to change the Congo from his personal fiefdom into a proper Belgian colony and to find other means of economic progress than terror. The formal cession probably contributed less than the exhaustion of rubber supplies and the development of other, less dramatically noxious economic activities to ending forced rubber collection.[47] But Leopold had been humiliated because of what he did to Africans. A campaign against the roundup of Africans in Angola for labor in the disease-ridden and lethal coffee plantations on the island of São Tomé followed, and in the 1920s Liberia became the object of a campaign against similar recruitment practices.[48]

The attack on Leopold—with all its echoes of nineteenth-century antislavery—focused on a bounded evil, contrasted to the benign appearance of market transactions. But such a contrast presumed what Leopold's minions could not: that Africans had already accepted the rational world of markets. The rubber companies needed labor to tap rubber more than the rubber tappers needed them. In extracting labor by terror, the companies created an aura around their victims—of the African irrationality that impeded rational Europeans from doing business, of the savagery of Africans that justified brutality. Some of the leading lights of the anti-Leopold campaign were from the merchant houses doing business with West Africans.[49] The deeper questions of the peculiar nature of capitalist economic rationality and the difficulties of transporting it to Africa lay unexamined.

The reformist critique of imperialism gone wrong helped to define the normality of colonial rule.[50] All the while, South Africa was reducing African land rights, uprooting squatters, and enforcing discipline on African workers through pass laws, control of residence, and other means. South African labor policy had long had its principled critics, but they had no sure handle to pry open the legalistic and systematic approach through which the choice of Africans as to whether or not to work for wages was being made for them. The visible signs of South Africa's economic growth were too powerful to leave the self-serving progressivism of the pioneers of mining capitalism vulnerable to attack.[51]

France and Britain, facing in most of Africa a situation where Africans could distance themselves from the "rational predicament" of wage labor, faced regular criticism from the purists of the labor market. The critics frequently used the word "slavery"—along with images of death and dehumanization that echoed those of antislavery propaganda—to dramatize policies that strayed beyond the bounds.[52] All regimes defended themselves by evoking public purpose—above all, the need to develop transportation networks to "open" Africa—to justify the provisional use of forced labor. French officials employed a military metaphor for forced public-works labor: the "deuxième portion du contingent," that is, the men leftover from military recruitment after the desired number of soldiers were sent off. They served their term and were paid a wage, as were conscripts, but they worked on roads and other public-works enterprises, usually under bad conditions. Yet another category of coerced labor went under the guise of *prestations*, or service of a villager to his local community and chief. But in fact official recruitment of unwilling laborers for private concerns—not just public service—continued in French Africa until 1946.[53] The Portuguese also employed a forced labor system that was severe, long-lasting, and barely covered up. The British insisted that they abhorred forced labor but practiced it nonetheless in the early decades of the century in mines in the Gold Coast and Rhodesia—and revived it extensively during World War II. Words like "recruitment" were carefully employed, but Africans in Rhodesia were not fooled: they used the word "Chibaro"—meaning "slave" in local languages—for laborers supplied to the mines by the government recruitment agency.[54]

But most Africans faced more indirect pressure. Relations between chiefs and people in African villages were nested in a complex web of affinity and power far more subtle than the distinction between slave and free labor. As a British official in Kenya put it, obtaining labor from a chief for the benefit of white settlers "depended on how far he could be induced to exceed his instructions."[55] This meant that critical questions concerning labor could not be posed forthrightly. The actual operations of the system took place covertly. For their part, opponents of forced labor usually phrased their critiques narrowly—against the use of official coercion for private profit or against the abuses of government recruitment—and did not penetrate the patterns of land seizure and power that actually shaped the conditions of labor.[56]

By the 1920s in Kenya—and at different times elsewhere—the free labor question was becoming less salient. A new equilibrium was reached, as much a consequence of the increasing modesty of European aspirations as of the fact that Africans had been forced by varying kinds of necessities to participate in labor and produce markets. The areas from which most export crops came were in fact quite limited, and the social relations of production in them were varied. The labor supply for areas such as the Central African mines, the Kenyan highlands settler farms, or the Ivory Coast plantations came from large catchment areas for relatively short periods of time—and not simply because Europeans wanted it this way. Whereas the classic pattern of capitalist development in Europe entailed the assertion of the bourgeoisie's control over workers' time, the pattern of labor force recruitment in interwar Africa came to depend more on colonial states' control over space.[57] A small demand for manpower required large numbers of potential laborers and worked most predictably when large regions were sufficiently impoverished that wage labor became part of the life cycle.

As colonial powers adjusted to the realization that their early ambitions would not be fulfilled and began to celebrate the wisdom of conserving African culture, free labor ideology became formalistic. But its exponents were close enough to exposing fundamental contradictions in colonial rule that their efforts generated controversy. The League of Nations agreed on a "Slavery Convention" in 1926, pledging to stamp out the vestiges of slavery and slave trading in the colonies. The convention asked the International Labour Organisation (ILO) to take a further step and conduct an investigation of "the best means of preventing forced or compulsory labour from developing into conditions analogous to slavery."[58]

The League of Nations was accepting the possibility that a practice of a member government—rounding up laborers to engage in a purpose that the government deemed appropriate—could be analogous to slavery.[59] The problem now was to draw a line, to define where labor became unfree. The invocation of the century-old tradition of antislavery in this context abstracted the dichotomy of free and coerced labor from the complex web of power and affinity in which laborers actually existed. This process of abstraction would carry considerable ideological weight: whatever was not declared coerced was therefore not analogous to slavery and would acquire the distinction of having been exonerated in terms of the only moral criteria the league and the ILO were applying to colonial labor. The ILO duly appointed a Committee of Experts who undertook this task.

Their labors resulted in the ILO's Forced Labour Convention of 1930. This was, in its own way, a radical document. It set as its goal the suppression of "forced or compulsory labour in all its forms within the shortest possible period" and declared that, effective immediately, such labor could not be used "for the benefit of private individuals, companies or associations." Forced labor meant "all work or service which is exacted from any person under the menace of any penalty and for which the said person has not offered himself voluntarily." Such labor could be used temporarily for public purpose, but the convention set out terms: laborers could work only for limited times and at going rates of pay. Member governments had the burden of implementing these regulations while striving to abolish the practice altogether.[60]

The Committee of Experts faced close debates and divided votes on key provisions; the International Labour Conference of 1930 passed the final version by a vote of 93 in favor, with 63 abstentions, including France, Belgium, and Portugal. Proponents of the measure stressed universal principle: the convention was a "definite and unqualified condemnation of the whole system of forced or compulsory labour." Its opponents accepted the principle but insisted that in confronting people "in different stages of civilisation" colonial governments needed flexibility to ensure that work necessary for the people's own good would get done; moreover, the people would benefit from "a period of habituation and education." Efforts to slow implementation and exempt private firms working on public-works projects were vigorously debated and defeated. The French delegation was itself divided, as government and employer representatives opposed the outright ban on forced labor for private purposes, while representatives of French workers supported it.[61]

Perhaps the most revealing insights into the assumptions behind this convention come from an opponent, René Mercier, who objected to the "assimilation of obligatory labor to slavery" while wondering what free labor really was. The convention "visualized above all 'man in himself,' like an entity, and not the native as he is, with his inheritance, his psychology, his customs, his social life, his 'climate.' "[62] In other words, banning forced labor assumed there was such a thing as free labor, that there existed individuals detached from community and culture who could stand alone in the labor market and make decisions. That argument assumed—although Mercier would not have said it this way—that capitalism had already remade culture, that Africans' access to the means of production were sufficiently compromised so that wage labor would be a preferable alternative to self-directed cultivation.[63] Mercier claimed to know "colonial reality," meaning that he knew the African was not the acultural, universal being the ILO assumed. He had a point in this regard, although his conclusion that the African's cultural uniqueness made him or her a legitimate target for coercion was based on its own dubious assumptions as well.

The French government, not interested in taking up the issue on such terms, refused, for reasons of state, to ratify the convention until 1937. It objected to internationalist meddling in what it regarded as a national military matter—the "deuxième portion du contingent"—or, in the case of its policy of allowing local rulers (French or African) to exact a few days local labor each year, as a "tax." In other words, French officials did not regard these forms as labor—important as they were for building railroads or maintaining roads—but put them into another category of legitimate government resource mobilization.[64]

The British government, however, ratified the convention promptly, thinking its colonies had already crossed the divide between coercion and its opposite. The conventions of 1926 and 1930 were mainly used to justify international pressure and occasional intervention, through league and ILO auspices, in the weaker governments in Africa whose practices were blatantly coercive and blatantly for private purposes—Liberia and Portuguese Angola in particular.[65] In France the convention plunged the labor question ever more deeply into a covert world where even secret official correspondence could not discuss it in a straightforward way, and from which it only emerged in 1946.[66]

Forced Labor in French Africa, 1930–1946

Forced labor continued to exist in French Africa both in the form of *prestations*, or pseudomilitary labor, and in the case of workers recruited by government officials and sent to private places of work.[67] There had already been scandals in the 1920s about the use of coerced labor by concession companies in French Equatorial Africa (particularly in lumbering) as well as in the government's construction of a railway in the French Congo, which had resulted in horrific mortality among laborers forcefully imported from another part of the region. The development of plantations in the Ivory Coast and later in Guinea would be based largely on coerced labor, and the most important public works project of the 1930s and 1940s, the Office du Niger in the French Sudan, would be the major consumer of forced labor for "public" purposes.[68]

Top officials claimed there was no recruitment for private purposes, but everyone in the hierarchy knew this was false. The white settlers, or colons, of the Ivory Coast, in particular, depended on laborers recruited by chiefs—under the eyes of French administrators—in the Upper Ivory Coast (known at various times as the colony of Upper Volta, and now the country of Burkina Faso). As the ILO pondered what became the convention of 1930, Governor-

General Carde noted the dilemma posed by universal norms and particular realities in relation to the proposed ban on forced labor for private enterprises: "This question is very delicate; the strict application of this rule could in effect have disastrous consequences for numerous established enterprises in French West Africa. It is thus necessary for us, while respecting the accepted principle, to push ourselves to avoid the deplorable effects which its pure and simple application would not fail to provoke." [69] Such a situation affected not only the public posture of the administration, but also the language of its internal debates. Silences spoke loudly. As one unusually honest inspection report described the operations of recruitment, "No written instruction was ever addressed to administrators on their conduct in this matter. And yet everyone knew the boss's wishes, everyone trembled for his promotion and did not dare formulate explicitly any criticism whatsoever." [70]

The Popular Front government of 1936–38 finally was willing to ratify the 1930 convention, as well as reduce its use of *prestations*.[71] It would not give up the *deuxième portion* and insisted that the convention did not apply to this kind of service; compulsion for public projects through the invocation of the analogy to military service was defended by the Left as well as the Right. Administrators, however, were told to desist from the use of coercion for the benefit of the colons.[72] They were asked to engage in an "apostolat du travail," that is, to preach the virtues of wage labor. These decisions reflected a government conscious of its progressive intent and aware of the hypocritical nature of its own discourse, a point emphasized by Governor-General Marcel de Coppet: "We lie in France, in Europe, in the entire world, in Geneva and at the International Labor Organization when regulations and circulars in hand, we speak of the organization of public works labor in the colonies. We dishonor our colonial administration and we demoralize our civil servants by asking them to apply, on paper only, regulations inapplicable in practice." [73]

There was also a recognition that violence ran up against its political limits —as well as posing severe demographic risks—at a point where the labor force was quite small, and that it was not a step to a more prosperous and less coercive future. Popular Front leaders believed that the only way to overcome present limits was to allow peasants to become more involved in commercial activities. Implicitly admitting the failure of French interventions, they saw no brighter hope for Africa's future than what they conceived of as the social and cultural formations of its past.[74]

But the new regime would only go so far. Wage labor was still needed for infrastructural projects and transport as well as for the existing settler farms, for elimination of this sector risked too much of the export revenue French

West Africa could boast of. Hence the importance of the "apostolat du travail." But in the far reaches of the Upper Ivory Coast it was not clear where the "apostolat du travail" ended and coercion began. Some local administrators tried to inform the Popular Front colonial minister of dubious practices, but his inquiries, through official channels, produced no results.[75] Indeed, the Popular Front was constrained by the code of silence developed by its predecessors: it was difficult to locate and stop practices that officially did not exist. Nor was it easy for Dakar or Paris to get tough with a territorial administration: the entire structure of colonial authority depended on a hierarchy of administrators who knew their natives and whose legitimacy was unquestioned. At the very least, the roundup of unwilling laborers for the colons became less overt under the Popular Front. It is much less clear that such practices ended.

As soon as a less agonized administration came to power in France in 1938, and as war and the need to augment production loomed, the situation degenerated. On the eve of World War II, war mobilization—and the usual complaint that voluntary labor was insufficient—became a rationale for sending signals through the bureaucracy that more men were wanted and fewer questions would be asked.[76] After France's defeat in 1940, the collaborationist Vichy regime ruled French West Africa until late 1942, and forced labor in this region reached unprecedented heights. Some 55,000 recruits per year were put to work in the Ivory Coast, 39,000 in Guinea. As France would not or could not send desirable manufactured goods to Africa, there were few incentives for Africans to work. Under Vichy, however, compulsion became more open, and colonial officials in France ridiculed anyone with scruples about enlisting African labor in the cause of national strength. Recruiting quotas were openly discussed, and the Vichy governor-general, Pierre Boisson, came under criticism for arguing that recruitment levels had reached the limits of what French West Africa could supply.[77]

Even after the Free French took over control of French West Africa, the imperatives of war production—now for the opposite side—and the belief that wartime commodity shortages exacerbated an African aversion to wage labor kept forced labor in place. Indeed, the ups and downs of French reliance on coercion both conceal and reflect an attitude toward Africans that was to a significant extent shared by both proponents and opponents of forced labor in the 1930s and early 1940s: that Africans were peculiar beings with deeply ingrained habits. Some took this to mean that economic progress would only come from compulsion. Others insisted that Africans were and would always be peasants, and officials had to reconcile themselves to that fact and adjust their approaches to agricultural expansion accordingly. The top officials of the new administration believed that forced labor was simultaneously dangerous and necessary: "Little habituated to fixed work hours, little interested in improving their situation by a painful discipline, they easily slip away to any prospects. It is impossible in such conditions, to think of implementing a development program based solely on the principle of free labor."[78]

That was the situation in February 1944, when Free French officials met in Brazzaville in the Congo to debate new directions in colonial policy for the postwar era. This was another moment when officials were acutely conscious of the need to articulate a progressive policy. Not only were wartime denunciations of infringements of "self-determination" ringing in their ears, but officials themselves, emerging from France's wartime debacle, needed a positive vision of their role. The Brazzaville conference was a strong reaffirmation of the morality of empire, now justified by the role of France in masterminding economic and social development. The conferees wanted to give Africans who played by the rules a voice in French institutions; as a result of such deliberations, elections were held in October 1945—with a limited franchise—and over twenty colonial representatives were sent to Paris to participate in drafting a new French constitution and to exercise legislative functions.[79]

While these decisions were being made, officials also debated forced labor. The Brazzaville conference heard the new governor of the Ivory Coast describe the horrors of forced labor. Conferees agreed that it was a demographic and economic disaster as well as a moral one; they feared an exodus of people from France's landlocked but populous colony of Upper Volta to the British colony of the Gold Coast in order to escape the manhunters of the administration. But officials were so convinced that Africans would not work for wages that they gave themselves five years to end forced labor. Recruitment levels were to be reduced by 20 percent each year, to zero the final year.[80]

In any event, forced labor was ended definitively in two years, not five. Brazzaville's time schedule collapsed in the extraordinary conjuncture of 1946. African colonies were now the site of political campaigns, and Africans were sitting in the legislature in Paris. In December 1945 a two-month-long strike began in French West Africa's leading port, Dakar; officials could only get the strikers back to work with large wage increases and, what is even more significant, by bringing to bear the entire apparatus of industrial relations used in France—in short, by acting as if the strikers were modern, industrial workers.[81] In the midst of all this, the manhunters were still operating.

Félix Houphouët-Boigny addressing a crowd of supporters in a neighborhood of Abidjan, capital of the Ivory Coast, in 1946. The law abolishing forced labor in French colonies, passed in April 1946, is known as the "Houphouët-Boigny law." (Courtesy Agence France Presse)

"The Slavery Which Is Still Practiced in Black Africa"

The African delegates in Paris forced French legislators to go on public record as to whether or not they wanted forced labor to be part of postwar French society. In February 1946 a group led by Félix Houphouët-Boigny—whose political base was a group of African cocoa planters in the Ivory Coast—wrote to the colonial minister: "Millions of men have sent us here giving us a precise mandate, to struggle with all our might to abolish the slavery which is still practiced in Black Africa by men, civil servants and civilians, who are traitors to France and her noble civilizing mission." They astutely tied their rhetoric to that with which France defended the morality of imperialism, while bringing the analogy to slavery into jarring juxtaposition.[82] This group, joined by the noted poet and West Indian deputy Aimé Césaire and others, soon submitted in proper form a bill whose principle article read simply, "Forced or obligatory labor is forbidden in the most absolute fashion in the overseas territories." This was what representation, however minoritarian, was all about. The legislators would have to examine their beliefs in a public forum.[83]

The proposed law went before a committee headed by Houphouët-Boigny, which soon issued a report stressing the abuses to which forced labor led and the dangerous political, social, and demographic consequences of forcing men to leave their villages for labor in distant areas. This document also invoked the image of slavery and of the *corvée*, or hard labor, of the ancien régime in France. Houphouët-Boigny, citing his own example, held up the possibility of African producers making a far larger contribution to exports than the white settlers could, and he offered the deputies the chance "to prove to the world that the France of the rights of man and of the citizen, the France of the abolition of slavery, remains always true to herself and could not contest or limit the liberty of any of the people living under her flag." The deputies took their opportunity, passing without debate what became known as the "loi Houphouët-Boigny." [84]

The colonial ministry, which did not oppose the bill, no doubt greeted its passage with relief. Backing off from the five-year plan represented a significant change in official perceptions. As recently as the summer of 1945, the governor-general of French West Africa had wondered whether production could be maintained without forced labor; he was not sure that free labor was a good thing for Africans after all, since they would lose "the ancestral contact with the land and this would mean the creation, full of hazards, of an indigenous proletariat, having lost its sense of landed property (in the customary sense), only counting on wages to live." [85] The governor-general was still caught up in the peculiarity-of-the-African argument, despite assertions that economic and social development was the raison d'être of the entire colonial project.

The change in official thinking came about largely because of African initiative. Specifically, it was the growth of an African political-cum-agricultural organization that showed a way out of the contradictory jumble of officials' modernizing aspirations for the future and their fear of the weight of the African past. For some years, most of the coffee and cocoa coming out of the Ivory Coast had been grown by African planters, despite the fact that the white colons were getting most of the attention and all the recruited labor. Officials began to take more of an interest in this group after 1944, when the government—having explicitly acknowledged the evils of forced labor, but ever willing to compromise on the process of abolishing it—was stonewalled by the colons, who refused to do anything to wean themselves from administration-supplied labor.[86]

The African planters, led by Houphouët-Boigny, had quietly organized themselves into the Société Agricole Africaine (SAA) in 1944 and established their own network for recruiting labor. Their standard procedure was a form of labor tenancy, usually referred to as *métayage*: the laborer received one-third of the value of coffee harvested and/or two-fifths of the value of cocoa, with a guaranteed monthly minimum, plus rations and free transport for the worker and family. Governor André Latrille, who had no love for the colons, began to see that the SAA was providing him a new card to play, and he even accompanied Houphouët-Boigny on a "propaganda tour" of the populous northern regions of the Ivory Coast, where labor was being sought, now voluntarily, for use in the more fertile south. Houphouët-Boigny later reported his pleasure at hearing an old chief, who had long served the French, say, "We want, with Houphouet, to try the experiment because it is very painful to us to recruit by force, each year, 6,500 of our young men, the majority of whom do not return." [87]

After years of intense recruitment for the colons, the regions most victimized were tense. To escape the mancatchers, many men were fleeing to the adjacent British territory of the Gold Coast to take jobs instead on African farms (on terms that provided, in fact, the model for those being offered in the Ivory Coast by the SAA). Governor Latrille noted that if caught and sent to colons' farms, workers had to endure conditions of "semi-slavery"; they could be disciplined only by coercive means—holding back food, "bad treatment," withholding of wages due—since being fired would be a blessing and not a sanction.[88] What was new about all this was that it was now taking place in the context of rural mobilization by an African organization and in the face of impending political campaigns and elections (first held in October 1945 and sending Houphouët-Boigny to Paris), not in the subterranean darkness where the labor question had resided before the war. The situation in the Upper Ivory Coast became so tense that recruitment had to be suspended there in January 1946.[89]

When Houphouët-Boigny and his colleagues introduced their bill into the Paris legislature, not long after the Dakar general strike had jarred officials' sense of control over another dimension of the labor question, the ministry apparently realized that it was being offered a way out of an impossible situation. It would not have to assume all of the political risks of going against governors' advice or the colons' wishes itself.

After the passage of the emancipation bill in April 1946, the SAA took on much of the burden of the transition in the Ivory Coast. When the European firms that supplied the railway with firewood stopped cutting—probably to demonstrate their continued need for forced labor—the SAA organized wood-cutting operations and networks to supply labor. In agriculture, as unwilling and angry workers left their white employers, African planters took up the slack. The government played its part by tripling the minimum wage, a move intended to shock the colons into a realization that their world had changed as much as to improve the labor supply (and which would not have affected the SAA's standard tenant-labor package). The government made available special stocks of cloth—the most important imported consumer item, and one in extremely scarce supply—to *ivoiriens* with ration cards issued through employers and thus available only to wage workers. The labor supply stabilized within a few months, while African farmers became increasingly important as producers and employers.[90]

The colons soon proved themselves an eminently forgettable part of the Ivory Coast economy. In the decade after 1946, cocoa and coffee exports from the Ivory Coast shot upward, and the Ivory Coast passed Senegal as the leading export economy of French West Africa. The great success story of postwar African agriculture was being written by the African planters and the tenant-laborers who worked for them.[91]

But within the wage labor sector, the myth of the peculiarity of the African did not go away so much as shift. Labor inspectors, themselves the vanguard of a new approach to the colonial labor question, still commented on the "indolent" and "unstable" workforce and considered instability and indiscipline as "infant diseases" or a "puberty crisis" (developmental metaphors are not exactly precise) of a new workforce. One report commented, "The primitive African has not yet acquired a taste for work and he is barely tempted to abandon his milieu, as well as his fields which bring him sufficient income, in order to go to a workplace where the discipline and the obligation for constant physical effort are contrary to his habits."[92] Governor Latrille tried to push even this view of African particularity out of the official mind: "[T]he old slander which said that the African was an incorrigible idler, incapable of working except under constraint, has been denied by the facts. For the African is not made differently from the rest of humanity. He knows how to appreciate the dignity of work done freely and he comes to offer his labor each time that one offers him remunerative prices."[93]

This was as much a fanciful projection of European norms as the opposite line was an old slander. But under the impact of new challenges such as the mobilization of workers in Dakar, as well as the putting to rest of the forced labor issue, it was a clear statement of the emerging direction in labor policy. The stress on stability and the attempt to transfer resources specifically to wage workers signaled the beginnings of an effort to define wage workers as a class and to try to wean them from the peculiarities of African culture. Hardly anyone had believed the old line that forced labor would "teach" Africans the virtues of work; rather, it had represented a de facto acceptance that Africans were attached to their own notions of economic life and could only be extracted from them temporarily and unwillingly. Now officials were beginning to act on the assumption that some Africans could be attracted to a life of wage labor and would learn new ways.[94]

What had actually happened in 1946 was not that Africans had suddenly become rational economic beings subject to the universal laws of the market, but that the SAA had organized a very specific labor system. The relatively prosperous and well-connected leaders of the SAA had their contacts in populated regions of the Ivory Coast, and they had something quite different from ordinary wage labor to offer their recruits: a form of labor tenancy that gave workers considerable control over work rhythms and how they used their own family's labor, as well as incentives to raise output. They were adapting to the Ivory Coast a form of labor mobilization worked out in the Gold Coast beginning in the late nineteenth century, with which people in the Ivory Coast's main labor "reservoir" had had considerable experience as they sought, through migration, alternatives to the regime of force in French Africa.[95]

French officials condescendingly noted that métayage was more suitable to African habits than the time discipline and time-based wages of European employers. But in 1946 they were not asking many questions about it, nor about the SAA's recruitment methods. One report did make a vague allusion to recruitment still being "far from the free labor which we wanted to install in the Ivory Coast," but it did not indicate who, if anyone, might have been bringing pressure, subtle or otherwise, against anyone else.[96]

If the idea of free labor shed little light on the specifics of how labor actually was organized, the opening of electoral politics left much in the shadows as well. Part of mobilization rested on the founding fathers of political movements positioning themselves as liberators in the most universal sense of the term. The "loi Houphouët-Boigny" became a cornerstone of the myth of emancipation in francophone West Africa. Political mobilization was just as particular in its linkage to social networks and to idioms of affinity as the SAA's labor recruitment methods. Houphouët-Boigny turned a network of African cocoa planters into a political machine and proved a master of the politics of clientelism; Léopold Senghor took the helm of Senegalese politics by his construction of a movement closely tied to Islamic brotherhoods, by his appeal to former subjects seeking to make real their admission to the category of citizen, and by his broadening of emancipatory rhetoric that held the imagination of younger educated men and women. Politically, economically, and socially, the uses of the universal were quite particular.

French officials freed themselves of slavery's analogue nearly a century after slavery itself had been abolished in the French colonies; they had ended the contradiction of defending colonial rule as an economically and socially progressive force while maintaining an institution that both assumed and perpetuated backwardness; they had freed their own civil service of the demoralizing task—of which junior officials had long complained—of supervising manhunts; and they had taken themselves out of a politically dangerous situation. Freed of the burden of directly intervening in the ambiguous world of rural social organization, they could take on an activist role in transforming the more bounded world of wage labor, particularly urban wage labor.

Beyond Forced Labor

The ending of forced labor was part of a remarkable conjuncture in 1946 that threw the labor question out of the narrow framework of free labor ideology and shook up the effort of the French government to redefine its imperial role for the postwar era. The emancipation act of April shares the spotlight with two other momentous events: the Dakar general strike of December 1945–February 1946 and the act of the French legislature in May abolishing the distinction between subject and citizen.

By March 1946, when Colonial Minister Moutet responded to the February letter about forced labor from the African deputies, he had accepted that the terms of discussion had changed. He said not a word to contradict the deputies' powerful argument comparing forced labor to slavery. Indeed, he thanked them for posing the issue in terms so respectful of the idea of France as an emancipatory nation. Moutet had two related issues on his mind: a proposed labor code for French overseas territories and the general strike that had just taken place in Senegal.

The labor code—regulating working hours and minimum wages, contracts, and rules for collective organization and bargaining—had been proposed in mid-1945, in a double form: one code for "subjects," another for "citizens." There had been objections to this from Senegal, on the grounds that anything other than a unitary code was racially discriminatory. The code had already been hung up over debates on whether its article proclaiming that labor must be voluntary should take effect within the Brazzaville time frame (by 1949) or within one year, as Houphouët-Boigny had argued.[97]

Then came the strike. It began in December 1945 in the port of Dakar and quickly spread from one group of workers to another, leading to rapid concessions and the rapid voicing of similar demands. For twelve days in January a well-run general strike paralyzed Dakar, and strikes broke out elsewhere in Senegal. The most important slogan of the strike was "equal pay for equal work," a notably concrete reinterpretation of the French claims for the unity of the French Empire. The strike was more of an overlapping and coordinated set of movements than a single one, with ordinary laborers seeking a livable wage, commercial workers a minimum wage equivalent to that of European workers, and civil servants full equality of benefits for all categories of workers. By early February workers had won the most important of their demands. The effects of the strike were powerful: officials feared that recourse to colonial muscle might drive workers out of Dakar, so they instead imported labor experts and techniques of labor organization directly from the metropole.[98]

Here were Africans acting in accordance with the idea of a "universal" worker. Here were citizens (those Africans historically associated with the old French colonies) and subjects (recent migrants from rural Senegal) striking side by side. And here was the French government having to accept a new reality, to concede that African workers and their families needed incomes and benefits of the same sort that French workers required, and to recognize that orderly bargaining with recognized trade unions was vital to the maintenance of order and continued production. In the months following the strike, the labor inspectors charged with managing employer-worker relations would become strong advocates of cooperation with African unions and of developing a predictable framework for labor relations. The inspectors, in the name of rational organization, became strong supporters of a new labor code, while the trade unions demanded such a code in the name of equality.

All the while, forced labor was still legal in French West Africa. One can understand why Moutet, in March 1946, was glad to let the deputies resolve the debate within the government over whether Africans were capable of becoming free laborers; he was already facing the reality of workers as political actors and as social beings. Moutet was no more interested in defending the distinction between citizen and subject—which had proven meaningless in the social crisis in Senegal—than he was in defending forced labor. He wanted the help of Houphouët-Boigny, Senghor, and their colleagues in writing a labor code that would apply to all workers, white or black, of any status, in French colonies, and he told them that repeal of the judicial regime that separated subjects from citizens was under study.

In April, therefore, the assembly voted for the emancipation of forced laborers, and in May it declared that the demeaning status of colonial "subject" no longer existed. All inhabitants of territory claimed by France were citizens. In both cases, African deputies took the initiative to bring the proposals before the Assemblée Nationale Constituante, the body elected to write a new constitution and to legislate on important issues in the meantime. Both measures formally repudiated the backward-looking colonialism of the past and suggested that France would remain imperial and become progressive at the same time.

The voice of the citizens would be mediated by the regulations of complex institutions, such as limitations on the franchise that stressed education and status (barriers, but not immutable ones), and the differential allocation of seats in representative bodies. Formulating the specifics of citizenship within the French Union would take much more debate than acceptance of the principle had required after the war: universal suffrage would come about ten years later; the distribution of legislative seats in accordance with population, not at all.[99]

The question of labor revealed the same tension of general principle and colonial specificity: once the field of application of a labor code was made universal, the stakes in each of its texts were very high. Such provisions as the forty-hour week or paid vacations would apply to workers of all origins, and the code was debated line by line for six years, passing in 1952 after yet another mobilization in Africa and in Paris. In the French legislature, Senghor and other African deputies argued in 1952 for a vigorous application of the principle of equivalence—that all workers be treated equally—whereas conservatives insisted that the particular nature of the African worker made such measures as paid vacations and family allowances difficult to apply. When one looks at citizenship and labor together, one sees just how dynamic the situation was in the postwar years, how basic was the challenge to established hierarchies posed by the application of concepts like equality and universality to specific struggles.

The laws of April and May 1946 marked the end of a long history, from the debates about the application of the rights of man to the issue of slavery in Saint Domingue in 1791, to the abolition of slavery in all French colonies in 1794 and its reinstatement in 1802, its final abolition in 1848 and the extension of citizenship to the "old" colonies, the halting measures against African slavery in the early 1900s, the conventions of the League of Nations and the ILO in 1926 and 1930 and the abortive attempt to curtail forced labor in 1936, to the efforts of colonial deputies since the time of World War I to force their colleagues to argue consistently about the meaning of citizenship in the

French republic.[100] Some debates seemed definitively settled in 1946: all inhabitants of the French Union would be citizens, and none would be subject to forced labor. Too definitively, perhaps: the rulers of France were soon wondering what they had wrought, as colonial citizens began to use the framework of citizenship to call into question every sort of inequality within what was once the French Empire and was now the French Union.

The French government's defense of empire was now linked to a universalism that was turning into demands for equality within all spheres of social life, publicly showcased in the Assemblée Nationale in Paris and through newspapers, trade unions, and other institutions that were now constitutionally protected.[101] One could still argue that the new debates would take place within terms defined by Europe. This is the gist—as noted in the Introduction to this volume—of much of the "postcolonial critique" of concepts such as citizenship. Indeed, such issues were raised at the time by participants in the debate. To Senghor, for example, engagement with France meant that Africans should assimilate what they saw as useful from French politics and culture, rather than "be assimilated" to the metropole's way of life. The implications of politics within a citizenship framework were taken up in a prescient legal thesis published in 1951 by a West African scholar, Doudou Thiam. He agreed with postcolonial theorists that citizenship was a powerful agent of cultural transformation, consistent with the "centralizing and unifying tendency" of French policy; it went against the notion, found in many African societies, that power was personal, emphasizing instead that the citizen was part of an institutional structure that operated in accordance with rules. Thiam was aware of the individualistic thinking intrinsic to the history of French citizenship: "To say to an African or a Malagasy that he is a French citizen, is it not to ask him in a sense to grow a new skin, to rid himself of the sum of the traditions that make up his personality?"

But for Thiam, the question was not rhetorical: he was also aware that the cultural meanings of the French Union were under debate. He cited Senghor's insistence in the constitutional assemblies that civilizations existed only in the plural: each person put an emphasis on different aspects of the human condition. The new constitution, Thiam argued, implied that individual rights had to be reconciled with distinct legal statuses and distinct senses of "nation" within the French Union—a person, for instance, was no less a citizen for marrying and conveying property under Islamic law (an issue still contested at the time in Algeria). The relationship between different sorts of "modern" and "traditional, customary" rights, he concluded, "is not simple." Thiam advocated a more social conception of citizenship, one that took account of what "overseas worlds" had to offer to French civilization; he wanted to see more "points of contact" develop within French citizenship, and he hoped to see "the loss of homogeneity" within French conceptions of citizenship.[102] He was certainly correct that these issues would be the focus of debate and that they would be complicated; they remained so within the territorial confines of France even in the 1990s. But it would be a mistake to assume that Thiam's cause was a lost one from the start—citizenship is a dynamic concept, whose meanings are not intrinsic to the construct but are shaped in political, social, and cultural debate and confrontation.

The free labor and citizenship enactments of April–May 1946 quickly expanded into a debate that went on until the passage of an inclusive labor code in 1952 and continued in various forms after that. The official vindication of free labor and citizenship could not be kept simply formal, simply legal; it also existed in relation to a social domain. The tension between the abstract principles of equivalence and the concrete issues at stake—wages and paid vacations—was important for making French officials consider the meaning of holding colonies in the political context of the postwar era. By 1952 they had found that equivalence meant that wage workers of all origins throughout the French Union had the right to the forty-hour week, paid vacations, a minimum wage sufficient to cover basic needs, and other benefits; workers' rights to join unions and to strike were guaranteed by law.[103]

In the end, citizenship, equality, and universalism proved to be ideas that were too compelling—too appealing to social movements and too hard for French elites to repudiate. By the mid-1950s, with the start of the Algerian war and the beginnings of efforts to devolve power to elected representatives in African colonies, the experiment in modernizing imperialism had failed. It had raised too many costs and provoked too many conflicts, and it had come aground on the unresolvable contradiction between the universalism of ideology in the Fourth Republic and the particularism of colonial rule. Few people would have predicted in 1946 that the French state would repudiate the unity of its own empire, but that was what the government had come to accept a decade later.

Just as Senghor, Houphouët-Boigny, and others had astutely manipulated a discourse about the French Revolution and emancipation in the forced labor debate, post-1946 labor politics involved the ability of African trade unions and politicians to invoke European social ideas—and to turn what officials thought would be an ideology of control into the basis for demands. The idea of the universal could be used to advocate not simply the particular model of European capitalism, but the particular interests of African workers.

The shift in the terms of the labor question took place at an international level, too. In 1944 the International Labour Organization cautiously moved beyond its long position that the question of free labor was the relevant one for colonies, whereas a wide variety of social issues was vital to regulating the labor question in "metropolitan" countries.[104] A resolution that year on "minimum standards of social policy in dependent territories" expressed the sense that metropolitan social legislation should be applied to dependencies. By that time Great Britain had been confronting waves of strikes in its empire and was trying to resolve them in a manner similar to that which would used by France in 1946, albeit on a more case-by-case basis. In 1947 the ILO adopted a formal convention on the extension of social legislation overseas. In the following years, the ILO became a site—comparable to the role played by the Berlin and Brussels conferences of the 1880s and 1890s—for expressing an international consensus on the need for "stabilizing" labor: that all workers should receive wages and/or family allowances sufficient to raise families without recourse to rural resources, that all people should benefit from a standard of living above a certain minimum level, and that all workers should have the right to organize and strike. The universal worker had come into being—as something more complex than a "free" individual.[105]

Free labor ideology still had its influence: the idea that South African workers were not truly free was a powerful image in the antiapartheid struggle, as are critiques of forms of contractual labor and child labor today. But one should not assume that the ascendancy of norms like a global minimum standard of living or a family wage are part of a linear history of continual progress. The attack on "urban bias" in the 1970s and arguments for "flexibility" in labor markets—characteristic of the neoliberalism of the 1980s and 1990s— entail a rejection of the ILO consensus of the 1950s. African states are now accused of paying urban workers too much and farmers too little, of failing to pay heed to the universal laws of the market; the argument that Africans behave in peculiar ways has appeared in a new form.

The consensus of the 1950s was as important for what it left out—any form of labor other than wage labor—as for what it included. A category like "informal sector," for example, is in effect a shorthand for forms of labor excluded from regulatory systems such as that of the French labor code of 1952.[106] Such categorizations have important implications: the 1952 code applied to forms of labor largely carried out at the time by males, leaving a sizable domain of economic activities done by females outside the legal definition of labor; such gender exclusions have had a crucial impact on the kinds of opportunities people have in both wage labor and commerce.

Beyond Imperialism

The story of the emancipation of 1946 reveals much more than the inadequacy of a neo-abolitionist conception of liberty progressively suppressing coercion. It illustrates how definitions of the politically possible are transformed in the process of political engagement. Forced labor, once defensible and ordinary in a colonial context, became unthinkable, and what was once unimaginable—the African as a worker, acquiring skill, supporting a family, and participating in labor organizations—became an accepted norm. When Britain and France tried to seize the postwar moment by setting out a development-oriented, progressive agenda for colonial rule, they quickly found that the agenda was not theirs to set. France, notably, could not prevent its assertion of universal citizenship from spilling over into a politics of social and economic equivalence, or prevent its embrace of social "progress" from spilling into an escalation of demands for political empowerment.

However much colonial powers tried to use the categories of citizen and worker to contain aspirations within Europe's concept of what "universal" was supposed to mean, trade unionists, political leaders, and ordinary workers and citizens in Africa were using, manipulating, and redefining those categories as they lived them. The power to define the terms of debate over international issues is not an equal one, but the antislavery, anticolonial, and antiapartheid movements all compelled profound changes in what kinds of political processes fell within universalistic norms and what kinds did not.[107] The Western roots of the categories of such movements are not the only, or necessarily the most important, aspect of the histories or present-day significance of these mobilizations. Most important is whether debate over the meanings and implications of citizenship and work can still be carried out.

Afterword

It is now just over 150 years since France, in the midst of its own revolutionary trauma in 1848, abolished slavery in its colonies. Much of the press coverage of this anniversary noted how absent this event had been from French discussions of the past. Acknowledging emancipation would have meant acknowledging slavery, especially the fact that slavery was still legal a half-century after the Revolution of 1789, annually commemorated as the starting point of the French republican tradition and the idea of citizenship. The Revolution had indeed abolished slavery in 1794, albeit under the duress of slave revolts and foreign invasions of plantation islands, but Napoleon had restored it in 1802.

In 1998 the president of France, Jacques Chirac, sought to move beyond the long neglect of the colonial side of France's emancipatory tradition. He did so by emphasizing that the emancipated slaves of 1848 passed directly into the category of "citizen." Apparently, their inferior status—as well as whatever bitterness their history had left them with—had disappeared unre-marked upon into the collective anonymity of being "French." For Chirac the emancipation of 1848 marked the "French model of integration." But the next day, newspapers reported that in Martinique—once a sugar colony, now a department of France—people who traced their ancestry to the slaves did not want their history to dissolve and, indeed, did not see the emancipation act as the primary focus of celebration. Instead, their focus was on the slave revolts that had taken place shortly before the emancipation decree, on the actions of slaves that helped to precipitate the action of the revolutionaries of Paris. And in Paris itself, one of the central issues of political debate in April of 1998 was the status of migrant workers—mostly from former French colonies, and mostly of African origin—who had labored for years in France while in an "irregular" immigration status, and many of whom were being deported out of France on chartered airplanes. A cartoon in Le Monde juxtaposed a picture, labeled 1848, of a black person breaking the chain that bound him to a white hand with an image, labeled 1998, of a black person chained to an airplane, the sign of the French model of exclusion.[1]

It is now just over fifty years since Frank Tannenbaum published his plea to white Americans to allow the descendants of slaves to achieve a fuller kind of citizenship than was then available to them, eighty years after their emancipation. It is just over fifty years as well since the French government decided to abolish the invidious distinction between subject and citizen and to eliminate forced labor in its empire, hoping to promulgate a more inclusive and dynamic notion of "France," a conception that would soon explode out of its boundaries.

It is tempting now to look back on the ensuing decades as a period when the stunted promises of liberation that were already the focus of concern in 1946—or 1848, or 1794, or 1863—were at last fulfilled. Jamaica, like the territories of French West Africa, acquired sovereignty. The civil rights movement in the United States achieved a genuine end to disfranchisement and made real progress in ending discrimination in education and public accommodations. The demeaning subordination of sugar workers in Cuba became the object of explicit government efforts at reform, even if those workers found that formal respect was not necessarily matched by effective political voice. And if one looks farther afield, one can point to the end of the apartheid regime in South Africa in 1994, an advance that marked both the first time that black South Africans could vote en masse and the end of restrictive labor and migration regulations that made seeking a job less than "free." One can point as well to the end of another project of modernization from above, which also involved immense amounts of forced labor in the name of a better future—the Soviet Union.

Yet as one looks beyond slavery to the various ways in which "analogous" conditions were addressed and to the question of what citizenship means for those emancipated, the picture is mixed. It becomes apparent that the search for legacies of past systems, for evidence that they have been diluted or overcome, is only one part of understanding the "beyond" in "beyond slavery." We need also to keep looking at the flow of history, examining how certain forms of social power once taken for granted became impossible while others emerged—with their own constraints as well as opportunities. The transition to new forms of social power offers the possibility of illuminating oppressive practices once obscured—but carries the risk of blinding us to others.

Sovereignty is now a virtually universal concept: everybody is a citizen of someplace. In 1946 this was not true: colonized people were subjects, not citizens. They were parts of empires, not states, and within those empires they were often treated as if they belonged to "tribes," not nations. Today, more than fifty years later, we may recognize diverse forms of belonging, we may even inscribe on some an "identity" that belies their dynamism and shifting meaning, but we link at least one form of belonging to a specific institutional structure—the nation-state. Indeed, much "subnational" struggle is in fact about redefining the boundaries of institutions to conform to alleged boundaries of affiliations. The citizenship construct thus remains a very powerful one, a mobilizing cry as well as an assertion of the normality of having political voice, of having rights.

But precisely because sovereignty has become generalized in a way that it was not before, there are certain questions that become harder to ask, and certain ways in which people and practices can become isolated from worldwide critique. The poverty of a Jamaican or a Malian in 1946 was a question that resonated across the British or French empires and opened London and Paris to criticism at home and abroad. But the poverty of a Jamaican or a Malian today is more often construed as a question for experts in famine relief. The International Labour Organization, from its founding until the fall of white supremacy in South Africa, focused international attention on forced labor and, later, on the difficult questions of the social protections people needed in an age of wage labor. But those questions are now more hidden behind walls of sovereignty: it has been argued that citizens themselves can demand that labor laws in their own countries be enforced. To insist that the international community might have a say could be considered an infringement of sovereignty, a new form of do-good imperialism, as much an exercise of power as the anti-slave-trade colonialism of the late nineteenth century.

At the same time, the national building blocks that make up the world economy are involved in connections that are, at the very least, far more rapid than before. The connections that the trade in slaves and plantation commodities of the sixteenth century pioneered are still evolving. One now finds Senegalese sweeping the streets of Paris, Turks working in German factories, Chinese toiling in Los Angeles sweatshops. And European, Japanese, and American firms draw on the labor power of these and other peoples in Africa, Latin America, and Asia, in the places where workers live or in still other "export platforms" to which workers migrate. Such workers thus escape both from the poverty of their places of origin as well as from the regulatory apparatus of the factory owners' home countries. Sovereignty is more widely distributed than ever before, yet it may well protect less.

Equally important, citizenship may be generalized, but millions of people are located away from their place of citizenship. The labor migrant and the refugee reveal as much about the world of nations as does the voting citizen located in his or her place of birth. The anxieties surrounding such migrants betray the disjuncture between the institutional and imaginary structure of nationhood and the reality of lives. And more than anxiety is in evidence. The skinheads of Germany and the followers of Jean-Marie LePen in France, as well as the anti-immigration forces in the United States, remind us that working and living in a place do not necessarily securely locate one there. The power of these movements, moreover, is not derived simply from debates over citizenship documents and issues of access to social welfare services—the question of race is fundamental. Representations of the Haitian refugee and of the Korean immigrant in American media are not the same, nor are representations of the Mozambican and of the Pole in Germany. Countries from which the victims of racial discrimination in Europe come may themselves discriminate against the nationals of their neighbors, or against people (like the Kurds in Turkey) classified in particular ethnic terms.

Neither the notion of citizenship nor the notion of a labor market that is both "free" and "global" quite gets at the social meanings of work, a problem that former slaves posed with extreme clarity in the aftermath of Jamaica's emancipation. The degrading experience of plantation labor, these former slaves showed, would not necessarily make wage labor an object of dislike and avoidance. But they were going to think about its significance in their own terms: to ask what the conditions of labor meant for the rhythms of their lives, for the possibilities of combining cash-earning with cropping activities, for the balance of their families' lives. They wanted to know what work meant for the changing communities they experienced, and they wanted to know what their status as workers or as members of a racial majority meant for their exercise of citizenship.

Much the same may be said of former slaves in the sugar regions of central Cuba. In 1899 Cayetano Quesada and Ciriaco Quesada, both members of an extended family of former slaves from the Santa Rosalía plantation, returned from three years of service in the rebel Ejército Libertador, where they had fought to defeat Spanish colonialism. Installing themselves on adjacent plots of land in the village of San Antón, Ciriaco raised horses and cattle while Cayetano planted a provision garden and harvested *palmiche* from the palm trees to feed his and his neighbors' pigs. These households cultivated the classic Caribbean food crops—maize, yams, plantains, beans—and some of their members worked for wages on the neighboring Soledad sugar plantation.[2] The balance they sought was a delicate one indeed, as it involved earning cash from the same sugar plantation whose expansion and prosperity threatened to encroach on the land they had carefully planted in food crops. To say that economic security was an issue for former slaves in Jamaica and Cuba, as it is for their descendants today, is to utter the most profound of understatements.

In the nineteenth century, in large part through the debates and interventions around slavery, Europe set itself up as the model for global society. Systems like slave labor would no longer be one of a number of techniques useful for the extraction of resources; the social process of production would be subject to scrutiny. Exploitation of resources and of labor power would be extended globally, but they would be linked to an ideology of progress, positing some sort of advance for the people who did the work. Such notions were often honored in the breach, but by the early twentieth century it was clear that an imperious Europe could not simply ignore them. Colonial economic policies and colonial rule itself were repeatedly challenged, sometimes within the colonizers' terms, but often in ways that questioned those terms themselves. The Jamaican produce grower and hawker could inject alternative notions of production and commerce into the reality of colonial life, even if policymakers would not understand or would deliberately avoid the implications of those questions.

Many of those alternative notions are still at issue. The sovereignty of former colonial states has not ended the question of whether the "world market" or the International Monetary Fund can dictate how social and economic structures will be shaped. The Nike shoe corporation may shift a plant from a country where labor laws and a labor movement ensure certain standards of compensation to another one whose government allows miserable working conditions, famine wages, and suppression of unions, but such actions can also give rise to cross-national movements attacking Nike at the same global level at which it operates.

Such transnational mobilization follows in the footsteps of a William Lloyd Garrison or a Frederick Douglass, who crossed the Atlantic to combat slavery in the name of free labor, or of a W. E. B. Du Bois, who saw that the worldwide oppression of people of color required mobilization on a Pan-African level. It also follows Nelson Mandela, who fought racial oppression by linking organization in townships to organization across continents, and who framed his arguments in a variety of idioms, from that of universal justice and citizenship to the language of a Xhosa migrant worker in Johannesburg. The question is not whether global connections and universalistic ideologies have intrinsic tendencies to expand or contract the realm of human freedom, but how those connections and ideologies are used in the specific struggles at hand.

The rapidity of international communications and the ability of multinational corporations to link production across the world has had an ironic impact on the global significance of the labor question. Europe in the nineteenth century set itself up as the model for the world. But today the wages and social benefits of a Salvadoran, of a Thai, or of an Egyptian set a standard of which the workers of France, Great Britain, Spain, or the United States need to be aware, while the productivity of a Japanese or Singaporan factory sets another sort of standard. Whether worldwide exchange is likely to be a force for upward or for downward leveling for the majority of the people who do the work is yet to be seen. We have moved far beyond slavery, but whether our insights have moved far enough to understand, let alone affect, the unfolding questions of labor and citizenship remains open to examination and debate at the end of a century of colonization and liberation, of forced labor and emancipation.

Notes

Introduction

1. Frank Tannenbaum, *Slave and Citizen: The Negro in the Americas* (New York: Knopf, 1956); Stanley M. Elkins, *Slavery: A Problem in American Institutional and Intellectual Life* (Chicago: University of Chicago Press, 1959). For a collection of essays and extracts that explain and critique this genre of comparative work, see Laura Foner and Eugene Genovese, eds., *Slavery in the New World: A Reader in Comparative History* (Englewood Cliffs, N.J.: Prentice-Hall, 1969).

2. This was done explicitly in A. G. Hopkins, *An Economic History of West Africa* (London: Longman, 1973), and Suzanne Miers and Igor Kopytoff, eds., *Slavery in Africa: Historical and Anthropological Perspectives* (Madison: University of Wisconsin Press, 1977). But the appearance in the 1980s and 1990s of a modest but significant number of studies showed that there was indeed something out there to study. See, in particular, Frederick Cooper, *From Slaves to Squatters: Plantation Labor and Agriculture in Zanzibar and Coastal Kenya, 1890–1925* (New Haven: Yale University Press, 1980); Suzanne Miers and Richard Roberts, eds., *The End of Slavery in Africa* (Madison: University of Wisconsin Press, 1988); Paul E. Lovejoy and Jan S. Hogendorn, *Slow Death for Slavery: The Course of Abolition in Northern Nigeria, 1897–1936* (Cambridge: Cambridge University Press, 1993); and Martin A. Klein, ed., *Breaking the Chains: Slavery, Bondage, and Emancipation in Modern Africa and Asia* (Madison: University of Wisconsin Press, 1993), as well as his *Slavery and French Colonial Rule* (Cambridge: Cambridge University Press, 1998).

3. The three authors of this volume have been caught up in these issues for some time, and the present work is in part a reflection on where our studies of the "beyond" have taken us—and what they have left in question. See Cooper, *From Slaves to Squatters*; Rebecca J. Scott, *Slave Emancipation in Cuba: The Transition to Free Labor, 1860–1899* (Princeton: Princeton University Press, 1985); and Thomas C. Holt, *The Problem of Freedom: Race, Labor, and Politics in Jamaica and Britain, 1832–1938* (Baltimore: Johns Hopkins University Press, 1992). Meanwhile, historians of the United States, whose voluminous writings on the Reconstruction era had tended to skirt the issues specified here, have taken them up in a serious and compelling way. An ambitious and pioneering example for the United States is *Freedom: A Documentary History of Emancipation, 1861–1867*, a collection of edited documents compiled by the Freedmen and Southern Society Project at the University of Maryland, directed initially by Ira Berlin and later by Leslie Rowland, and published by Cambridge University Press. Volumes include Ira Berlin, ed., Joseph P. Reidy and Leslie S. Rowland, assoc. eds., *The Black Military Experience* (1982); Ira Berlin, Barbara J. Fields, Thavolia Glymph, Joseph P. Reidy, and Leslie S. Rowland, eds., *The Destruction of Slavery* (1985); Ira Berlin, Thavolia Glymph, Steven F. Miller, Joseph P. Reidy, Leslie Rowland, and Julie Saville, eds., *The Wartime Genesis of Free Labor: The Lower South* (1990); and Ira Ber-

lin, Steven F. Miller, Joseph P. Reidy, and Leslie Rowland, eds., *The Wartime Genesis of Free Labor: The Upper South* (1993). These volumes have been accompanied and followed by important monographs, including Barbara Jeanne Fields, *Slavery and Freedom on the Middle Ground: Maryland during the Nineteenth Century* (New Haven: Yale University Press, 1985); Julie Saville, *The Work of Reconstruction: From Slave to Wage Laborer in South Carolina, 1860–1870* (Cambridge: Cambridge University Press, 1994); and Leslie A. Schwalm, *A Hard Fight for We: Women's Transition from Slavery to Freedom in South Carolina* (Urbana: University of Illinois Press, 1997). Contributions to the understanding of free labor as a system in the U.S. South are now numerous, including Gerald R. Jaynes, *Branches without Roots: Genesis of the Black Working Class in the American South, 1862–1882* (New York: Oxford University Press, 1986), Eric Foner, *Nothing But Freedom* (Baton Rouge: Louisiana State University Press, 1982), and Gavin Wright, *Old South, New South: Revolutions in the Southern Economy since the Civil War* (New York: Basic Books, 1986). A recent important work on Brazil after emancipation is Hebe Maria Mattos de Castro, *Das cores do silêncio: os significados da liberdade no sudeste escravista—Brasil século XIX* (Rio de Janeiro: Arquivo Nacional, 1995), and a collection of essays on Cuba is in press, edited by Fernando Martínez Heredia, Orlando García Martínez, and Rebecca J. Scott, titled *Espacios, silencios, y los sentidos de la libertad: Cuba, 1878–1912* (Havana: Editorial UNIÓN, forthcoming). For an earlier collection with a comparative focus, see Frank McGlynn and Seymour Drescher, eds., *The Meaning of Freedom: Economics, Politics, and Culture after Slavery* (Pittsburgh: University of Pittsburgh Press, 1992). For a listing of the secondary as well as primary literature, see Rebecca J. Scott, Thomas C. Holt, and Frederick Cooper, eds., Aims McGuinness, assoc. ed., *Societies after Slavery: A Select Annotated Bibliography of Printed Sources on the British West Indies, British Colonial Africa, South Africa, Cuba, and Brazil* (Ann Arbor: University of Michigan Press, forthcoming).

4. Igor Kopytoff and Suzanne Miers, "African 'Slavery' as an Institution of Marginality," in Miers and Kopytoff, *Slavery in Africa*, 17.

5. Igor Kopytoff, "The Cultural Context of African Abolition," in Miers and Roberts, *End of Slavery in Africa*, 485–506.

6. See Orlando Patterson, *Slavery and Social Death: A Comparative Study* (Cambridge: Harvard University Press, 1982), and Moses Finley, *Classical Slavery* (London: Frank Cass, 1987).

7. For a survey, see Paul E. Lovejoy, *Transformations in Slavery: A History of Slavery in Africa* (Cambridge: Cambridge University Press, 1983).

8. Quoted in Suzanne Miers, *Britain and the Ending of the Slave Trade* (New York: Africana Publishing Corporation, 1975), 11. On the changing importance of antislavery discourse in nineteenth-century European thought—and the varying degrees of temporizing in acting in terms of that discourse—see David Brion Davis, *Slavery and Human Progress* (New York: Oxford University Press, 1984), and Seymour Drescher, *Capitalism and Antislavery: British Mobilization in Comparative Perspective* (New York: Oxford University Press, 1987). The relationship of antislavery to politics, particularly to Europe's revolutionary mobilizations, is a major theme of Robin Blackburn, *The Overthrow of Colonial Slavery, 1776–1848* (London: Verso, 1988).

9. Orlando Patterson, *Freedom in the Making of Western Culture* (New York: Basic Books, 1991), xiii.

10. Ibid., 3–4.

11. On the intertwining of emancipation and republican ideology, see, most recently,

Laurent Dubois, "A Colony of Citizens: Revolution and Slave Emancipation in the French Caribbean, 1789–1802" (Ph.D. diss., University of Michigan, 1998) and *Les esclaves de la République: L'histoire oubliée de la première émancipation, 1789–1794* (Paris: Calmann-Lévy, 1998).

12. See Eugene D. Genovese, *From Rebellion to Revolution: Afro-American Slave Revolts in the Making of the Modern World* (Baton Rouge: Louisiana State University Press, 1979). Michel-Rolph Trouillot gives another reading, calling attention to the "war within the war," the action of guerrilla bands of African-born slaves against both the French and Haitian leaders who sought to continue a plantation economy or compromise the island's political autonomy from the French Empire. See Michel-Rolph Trouillot, "The Three Faces of Sans Souci: Glory and Silences in the Haitian Revolution," in *Silencing the Past: Power and the Production of History* (Boston: Beacon Press, 1995). For C. L. R. James, in *The Black Jacobins: Toussaint L'Ouverture and the San Domingo Revolution*, 2d ed. (New York: Random House, 1963), the revolution marked a defining precedent for a socially radical, racially self-conscious movement, of direct relevance to James's own politics in the 1930s. See also Carolyn Fick, *The Making of Haiti: The Saint Domingue Revolution from Below* (Knoxville: University of Tennessee Press, 1990).

13. See Julius Scott, "A Common Wind: Currents of Afro-American Communication in the Age of the Haitian Revolution" (Ph.D. diss., Duke University, 1986).

14. For a penetrating overview of this phenomenon, see Paul Farmer, *The Uses of Haiti* (Monroe, Maine: Common Courage Press, 1994).

15. The problem posed by colonization in the age of universal reason was not simply the fact of imposing European rule, but the act of reproducing it. The continuity of colonial rule—of the people of one territory over people regarded as different—required the reproduction of markers of difference, be they linguistic, racial, or cultural. Colonial regimes went to great lengths to preserve the coherence of the colonizing group from dilution through intermarriage or through its members "going native," and they had to be careful to ensure that whatever the extent to which members of the colonized group became converted to Christianity or assimilated to Western culture, the colonized collectivity as a whole remained clearly demarcated. Colonization was threatened both by a failure to maintain boundaries and by the rigidities that the boundaries imposed. These themes are treated at length in Frederick Cooper and Ann Laura Stoler, eds., *Tensions of Empire: Colonial Cultures in a Bourgeois World* (Berkeley: University of California Press, 1997), especially in the introduction and in the article by Stoler included in the volume.

16. Fields, *Slavery and Freedom*, 193.

17. Among historians of India, the issue is a acute one, for it raises the question of whether a "postcolonial" state can find its own way of organizing political life or is stuck with the structures of state and citizenship originating in the West. The citizenship debate is thus most vividly addressed in the political writings of Indian intellectuals such as Dipesh Chakrabarty, "Modernity and Ethnicity in India: A History of the Present," *Economic and Political Weekly* 30 (30 December 1995): 3373–80, and Partha Chatterjee, "Secularism and Toleration," *Economic and Political Weekly* 29 (9 July 1994): 1768–77. The argument about the representation of groups claiming cultural distinction within Western democracies has also entailed debate. The question that advocates for the participation of groups, as such, in democratic polities have had the most difficulty facing is the problem of boundaries: How does one define groups whose existence is historically contingent, whose members may have multiple affiliations, and whose claim to represent individual members may be disputed by individuals seeking to exercise an "exit option" from

those groups? For a thoughtful initial analysis, see Will Kymlicka, *Multicultural Citizenship: A Liberal Theory of Minority Rights* (Oxford: Clarendon, 1995).

18. The postcolonial critiques of concepts such as citizenship, liberal democracy, and the state owe much to the work of Michel Foucault. For a vigorous exposition of the underpinnings of such arguments, see Dipesh Chakrabarty, "Postcoloniality and the Artifice of History: Who Speaks for 'Indian' Pasts?" *Representations* 37 (1992): 1–26.

19. Margaret R. Somers, "Citizenship and the Place of the Public Sphere: Law, Community, and Political Culture in the Transition to Democracy," *American Sociological Review* 58 (1993): 587–620.

20. For a pointed discussion of these issues in the United States, see Elsa Barkley Brown, "Negotiating and Transforming the Public Sphere: African American Political Life in the Transition from Slavery to Freedom," *Public Culture* 7 (Fall 1994): 107–46.

21. Uday Mehta, "Liberal Strategies of Exclusion," *Politics and Society* 18 (1990): 427–54; Rogers Brubaker, *Citizenship and Nationhood in France and Germany* (Cambridge: Harvard University Press, 1992).

22. Carole Pateman, *The Sexual Contract* (Stanford: Stanford University Press, 1988); Nancy Fraser and Linda Gordon, "Contract versus Charity: Why Is There No Social Citizenship in the United States?" *Socialist Review* 22, no. 3 (1992): 34–67.

23. See Linda K. Kerber, *Women of the Republic: Intellect and Ideology in Revolutionary America* (Chapel Hill: University of North Carolina Press, 1980); Joan B. Landes, *Women and the Public Sphere in the Age of the French Revolution* (Ithaca: Cornell University Press, 1988); Leora Auslander, *Taste and Power: Furnishing Modern France* (Berkeley: University of California Press, 1996); Pateman, *Sexual Contract*. A suggestive recent contribution is Jennifer Heuer, "Foreigners, Families and Citizens: Contradictions of National Citizenship in France, 1789–1830" (Ph.D. diss., University of Chicago, 1998).

24. The pioneering recent work on this subject is Ada Ferrer, *Insurgent Cuba: Race, Nation, and Revolution, 1868–1898* (Chapel Hill: University of North Carolina Press, 1999). An important earlier work is Jorge Ibarra, *Ideología mambisa* (Havana: Instituto Cubano del Libro, 1972).

25. Sidney Mintz, *Sweetness and Power: The Place of Sugar in Modern History* (New York: Penguin, 1985); Dale Tomich, *Slavery in the Circuit of Sugar: Martinique and the World Economy, 1830–1848* (Baltimore: Johns Hopkins University Press, 1990).

26. Report of the Select Committee on the Extinction of Slavery throughout the British Dominions, *Parliamentary Papers*, 1831–32, 20:721 (hereafter cited as PP).

27. Henry Taylor, quoted in Holt, *Problem of Freedom*, 45.

28. James Stephen, 1832, quoted in Davis, *Slavery and Human Progress*, 218. See also Davis's discussion of these issues, 214–19.

29. Thomas Fowell Buxton, quoted in David Eltis, *Economic Growth and the Ending of the Transatlantic Slave Trade* (New York: Oxford University Press, 1987), 21; E. G. Stanley, Circular Despatch to Governors, 20 May 1833, 13 June 1833, in PP, 1835, L, 1:4, 46. Apprenticeship caused anxiety in its nonmetaphorical, British context as well. Adam Smith thought its restrictions compromised market principles and induced inefficiency; he equally strongly opposed it as an unfair imposition of the powerful upon the vulnerable, administered by the whims of magistrates, masters, overseers, and churchwardens. See Emma Rothschild, "Adam Smith, Apprenticeship and Insecurity," discussion paper, Centre for History and Economics, Cambridge University, July 1994.

30. Robert W. Fogel, *Without Consent or Contract: The Rise and Fall of American Slavery* (New

York: Norton, 1989), 229; Holt, *Problem of Freedom*. Other fine studies of West Indian emancipation are Alan H. Adamson, *Sugar without Slaves: The Political Economy of British Guiana, 1838–1904* (New Haven: Yale University Press, 1972), and Walter Rodney, *A History of the Guyanese Working People, 1881–1905* (Baltimore: Johns Hopkins University Press, 1981). An overview and a comparison—although one in need of further revision—is William A. Green, *British Slave Emancipation: The Sugar Colonies and the Great Experiment, 1830–1865* (Oxford: Clarendon Press, 1976).

31. Glenelg, dispatch, 30 January 1836, PP, 1836, XLVIII, 166:58–60, quoted in Holt, *Problem of Freedom*, 74.

32. Bernard Semmel, *Jamaican Blood and Victorian Conscience: The Governor Eyre Controversy* (Boston: Houghton Mifflin, 1963).

33. On the increasing conservatism of abolitionism and the transformations in racism, see Miers, *Britain and the Ending of the Slave Trade*; Christine Bolt, *Victorian Attitudes to Race* (London: Routledge, Kegan Paul, 1971); Howard Temperley, *British Anti-Slavery, 1833–1870* (London: Longman, 1972); Douglas Lorimer, *Colour, Class and the Victorians: English Attitudes to the Negro in the Mid-Nineteenth Century* (Leicester: Leicester University Press, 1978); and Philip D. Curtin, *Image of Africa: British Ideas and Action* (Madison: University of Wisconsin Press, 1964). French leaders read the experience of British emancipation in negative terms. See Lawrence C. Jennings, *French Reaction to British Slave Emancipation* (Baton Rouge: Louisiana State University Press, 1988).

34. Hugh Tinker, *A New System of Slavery: The Export of Indian Labour Overseas, 1830–1920* (London: Oxford University Press for the Institute of Race Relations, 1974); P. C. Emmer, ed., *Colonialism and Migration: Indentured Labour before and after Slavery* (Dordrecht: Nijhoff, 1986); David Northrup, *Indentured Labor in the Age of Imperialism, 1834–1922* (Cambridge: Cambridge University Press, 1995). Modern historians have followed publicists who raised the first scandals about indentured labor in stressing the analogy to slavery. See Hugh Tinker and James Duffy, *A Question of Slavery* (Oxford: Oxford University Press, 1967).

35. See Robert Miles, *Capitalism and Unfree Labour: Anomaly or Necessity?* (London: Tavistock, 1987).

36. *United States v. Cruikshank et al.*, 92 U.S. 542 (1875). This decision, echoing *Minor v. Happersett*, 88 U.S. 162 (1875), emphasized that the right to vote in the United States comes from the states, though "the right of exemption from the prohibited discrimination comes from the United States." For a detailed discussion of the precise steps by which the meaning of the Fifteenth Amendment was pared down and disfranchisement contemplated with judicial equanimity, see Samuel Issacharoff, Pamela Karlan, and Richard Pildes, *The Law of Democracy* (Westbury, N.Y.: Foundation Press, 1998).

37. Ada Ferrer, "Social Aspects of Cuban Nationalism: Race, Slavery, and the Guerra Chiquita, 1879–1880," *Cuban Studies* 21 (1991): 37–56, and Ferrer, *Insurgent Cuba*. Antiimperialism, antislavery, and antiracism did not necessarily go together. Another nationalist current in Spain's Caribbean colonies, Puerto Rico as well as Cuba, argued for the ending of slavery on the grounds that it would "whiten" the population of the islands and make for a smoother evolution in the relation of Spain to its Caribbean offshoots. See Christopher Schmidt-Nowara, "The Problem of Slavery in the Age of Capital: Abolitionism, Liberalism, and Counter-Hegemony in Spain, Cuba, and Puerto Rico, 1833–1886" (Ph.D. diss., University of Michigan, 1995) and *Empire and Antislavery: Spain, Cuba, and Puerto Rico, 1833–1874* (Pittsburgh: University of Pittsburgh Press, 1999).

38. See Ada Ferrer, "The Silence of Patriots: Race and Nationalism in Martí's Cuba," in *José Martí's "Our America": From National to Hemispheric Cultural Studies*, ed. Jeffrey Belnap and Raúl Fernández (Durham, N.C.: Duke University Press, 1998), 228–49; Rebecca J. Scott, " 'The Lower Class of Whites' and 'The Negro Element': Race, Social Identity, and Politics in Central Cuba, 1899–1909," in *La Nación Soñada: Cuba, Puerto Rico y Filipinas ante el 98*, ed. Consuelo Naranjo Orovio et al. (Aranjuez, Spain: Editorial Doce Calles, 1996); Aline Helg, *Our Rightful Share: The Afro-Cuban Struggle for Equality, 1886–1912* (Chapel Hill: University of North Carolina Press, 1995); and Ferrer, *Insurgent Cuba*. For a careful study of the twentieth century that qualifies the notion of silence, see Alejandro de la Fuente, "With All and For All: Race, Equality, and Politics in Cuba, 1900–1930" (Ph.D. diss., University of Pittsburgh, 1996).

39. A particularly interesting example of this challenge at a scholarly level is the work of Walterio Carbonell, *Como surgió la cultura nacional* (Havana: Ediciones Yaka, 1961). Carbonell's own trajectory illustrates the risks of such challenge; he was jailed in the 1960s. See also de la Fuente, "With All and For All," and his essay "Myths of Racial Democracy: Cuba, 1900–1912," forthcoming in *Latin American Research Review*.

40. See the *New Orleans Times Democrat*, 3 October 1887, transcribed in *Historical Military Data on Louisiana Militia July 1–Dec. 31, 1878*, Library, Jackson Barracks, New Orleans, and the *Weekly Thibodaux (La.) Sentinel*, 15 October 1887.

41. *Weekly Thibodaux Sentinel*, 17 September 1887.

42. Mary W. Pugh to Edward F. Pugh, 25 November 1887, Folder 1, Mary W. Pugh Papers, Louisiana and Lower Mississippi Valley Collection, Louisiana State University, Baton Rouge (hereafter cited as LLMVC).

43. The changing self-portrayals of colonial regimes—in which slavery is an important but not exclusive consideration—have been spelled out in relation to the two most powerful empires of the late nineteenth and early twentieth centuries in Anne Phillips, *The Enigma of Empire: British Policy in West Africa* (Bloomington: Indiana University Press, 1989), and Alice Conklin, *A Mission to Civilize: The Republican Idea of Empire in France and West Africa, 1895–1930* (Stanford: Stanford University Press, 1997). The importance of these "decentralized despotisms" and the idea of the colonial "subject" that lay within them is emphasized by Mahmood Mamdani, although in a way that treats them as a timeless essence of colonial rule, thus missing the dynamics of the origins and the coming apart of such policies. See *Citizen and Subject: Contemporary Africa and the Legacy of Late Colonialism* (Princeton: Princeton University Press, 1996).

44. There are strong parallels between the kind of order of work and family that the "emancipators" were trying to impose in the Cape region of South Africa and in the British West Indies, as well as among the alternatives emerging among the former slaves themselves. See Holt's chapter in this volume and Pamela Scully, *Liberating the Family? Gender and British Slave Emancipation in the Rural Western Cape, South Africa, 1823–1853* (Portsmouth, N.H.: Heinemann, 1997).

45. The quotation is from John Phillips, cited in Stanley Trapido, "The Emergence of Liberalism and the Making of 'Hottentot Nationalism,' 1815–1834," paper for the Institute of Commonwealth Studies Postgraduate Seminar, 23 February 1990, 3–4, 16. Laborers from these communities themselves used the language of equality before the law to demand a more equitable participation in labor markets. But South African settlers, as they expanded their farming and herding activities beyond the Cape, devised numerous ways—from apprenticeship to kidnapping—to extract labor from communi-

ties and to develop mechanisms of control that could be labeled something other than slavery. See the studies collected in Elizabeth A. Eldredge and Fred Morton, eds., *Slavery in South Africa: Captive Labor on the Dutch Frontier* (Boulder, Colo.: Westview, 1994), and Nigel Worden and Clifton Crais, eds., *Breaking the Chains: Slavery and Its Legacy in the Nineteenth Century Cape Colony* (Johannesburg: Witwatersrand University Press, 1994).

46. Keletso Atkins, *The Moon Is Dead! Give Me My Money!: The Cultural Origins of an African Work Ethic, Natal, South Africa, 1843–1900* (London: Heinemann, 1993); Colin Bundy, *The Rise and Fall of the South African Peasantry* (London: Heinemann, 1979).

47. Frederick Cooper has written about these issues inside and outside South Africa in "Peasants, Capitalists, and Historians: A Review Article," *Journal of Southern African Studies* 7 (1981): 284–314, and "Africa and the World Economy," in *Confronting Historical Paradigms: Peasants, Labor, and the Capitalist World System in Africa and Latin America*, ed. Frederick Cooper et al. (Madison: University of Wisconsin Press, 1993), 84–201. On the ideology of African particularity in South Africa, as well as its institutional manifestations, see Ivan Evans, *Bureaucracy and Race: Native Administration in South Africa* (Berkeley: University of California Press, 1997).

48. Cooper's chapter will touch on this part of the story, but it is at the center of his book *Decolonization and African Society: The Labor Question in French and British Africa* (Cambridge: Cambridge University Press, 1996).

The Essence of the Contract

1. Glenelg to Governors of the West India Colonies, 6 November 1837, in "Papers in Explanation of the Measures Adopted For Giving Effect to the Act For the Abolition of Slavery," Great Britain, PP, 1837–38, 154-I, 49:9-11.

2. Earl Grey to Charles Grey, 16 March 1849, Richard Hart Collection, National Library of Jamaica, Kingston.

3. Although the British West Indies have been compared unfavorably with the United States with respect to the extent that freedmen enjoyed political rights, we must be careful not to exaggerate the differences by taking the cases out of their respective temporal and institutional contexts. After all, universal suffrage for white males was only just beginning to be broached in North America at the time of British emancipation, and the West Indies were in a colonial relationship with the central government. Nevertheless, their histories are actually comparable from a policy perspective. For a contrary view, see Eric Foner, *Nothing But Freedom* (Baton Rouge: Louisiana State University Press, 1982).

4. The first legal acts of emancipation occurred between the 1780s and the 1810s in the northern United States, Haiti, and the liberated Spanish colonies in Central and South America. Each of these was preceded by revolutionary warfare, and declarations of emancipation were generally followed by some form of unfree labor for a period of years. For Tocqueville's remarks, see Alexis de Tocqueville, *Democracy in America*, ed. J. P. Mayer and Max Lerner (New York: Harper and Row, 1966), 315.

5. Popular, and sometimes scholarly, explanations of such phenomena generally take the form "racism, endemic to a slave society, reasserted itself after a brief hiatus," or, more colloquially, "racism raised its ugly head." The implication of an argument in that form, however, is that racism appears as an autonomous, even innate quality of societies or individuals rather than a historically determined aspect of social relations. The difficulties such modes of argument pose for historical explanation—or, more important,

for social change—are suggested by Barbara Jeanne Fields, "Slavery, Race and Ideology in the United States of America," *New Left Review* 181 (May/June 1990): 95–118.

6. This point has been established most persuasively by David Brion Davis, *The Problem of Slavery in the Age of Revolution, 1770–1823* (Ithaca: Cornell University Press, 1975).

7. In Jamaica, Governor Sligo, with Glenelg's approval, did encourage colored representatives in the assembly to organize as an incipient government party, but that policy was embraced reluctantly, pursued inconsistently, and lasted for only a brief time. See Thomas C. Holt, *The Problem of Freedom: Race, Labor, and Politics in Jamaica and Britain, 1832–1938* (Baltimore: Johns Hopkins University Press, 1992), chap. 7.

8. The electoral system and voting qualifications for Great Britain had just been revised the year before slavery emancipation was enacted. The new system enfranchised £10 householders in the boroughs and forty-shilling freeholders in the counties. Although the electorate was thereby increased by an estimated 50 percent, most of the adult male population was still excluded. In England, about one in five adult men was now eligible to vote; in Scotland, one in eight; in Ireland, one in twenty. See Asa Briggs, *The Age of Improvement, 1783–1867* (London: Longmans, Green, 1959), 261–68.

9. Holt, *Problem of Freedom*, chap. 7.

10. The literature on this topic is extensive and growing, but a succinct introduction can be found in E. J. Hobsbawm, *Nations and Nationalism since 1780: Programme, Myth, Reality,* 2d ed. (Cambridge: Cambridge University Press, 1990); Benedict Anderson, *Imagined Communities: Reflections on the Origin and Spread of Nationalism* (London: Verso, 1983); and Hagen Schulze, *States, Nations and Nationalism: From the Middle Ages to the Present* (Oxford: Blackwell, 1994).

11. Orlando Patterson, *Slavery and Social Death: A Comparative Study* (Cambridge: Harvard University Press, 1982), 209–61.

12. See Thomas Jefferson, *Notes on the State of Virginia,* ed. William Peden (Chapel Hill: University of North Carolina Press, 1955), 138–43.

13. For British developments in this regard, see Leonore Davidoff and Catherine Hall, *Family Fortunes: Men and Women of the English Middle Class, 1780–1850* (Chicago: University of Chicago Press, 1991), esp. 25, 180–92, 229. See also Catherine Hall, *White, Male and Middle-Class: Explorations in Feminism and History* (New York: Routledge, 1988).

14. The general point here has been established beyond dispute by Davis, *Problem of Slavery in the Age of Revolution.* See different but complementary formulations in Seymour Drescher, *Capitalism and Antislavery: British Mobilization in Comparative Perspective* (New York: Oxford University Press, 1987), and Eric Williams, *Capitalism and Slavery* (Chapel Hill: University of North Carolina Press, 1944). For a more detailed review of this literature, see Thomas C. Holt, "Explaining Abolition," *Journal of Social History* 24 (Fall 1990): 371–78.

15. There is an extensive literature on this subject, but the following passages have drawn most heavily on Jürgen Habermas, *The Structural Transformation of the Public Sphere: An Inquiry into a Category of Bourgeois Society,* trans. Thomas Burger (1962; reprint, Cambridge: MIT Press, 1989), chaps. 1–15, and on the incisive critique of Habermas by Nancy Fraser, "What's Critical about Critical Theory? The Case of Habermas and Gender," in her *Unruly Practices: Power, Discourse and Gender in Contemporary Social Theory* (Minneapolis: University of Minnesota Press, 1989), 113–43. I am also indebted to C. B. Macpherson, *The Political Theory of Possessive Individualism: Hobbes to Locke* (Oxford: Clarendon, 1962) and *Democratic Theory: Essays in Retrieval* (Oxford: Clarendon, 1973); Albert O. Hirschman, *The Passions and the Interests: Political Arguments for Capitalism before Its Triumph* (Princeton: Princeton Univer-

sity Press, 1977); and Carole Pateman, *The Sexual Contract* (Stanford: Stanford University Press, 1988).

16. See Joyce Appleby, "Ideology and Theory: The Tension between Political and Economic Liberalism in Seventeenth-Century England," *American Historical Review* 81 (June 1976): 499–513.

17. Habermas, *Structural Transformation*, 43–51 (quotes on 43 and 51).

18. On the timing of the emergence of the public sphere, see Habermas, *Structural Transformation*, 24–26. Consideration of the timing and impact of this invention of "publicity" could give new meaning to Seymour Drescher's evidence about the timing and character of abolitionist mobilization (see *Capitalism and Antislavery*, esp. chap. 4).

19. French revolutionaries wrestled with their own version of this problem. See William H. Sewell Jr., "Le citoyen/la citoyenne: Activity, Passivity, and the Revolutionary Concept of Citizenship," in *The French Revolution and the Creation of Modern Political Culture*, ed. Colin Lucas (Oxford: Pergamon Press, 1988), 2:105–23.

20. In addition, as Fraser points out, it assumed a male subject and a masculine-style discourse. See "What's Critical about Critical Theory?," 126–27, 129.

21. In their different ways both Marx and John Stuart Mill recognized this paradox in liberal democracy. See Habermas, *Structural Transformation*, 122–40, and Graeme Duncan, *Marx and Mill: Two Views of Social Conflict and Social Harmony* (Cambridge: Cambridge University Press, 1973). Also see Holt, *Problem of Freedom*, 3–9.

22. Uday S. Mehta labels such criteria of inclusion "the anthropological minimum." See his "Liberal Strategies of Exclusion," *Politics and Society* 18, no. 4 (1990): 427–54.

23. The "residuum" in England and the Irish Catholics are cases in point. See, respectively, Gareth Stedman Jones, *Outcast London: A Study in the Relationship between Classes in Victorian Society* (New York: Pantheon, 1984), and L. Perry Curtis Jr., *Apes and Angels: The Irishman in Victorian Caricature* (Newton Abbot, England: Davis and Charles, 1971). Interesting contemporary linkages were made between race and class exclusions by London observer Henry Mayhew (see Cheryl Marguerit Cassidy, "Islands and Empires: A Rhetorical Analysis of the Governor Eyre Controversy, 1865–1867" [Ph.D. diss., University of Michigan, 1988], chap. 1).

24. [Sligo], *Jamaica under the Apprenticeship System* (London: J. Andrews, 1838), in Joseph Beldam Papers, MST321R, no. 28, National Library of Jamaica, Kingston.

25. [Taylor], "Memorandum on the Course to be Taken with the West Indian Assemblies," 19 January 1839, Colonial Office 884/II, Public Record Office, Kew, England.

26. *Autobiography of Henry Taylor, 1800–1875* (London: Longmans, Green and Company, 1885), 1:246–49.

27. [Taylor], "Memorandum."

28. *Morning Journal* (Kingston), 17 August 1838.

29. Holt, *Problem of Freedom*, 78.

30. Fraser, "What's Critical about Critical Theory?," 124–25.

31. James Anthony Froude, *The English in the West Indies, or The Bow of Ulysses* (1888; reprint, New York: Charles Scribner's Sons, 1900), 286–87.

32. Glenelg to Governors of the West India Colonies, 30 January 1836, in PP, 1836, XLVIII, 166:58–60.

33. Ibid.

34. Ibid.

35. Elgin to Stanley, 5 August 1845 (confidential), CO 137/284.

36. [Sligo], *Jamaica under the Apprenticeship System*.

37. Elgin to Stanley, 5 August 1845 (confidential).

38. Elgin to Stanley, 20 April 1843, no. 112, CO 137/273.

39. Elgin to Stanley, 5 August 1845 (confidential).

40. Ibid.

41. Elgin to Stanley, 20 April 1843, no. 112.

42. Elgin to Stanley, 5 August 1845 (confidential).

43. Elgin to Stanley, 23 October 1844, no. 119, CO 137/280. Stanley expressed his hearty concurrence with Elgin's views (Stanley to Elgin, 24 November 1844, no. 303, CO 137/280).

44. Journal of Henry John Blagrove, 1841–42, 3 July 1841, Jamaica Archive, Spanish Town.

45. "Reply of Assembly to the Governor," 23 October 1845, encl. with Elgin to Stanley, 23 October 1845, no. 90, CO 137/285.

46. Elgin to Stanley, 15 January 1845, no. 5, CO 137/283; Charles Grey to Earl Grey, 20 September 1847, no. 91, CO 137/293.

47. Charles Grey to Earl Grey, 20 September 1847, no. 91. On the Methodists' early support for industrial education, see James M. Phillipo to Sligo, 24 October 1835, encl. with Sligo to Glenelg, 25 October 1835, no. 174.

48. Barkly to Henry Labouchere, 18 March 1856, no. 47, CO 137/331.

49. Darling to Stanley, 25 May 1858, no. 77, CO 137/337; Darling to E. B. Lytton, 21 July 1859, no. 90, CO 137/345.

50. See Holt, *Problem of Freedom*, chap. 6.

51. The freedpeople's alternative worldviews and modes of resistance are discussed in more detail in chapters 5 and 8 of Holt, *Problem of Freedom*.

52. *Colonial Standard* (Kingston), 12 January 1850.

53. Barkly to Labouchere, 21 April 1856, no. 57, CO 137/331.

54. PP, 1854 [1848], 43:39–40, 96.

55. Eyre to Cardwell, 6 August 1864, no. 234, CO 137/384. For further discussions of the gender dynamics of this crisis, see Catherine Hall, *White, Male, and Middle-Class*, 255–95.

56. There is no evidence of any disagreement within the Colonial Office over this soon-to-be controversial dispatch. Enclosed with Eyre to Cardwell, 25 April 1865, no. 117, CO 137/390.

57. *Hansard*, 3d ser., House of Lords, 181 (1866):131, 133.

58. Comparable to this discourse on the colonial "other" are Henry Mayhew's contemporaneous observations on the London underclass, in which he links in the same sentence "repugnance to regular labour," "extraordinary powers of enduring privation," "love of libidinous dances," "delight in warfare," and "absence of chastity among his women" (quoted in Cassidy, "Islands and Empire," 19).

59. See especially Amy Dru Stanley, *From Bondage to Contract: Wage Labor, Marriage and the Market in the Age of Emancipation* (Cambridge: Cambridge University Press, 1998), and Peter W. Bardaglio, *Reconstructing the Household: Families, Sex, and the Law in the Nineteenth-Century South* (Chapel Hill: University of North Carolina Press, 1995). For the initiatives of freedwomen themselves, see Leslie A. Schwalm, *A Hard Fight for We: Women's Transition from Slavery to Freedom in South Carolina* (Urbana: University of Illinois Press, 1997).

60. See especially Glenda E. Gilmore, *Gender and Jim Crow: Women and the Politics of White Supremacy* (Chapel Hill: University of North Carolina Press, 1996); Laura F. Edwards, *Gendered Strife and Confusion: The Political Culture of Reconstruction* (Urbana: University of Illinois Press, 1997); and Hannah Rosen, "The Gender of Reconstruction: Exploring the Meaning of Sexual Violence in the Context of Postemancipation Politics" (Ph.D. diss., University of Chicago, 1999).

61. Holt, *Problem of Freedom*, 64–65.

62. Ibid., chap. 5.

Fault Lines, Color Lines, and Party Lines

1. On this phenomenon in France and the Caribbean, see Laurent Dubois, "A Colony of Citizens: Revolution and Slave Emancipation in the French Caribbean, 1789–1802" (Ph.D. diss., University of Michigan, 1998), a portion of which has appeared in French as *Les Esclaves de la République: L'histoire oubliée de la première émancipation, 1789–1794* (Paris: Calmann-Lévy, 1998). On Britain and the West Indies, see Thomas C. Holt, *The Problem of Freedom: Race, Labor, and Politics in Jamaica and Britain, 1832–1938* (Baltimore: Johns Hopkins University Press, 1992), and his essay in this volume. On Spain and the Spanish Antilles, see Christopher Schmidt-Nowara, *Empire and Antislavery: Spain, Cuba, and Puerto Rico, 1833–1874* (Pittsburgh: University of Pittsburgh Press, 1999). On Cuba, see Ada Ferrer, *Insurgent Cuba: Race, Nation, and Revolution, 1868–1898* (Chapel Hill: University of North Carolina Press, 1999).

2. The pairing of the terms "livelihood" and "resistance" is borrowed from Gavin Smith, *Livelihood and Resistance: Peasants and the Politics of Land in Peru* (Berkeley: University of California Press, 1989).

3. For a careful analysis of this process, and a revealing set of documents, see *Freedom: A Documentary History of Emancipation, 1861–1867*, ser. 1, vol. 1, *The Destruction of Slavery*, ed. Ira Berlin, Barbara J. Fields, Thavolia Glymph, Joseph P. Reidy, and Leslie S. Rowland (Cambridge: Cambridge University Press, 1985), chap. 4; and *Freedom*, ser. 1, vol. 3, *The Wartime Genesis of Free Labor: The Lower South*, ed. Ira Berlin, Thavolia Glymph, Steven F. Miller, Joseph P. Reidy, Leslie S. Rowland, and Julie Saville (Cambridge: Cambridge University Press, 1990), chap. 2.

4. See the testimony of John J. Moore, New Orleans, 8 June 1869, in U.S. House of Representatives, "Testimony Taken by the Sub-Committee of Elections in Louisiana," 41st Cong., 2d sess., 1870, House Miscellaneous Document 154, pt. 1, 634–42.

5. For discussions of Banks's policy, see Berlin et al., *Wartime Genesis*, 363–66, and John Rodrigue, "Raising Cane: From Slavery to Free Labor in Louisiana's Sugar Parishes, 1862–1880" (Ph.D. diss., Emory University, 1993), 168–71.

6. For an analysis of the "labor companies" under which former slaves produced foodstuffs and market crops, see Paul Eiss, "A Share in the Land: Freedpeople and the Government of Labour in Southern Louisiana, 1862–1865," *Slavery and Abolition* 19 (1998): 46–89. See also Rodrigue, "Raising Cane." On the prior "slaves' economy," see Roderick A. MacDonald, *The Economy and Material Culture of Slaves: Goods and Chattels on the Sugar Plantations of Jamaica and Louisiana* (Baton Rouge: Louisiana State University Press, 1993).

7. See Monthly Report of Capt. C. E. Wilcox, Asst. Inspr. Freedmen, Parish of Lafourche, La., 31 January 1866, and Hqtrs. BRFAL, State of Louisiana, Inspection Report

for January, February, March 1866. Both in RG 105, Records of the Bureau of Refugees, Freedmen, and Abandoned Lands, U.S. National Archives (hereafter cited as USNA), reproduced on Roll 28, Microfilm Publication M1027.

8. See Monthly Report of 1st Lieut. J. S. Wadsworth, Asst. Inspr. Freedmen, for the Parish of Terrebonne, for the month ending 30 April 1866, Roll 28, M1027, USNA; and Monthly Report of George A. Ludlow, Asst. Inspr. Freedmen, for the Parish of Terrebonne, La., for the month ending 31 July 1866, Roll 29, M1027, USNA.

9. See Diary, 1866, vol. 1, entries for April 2 and August 24, in Box 2, Alexandre E. DeClouet and Family Papers, LLMVC.

10. See the entries for Thomas Cage, John J. Moore, and Isaac Sutton in Eric Foner, *Freedom's Lawmakers: A Directory of Black Officeholders during Reconstruction*, rev. ed. (Baton Rouge: Louisiana State University Press, 1996). See also Charles Vincent, *Black Legislators in Louisiana during Reconstruction* (Baton Rouge: Louisiana State University Press, 1976), 118.

11. Testimony of John J. Moore, 8 June 1869.

12. See Diary, 1868, vol. 3, entries for April 1868, in Box 2, Alexandre E. DeClouet and Family Papers, LLMVC.

13. The quoted phrase on the provisions of the 1868 constitution is from the opinion of Judge John Minor Wisdom, Fifth Circuit Court of Appeals (New Orleans), in *United States v. State of Louisiana*, 225 F. Supp. 353 (1963). On the elections of 1868, see Ted Tunnell, *Crucible of Reconstruction: War, Radicalism and Race in Louisiana, 1862–1877* (Baton Rouge: Louisiana State University Press, 1984), chaps. 6, 8. See also Joe Gray Taylor, *Louisiana Reconstructed, 1863–1877* (Baton Rouge: Louisiana State University Press, 1974), 151–55.

14. Many of the former slaves on the DeClouet plantations departed at the beginning of 1870, and DeClouet hired "Virginia men" to replace them. Several left within less than a month, and others left after a wage settlement in March. See Diary, 1869–70, vol. 5, entries for early 1870, in Box 2, Alexandre E. DeClouet and Family Papers, LLMVC.

15. This information comes from the excellent case study by J. Paul Leslie, "Laurel Valley Plantation, 1831–1926," in *The Lafourche Country: The People and the Land*, ed. Philip D. Uzee (Lafayette: Center for Louisiana Studies, University of Southwestern Louisiana, 1985), 206–24. On Acadians in the bayou country, see Carl A. Brasseaux, *Acadian to Cajun: Transformation of a People, 1803–1877* (Jackson: University Press of Mississippi, 1992).

16. See Jean Ann Scarpaci, "Immigrants in the New South: Italians in Louisiana's Sugar Parishes, 1880–1910," *Labor History* 16 (Spring 1975): 165–83.

17. For rough estimates of the number of Italian workers, see Scarpaci, "Immigrants in the New South." See also the manuscript returns of the 1870 and 1880 censuses for Lafourche and Terrebonne Parishes in Microfilm Publications 593 and T9, USNA. A detailed discussion of race and occupation in the Louisiana sugar parishes will appear in Rebecca J. Scott, "Degrees of Freedom: Society after Slavery in Louisiana and Cuba, 1862–1914," chap. 5, in preparation.

18. For a discussion of the South as a regional labor market, see Gavin Wright, *Old South, New South: Revolutions in the Southern Economy since the Civil War* (New York: Basic Books, 1986), chap. 4. On wages in sugar, see Rodrigue, "Raising Cane," 431–48.

19. For an overview, see Mark Schmitz, "The Transformation of the Southern Cane Sugar Sector, 1860–1930," *Agricultural History* 53 (January 1979): 270–85. For the 1861 crop, see Noel Deerr, *The History of Sugar*, 2 vols. (London: Chapman and Hall, 1949), 1:250.

20. William Ivy Hair, *Bourbonism and Agrarian Protest: Louisiana Politics, 1877–1900* (Baton Rouge: Louisiana State University Press, 1969), 37–38.

21. For a pioneering discussion of this phenomenon, see Joseph P. Reidy, "Sugar and Freedom: Emancipation in Louisiana's Sugar Parishes" (paper presented at the annual meeting of the American Historical Association, Washington, D.C., December 1980).

22. Letter from H. O. Colomb, dated 9 January 1974, printed in the *New Orleans Daily Picayune*, 11 January 1874. For a general discussion of the fate of planter combinations, see Ralph Shlomowitz, " 'Bound' or 'Free'? Black Labor in Cotton and Sugarcane Farming, 1865–1880," *Journal of Southern History* 50 (November 1984): 569–96.

23. The strike is described in detail in the *New Orleans Daily Picayune*, 14, 15, 16, 18, and 20 January 1874. It is also traced carefully by John Rodrigue in "Raising Cane," 454–62.

24. See Eiss, "A Share in the Land."

25. See Holt, *Problem of Freedom.*

26. See Roger Wallace Shugg, "Survival of the Plantation System in Louisiana," *Journal of Southern History* 3 (August 1937): 311–25, and Tunnell, *Crucible of Reconstruction.* Tunnell argues that "the black majority voted twenty-five to eleven against the 150-acre restriction" (133). However, grouping the *gens de couleur* together with the freedmen as "black" somewhat confuses the picture.

27. Quoted in J. Carlyle Sitterson, *Sugar Country: The Cane Sugar Industry in the South, 1753–1950* (Lexington: University of Kentucky Press, 1953), 246.

28. See Shlomowitz, " 'Bound' or 'Free.' "

29. See Tunnell, *Crucible of Reconstruction*, 151–72.

30. See Otis Singletary, *Negro Militia and Reconstruction* (Austin: University of Texas Press, 1957), 13–14, 66–80. For an intriguing portrait of the former Confederate general, see William Garrett Piston, *Lee's Tarnished Lieutenant: James Longstreet and His Place in Southern History* (Athens: University of Georgia Press, 1987).

31. See the hostile account in the *New Orleans Bulletin*, 9 August 1874, transcribed in *Historical Military Data on Louisiana Militia, Jan. 1–Dec. 31, 1874–76*, Library, Jackson Barracks, New Orleans. On the militia in Louisiana, see Singletary, *Negro Militia and Reconstruction*, 13–14, 66–80. Singletary is mistaken, however, in his view that African American militia activity in Louisiana was confined to New Orleans "and never spread to the provinces" (80).

32. In two recent essays, Lawrence Powell has carefully traced this process of white supremacist mobilization through the wards of New Orleans to its culmination, after initial setbacks, in the precipitous "Battle of Canal Street" in September 1874. See "The Battle of Canal Street: An Upper-Class Dream of Power and Preferment" (paper presented at the annual meeting of the Organization of American Historians, Toronto, Canada, April 25, 1999) and "Reinventing Tradition: Liberty Place, Historical Memory, and Silk-Stocking Vigilantism in New Orleans Politics," in *From Slavery to Emancipation in the Atlantic World*, ed. Sylvia Frey and Betty Wood, a special issue of *Slavery and Abolition* (London) 20 (April 1999): 127–49.

33. See *Annual Report of the Adjutant General of the State of Louisiana For the Year ending December 31st, 1874* (New Orleans: The Republican Office, 1875), 24, 27, and 47 (typescript held at the Library, Jackson Barracks, New Orleans).

34. See the *New Orleans Times Democrat*, 3 October 1887, transcribed in *Historical Military Data on Louisiana Militia July 1–Dec. 31, 1878*, Library, Jackson Barracks, New Orleans.

35. *Historical Military Data on Louisiana Militia July 1–Dec. 31, 1878*, 87–94.

36. See Sheet 38, First Ward, Terrebonne Parish, vol. 16, Louisiana, *Tenth Census of the United States, 1880*, reproduced on Roll 472, Microfilm Publication T9, USNA.

37. *New Orleans Times Democrat*, 3 October 1887, transcribed in *Historical Military Data on Louisiana Militia July 1–Dec. 31, 1878*, Library, Jackson Barracks, New Orleans. Benjamin Lewis's name was at times transposed as Lewis Benjamin.

38. For a detailed analysis of collective action in the region, from which several of these paragraphs are drawn, see Rebecca J. Scott, " 'Stubborn and Disposed to Stand Their Ground': Black Militia, Sugar Workers, and the Dynamics of Collective Action in the Louisiana Sugar Bowl, 1863–87," in Frey and Wood, *From Slavery to Emancipation*, 103–26. On Junius Bailey, see A. E. Perkins, *Who's Who in Colored Louisiana* (Baton Rouge: Douglas Loan Company, 1930). I am also very grateful to Professor Jeffrey Gould for allowing me to make use of his pioneering unpublished essay, " 'Heroic and Vigorous Action': An Analysis of the Sugar Cane Workers' Strike in Lafourche Parish, November, 1887." I have inferred something of Junius Bailey's demeanor from the biographical sketch in Perkins and from the tone of his communications during the 1887 strike, cited below.

39. The early events of the strike in St. Charles Parish are described in the *New Orleans Democrat*, 19 March 1880, reprinted in the *St. Charles Herald*, 15 February 1973, 22. I thank Robert Paquette for calling this item to my attention. See also Hair, *Bourbonism*, 173, citing *New Orleans Daily Picayune*, 29, 31 March 1880. For a detailed reconstruction, see Rodrigue, "Raising Cane," 573–91. On the strike in St. Bernard Parish, see Gould, " 'Heroic and Vigorous Action.' "

40. See Gould, " 'Heroic and Vigorous Action,' " and Melton Alonza McLaurin, *The Knights of Labor in the South* (Westport, Conn.: Greenwood Press, 1978), esp. chap. 7.

41. Information on membership of local assemblies is contradictory and needs further work. I have drawn on Gould, " 'Heroic and Vigorous Action,' " and on Jonathan Garlock, *Guide to the Local Assemblies of the Knights of Labor* (Westport, Conn.: Greenwood Press, 1982). I suspect, however, that the compilation and coding of data for the Garlock volume may have compressed vernacular racial categories into a black/white dichotomy.

42. The description of local leaders is based on an examination of the signatories of petitions that appeared in the press and on the evidence compiled by Jeffrey Gould and described in " 'Heroic and Vigorous Action.' "

43. I am drawing here on the concept of "marking" and its importance in blocking or facilitating racist practice, as analyzed by Thomas C. Holt in "Marking: Race, Race-Making, and the Writing of History," *American Historical Review* (February 1995): 1–20.

44. The first case is to be found in the volume labeled "Criminal Cases, Vol. A, District Court, Parish of Lafourche," 384, 385. The second is found among the loose documents titled "Criminal Cases, 1887." All are in the Courthouse Annex, Thibodaux, Louisiana. I thank Barbara Lee and other staff members of the office of the Clerk of the Court for their assistance in locating these materials. I have reconstructed the events of 1887 in greater detail in " 'Stubborn and Disposed to Stand Their Ground,' " and portions of the following pages are taken from that essay.

45. *The State of Louisiana v. Peter Young* and *The State of Louisiana v. Amos Johnson*, Criminal Cases, 1887, Clerk of the Court, Parish of Lafourche, Courthouse Annex, Thibodaux, Louisiana.

46. I was startled to come across an envelope filled with such slips, dated from the

months surrounding the 1887 strikes, in the documents of Melodia Plantation, located outside of Thibodaux. They are included in Box 7, J. Wilson Lepine Collection, in the Allen J. Ellender Archives, Ellender Memorial Library, Nicholls State University, Thibodaux, Louisiana.

47. The text of the demands can be found in the *New Orleans Daily Picayune*, 30 October 1887. The description of the strike that follows is based on the newspapers, report, and manuscripts cited below, and on Hair, *Bourbonism*, esp. 175–84; Jeffrey Gould, "The Strike of 1887: Louisiana Sugar War," *Southern Exposure* 12 (November–December 1984): 45–55; Gould, " 'Heroic and Vigorous Action' "; and Covington Hall, "Labor Struggles in the Deep South," unpublished typescript in the Labadie Collection, Harlan Hatcher Library, University of Michigan, Ann Arbor.

48. See the *New Orleans Daily Picayune*, 31 October 1887, for the resolutions of the meeting of "influential people" in Thibodaux and of a committee headed by Hon. Don Caffery in St. Mary Parish.

49. See *Report of Brig-Gen. William Pierce Commanding State Troops in the Field in District from Berwick's Bay to New Orleans to General G. T. Beauregard, Adjutant General of the State of Louisiana. November 28th, 1887* (Baton Rouge: Leon Jastremski, State Printer, 1887), 3.

50. The *New Orleans Daily Picayune* reported on 2 November 1887 that "it is intimated that over 10,000 laborers in this district quit work this morning." The *Weekly Pelican*, a Republican newspaper from New Orleans, reported on 5 November 1887 that "ten thousand laborers throughout the sugar district are on strike. Fully nine-tenths of these laborers are colored men and all are members of the Knights of Labor organizations." Although the claim that nine-tenths were "colored men" seems to imply that one-tenth were white men, I have found no direct evidence that permits a more precise estimate of the number of white strikers.

51. *New Orleans Daily Picayune*, 2 November 1887.

52. See the *New Orleans Daily Picayune*, 31 October, 2 November 1887.

53. See *Report of Brig-Gen. William Pierce*, 4, and French-language section of the *Weekly Thibodaux Sentinel*, 5 November 1887. ("A peu près 500 grévistes noirs, blancs, et curieux assaistaient au débarquement de la force armée.")

54. *Report of Brig-Gen. William Pierce*, 11.

55. Hall, "Labor Struggles."

56. An article the year before in the French-language pages of the *Weekly Thibodaux Sentinel* described the numerous "petits habitants" of lower Bayou Lafourche, noting that they harvested a first crop of potatoes and a second crop of corn and sweet potatoes. *Weekly Thibodaux Sentinel*, 24 July 1886.

57. This observation on the distinction between upper and lower Lafourche is Jeffrey Gould's, in "Strike of 1887" and " 'Heroic and Vigorous Action.' "

58. The name of the town is variously reported as Patterson, Pattersonville, and Pattersville.

59. Gould, "Strike of 1887," 51, describes the posse as being led by A. J. Frere, a Knights of Labor member. According to Hall, the posse was initially reported to be led by "Don Caffery, a prominent planter and politician of St. Mary's," who denied such leadership, attributing it to another planter, Col. E. M. Dubroca. Caffery did say that he had assumed command of part of the posse to round up "rioters." See Hall, "Labor Struggles."

60. A. G. Frere appears both as a signatory of the declaration dissociating Local 6295 in Franklin, St. Mary Parish, from the strike call and among the posse that fired on

workers in Pattersonville. See *New Orleans Daily Picayune*, 31 October 1887, and Gould, "Strike of 1887," 51. (Gould lists him as "K of L white delegate A. J. Frere," but I presume that this is the same person.)

61. D. Caffery, Franklin, Louisiana, to "my dear son," 11 November 1887, in vol. 6, Donelson Caffery and Family Papers, LLMVC.

62. See *Report of Brig-Gen. William Pierce*, 9.

63. Cited in Hall, "Labor Struggles," pt. 2, p. 7.

64. *Report of Brig-Gen. William Pierce*, 21, 27–34. The men from Shreveport seem to have been perceived as something very similar to white supremacist "bulldozers." See the reference to "Shreveport guerrillas" in the *New Orleans Weekly Pelican*, 26 November 1887.

65. Mary W. Pugh to Edward F. Pugh, 25 November 1887, in Folder 1, Mary W. Pugh Papers, LLMVC.

66. See ibid.

67. Ibid.

68. Ibid.

69. Hair, *Bourbonism*, 181–82.

70. Hall, "Labor Struggles," pt. 2, p. 11.

71. On the concept of voice, see Albert O. Hirschman, *Exit, Voice, and Loyalty: Responses to Decline in Firms, Organizations, and States* (Cambridge: Harvard University Press, 1970), and *A Propensity to Self-Subversion* (Cambridge: Harvard University Press, 1995), chap. 1.

72. Hall, "Labor Struggles," identifies Jim Brown. The census entry is for Sheldon Guthrie, age 38, white male, "farms on shares"; Roselia Guthrie, age 23, mulatto female; and their daughter, Sarah Guthrie, age 2. See Entry #80, Tenth Ward, Lafourche Parish, Louisiana, *Tenth Census of the United States, 1880*, Roll 472, Microfilm Publication T9, USNA.

73. See U.S. House, "Testimony Taken by the Sub-Committee of Elections in Louisiana," 41st Cong., 2d sess., 1870, House Miscellaneous Document 154, pt. 1, 698–99. Also cited in Tunnell, *Crucible of Reconstruction*, 114. On Esnard, see Foner, *Freedom's Lawmakers*.

74. Quoted in the *New Orleans Weekly Pelican*, 15 October 1887.

75. Hall, "Labor Struggles."

76. Memoir of Florence Dymond, folios 164–67, Folder 351, Mss. 228, Dymond Family Papers, Historic New Orleans Collection, New Orleans, Louisiana. Perhaps with an eye to future readers, someone has penciled corrections in the memoir, changing "carpetbag" to "republican" and "as black as the ace of spades" to "a negro, unknown to us or our resident negroes."

77. See David Roediger, *Toward the Abolition of Whiteness: Essays on Race, Politics, and Working Class History* (London: Verso, 1994), chaps. 1, 5, and 10, and Eric Arnesen, *Waterfront Workers of New Orleans: Race, Class and Politics, 1863–1923* (New York: Oxford University Press, 1991).

78. James H. Blodgett, *Wages of Farm Labor in the United States: Results of Twelve Statistical Investigations, 1866–1902*, U.S. Department of Agriculture, Bureau of Statistics, Miscellaneous Series, Bulletin No. 26 (Washington, D.C.: Government Printing Office, 1903), 38.

79. The total number of farms whose primary product was sugar was 3,870. *Twelfth Census of the United States, Taken in the Year 1900*, vol. 5, *Agriculture*, pt. 1, *Farms, Live Stock, and Animal Products* (Washington, D.C.: United States Census Office, 1902), 23.

80. "Louisiana Sugar News," in *Louisiana Planter and Sugar Manufacturer*, 9 August 1919, 86. I am grateful to Catherine LeGrand for bringing this document to my attention.

81. For a portrait of the often suffocating world of Louisiana sugar plantations in the first half of the twentieth century, see the fiction of Ernest Gaines, especially the collection of short stories titled *Bloodline* (New York: Norton, 1976). On the importance of public spaces for the mobilization of opposition, see Robin D. G. Kelley, *Race Rebels* (New York: Free Press, 1994). For a brilliant discussion of public action, see Elsa Barkley Brown, "Negotiating and Transforming the Public Sphere: African American Political Life in the Transition from Slavery to Freedom," *Public Culture* 7 (1994): 107–46.

82. See Rebecca J. Scott, *Slave Emancipation in Cuba: The Transition to Free Labor, 1860–1899* (Princeton: Princeton University Press, 1985), and Ferrer, *Insurgent Cuba.*

83. On selective repression, see Ada Ferrer, "Social Aspects of Cuban Nationalism: Race, Slavery, and the Guerra Chiquita, 1879–1880," *Cuban Studies* 21 (1991): 37–56.

84. For figures, see Scott, *Slave Emancipation*, 22, 87.

85. See Manuel Ma. de Vivanco to Manuel Blanco, 7 November 1877, Colección Manuscrita Julio Lobo, Biblioteca Nacional José Martí, Havana, Cuba (hereafter cited as CML, BNC).

86. The correspondence from Santa Rosalía for this period is located in CML, BNC.

87. Edwin F. Atkins, *Sixty Years in Cuba* (1926; reprint, New York: Arno Press, 1980), 92. Atkins does not specify the date of the incident, but it was presumably prior to his purchase of Soledad in 1884.

88. See Pedro García to Manuel Blanco, 15 March 1885, in Item No. 9a, "Cartas de varias personas dirigidas a Manuel Blanco propietario del ingenio Santa Rosalía," CML, BNC.

89. See Fe Iglesias García, "La concentración azucarera y la comarca de Cienfuegos," in Fernando Martínez Heredia, Orlando García Martínez, and Rebecca J. Scott, eds., *Espacios, silencios, y los sentidos de la libertad: Cuba, 1878–1912* (Havana: Editorial UNIÓN, forthcoming).

90. For summaries of the evolution of Cuban sugar production, see Rebecca J. Scott, "Defining the Boundaries of Freedom in the World of Cane: Cuba, Brazil, and Louisiana after Emancipation," *American Historical Review* 99 (February 1994): 70–102, and Alan Dye, *Cuban Sugar in the Age of Mass Production: Technology and the Economics of the Sugar Central, 1899–1929* (Stanford: Stanford University Press, 1998), chap. 6.

91. Contract cane farming loomed larger in Cuba than in southern Louisiana, offering another mechanism for incorporation into the labor force in sugar. In Santa Clara as in Louisiana, however, white renters seem to have had an edge in obtaining tenancies. See Scott, *Slave Emancipation*, chaps. 10 and 11.

92. On Santa Rosalía, see "Libro No. 3 perteneciente al Ingenio Sta Rosalía propiedad de Dn Manuel Blanco y Ramos," Archivo Provincial de Cienfuegos, Cienfuegos, Cuba. On Soledad, see E. F. Atkins to Alvey A. Adee, Acting Secretary of State, August 1895, in "1901–1907 Letterbook E. F. Atkins," Atkins Family Papers, Massachusetts Historical Society, Boston (hereafter cited as AFP, MHS). See also pp. 118–29 and 207 of deposition of Edwin F. Atkins, Claim 387 (Atkins), Pt. 1, U.S./Spain Treaty Claims, Entry 352, RG 76, USNA.

93. This unfolding of prosperity and peril is vividly reflected in the correspondence of the successive administrators of Soledad Plantation. I thank Kathleen López and David Sartorius for their assistance in cataloging and transcribing portions of this voluminous material, held in AFP, MHS.

94. A classic account of the battle of Mal Tiempo and its effect on the region is to be found in José Miró Argenter, *Cuba: Crónicas de la Guerra*, 2 vols. (Havana: Editorial Lex, 1945), 1:168–80.

95. This discrimination is traced and carefully analyzed by Ferrer in chapter 6 of *Insurgent Cuba*. See also Aline Helg, *Our Rightful Share: The Afro-Cuban Struggle for Equality, 1886–1912* (Chapel Hill: University of North Carolina Press, 1995).

96. The analysis of racial categories in the Ejército Libertador is fraught with difficulties, though the work of Ada Ferrer, Orlando García Martínez, and Michael Zeuske, including the essays forthcoming in Martínez Heredia, García Martínez, and Scott, *Espacios*, provides important new insights. For my own initial efforts to understand the interplay between wartime service by former slaves and subsequent claims of rights, see "Race, Labor, and Citizenship in Cuba: A View from the Sugar District of Cienfuegos, 1886–1909," *Hispanic American Historical Review* 78 (November 1998): 687–728.

97. For a detailed examination of the insurgency on Soledad and Santa Rosalía, see Rebecca J. Scott, "Reclaiming Gregoria's Mule: The Meanings of Freedom in the Arimao and Caunao Valleys, Cienfuegos, Cuba, 1880–1899," *Past and Present*, forthcoming.

98. Williams's phrase "sitio negroes" seems to refer to former slaves and their kin who worked on land denominated the *sitio*, devoted to food crops and located outside the *batey*, or central mill yard. See Atkins, *Sixty Years*, 184–88. I am grateful to William Christian Jr. and to Olga Pérez Ponvert for helping me to puzzle out this phrase.

99. Atkins, *Sixty Years*, 192–93.

100. See José Rogelio Castillo, *Autobiografía del General José Rogelio Castillo* (Havana: Editorial de Ciencias Sociales, 1973), 149. On the development of the war in Cienfuegos, see Orlando García Martínez, "La Brigada de Cienfuegos: Un análisis social de su formación," forthcoming in Martínez Heredia, García Martínez, and Scott, *Espacios*.

101. Atkins, *Sixty Years*, 202. The enlistment list is in "Documentos relativos a la Inspección General del Ejército. Expediente que contiene la relación de jefes, oficiales, clases y soldados y el estado de las armas y animales de la Brigada de Cienfuegos. 27 de Noviembre de 1896," inventario 1, exp. 60, Colección de documentos del Ejército Libertador Cubano, Archivo Provincial de Santa Clara, Santa Clara, Cuba. I am grateful to Michael Zeuske and Orlando García Martínez for sharing their photocopies of these documents.

102. "Documentos relativos . . . Brigada de Cienfuegos. 27 de Noviembre de 1896." Quesada was the surname of the former owner of Santa Rosalía, José Quesada. Most former slaves on the estate took that surname when they became free.

103. Caridad Quesada of Cienfuegos, Cuba, the niece of Cayetano Quesada, recalled family stories in a session of the Taller de Historia, Cienfuegos, 3–5 March 1998. Ramona Quesada de Castillo, Gerardo Quesada, and Francisco Quesada, all children of Cayetano Quesada, shared their memories of their father in an interview by the author in Cienfuegos, June 1998. The activities of Ramos Quesada are outlined in an essay by David Sartorius, "Conucos y subsistencia: El caso de Santa Rosalía," forthcoming in Martínez Heredia, García Martínez, and Scott, *Espacios*.

104. Alcaldía Municipal de Cruces, "Relación de las fincas quemadas en todo ó parte por los insurrectos, 15 Sept. 1897," Legajo K-20, División 3a, Sección 2a, Archivo General Militar, Segovia, Spain.

105. I would like to thank Louis Pérez for sharing with me some of his ideas about the role of the pro-Spanish guerrillas in 1895–98 and in the violence that followed the war. For information on the guerrilla forces in Cienfuegos, see the testimony of Pau-

lino Castro y Rodriguez, a country laborer from Camarones who served as a guide for the Spaniards, in deposition of Paulino Castro y Rodriguez, beginning 24 February 1904, Claim 293 (Hormiguero), Pt. 3, U.S./Spain Treaty Claims, Entry 352, RG 76, USNA. See also the deposition of Peter M. Beal, in Claim 250 (Beal), ibid. One guerrilla unit was located on Santa Rosalía itself. See the wartime correspondence in CML, BNC.

106. Elías Ponvert of Hormiguero recalled the creation of a small village of cane farmers, women, and children within the confines of his estate, protected by a ditch and by a force of Spanish soldiers assigned to the estate. See the deposition of Elías Ponvert, beginning 25 January 1904, in Claim 293 (Hormiguero), Pt. 1, U.S./Spain Treaty Claims, Entry 352, RG 76, USNA. On *reconcentración* and its consequences, see Francisco Pérez Guzmán, *Herida profunda* (Havana: Ediciones UNIÓN, 1998).

107. The recent research of Orlando García Martínez and Michael Zeuske emphasizes the importance of the *zona fortificada* around the richest areas of Cienfuegos, which Zeuske argues limited the recruitment of former slaves to the insurgency. See Orlando García Martínez, "La Brigada de Cienfuegos," and Michael Zeuske, "Movilización afrocubana y clientelas en un hinterland cubana: Cienfuegos entre colonia y república (1895–1912)," both forthcoming in Martínez Heredia, García Martínez, and Scott, *Espacios*.

108. The centenary of 1898 occasioned many publications on the period of the war, including Louis A. Pérez Jr., *The War of 1898: The United States and Cuba in History and Historiography* (Chapel Hill: University of North Carolina Press, 1998), and Juan Pan-Montojo, coord., *Más se perdió en Cuba: España, 1898 y la crisis de fin de siglo* (Madrid: Alianza Editorial, 1998). See also the November 1998 special number of the *Hispanic American Historical Review* (78, no. 4) and the Winter 1999 special number of the *Radical History Review* (73), titled *Islands in History*.

109. One of the most subtle discussions of Cuban racial ideology is to be found in Verena Martinez-Alier, *Marriage, Class, and Colour in Nineteenth-Century Cuba* (Cambridge: Cambridge University Press, 1974).

110. See Atkins, *Sixty Years in Cuba*, 112, and chaps. 21–23.

111. I am very grateful to Caridad Quesada, Araceli Quesada, and other members of the Quesada family of Cienfuegos; to Tomás Pérez y Pérez, formerly of Soledad, later of Cienfuegos; and to Fermín Tellería, Blas Pelayo, and Santiago Pelayo, for sharing their recollections in interviews in 1997, 1998, and 1999. I also thank Leonardo Alomá, Modesto Hernández, and Sebastian Asla Cires for teaching me a great deal about the workings of Santa Rosalía and Soledad, in the distant as well as the recent past. The correspondence of the administrator of Santa Rosalía in 1899 is in the personal collection of Orlando García Martínez, Cienfuegos, Cuba.

112. Cayetano Quesada's service record is in his pension request, Legajo 477, Juzgado de Primera Instancia de Cienfuegos, Archivo Provincial de Cienfuegos. Information on his small farm comes from Ramona Quesada de Castillo, Evelio Castillo, Gerardo Quesada, and Francisco Quesada, interviews by the author, Cienfuegos, June 1998. A reference to the family as *precaristas* (squatters) appears in a 1959 document in Legajo 620, Soledad Papers, Fondo ICEA, Archivo Nacional de Cuba, Havana.

113. Atkins, *Sixty Years*, 297, 301. A vivid portrait of the prospects for economic recovery, combined with an unusually forthright recommendation of direct government aid to farmers, is found in the report of Brigadier General James H. Wilson in *Civil Report of Major-General John R. Brooke, U.S. Army, Military Governor, Island of Cuba* (Washington, D.C.: Government Printing Office, 1900).

114. The details of the conflict over the mule are recounted in the letters of Constantino Pérez to Manuel García, 17, 18, and 19 August 1899, in Correspondencia, Santa Rosalía, in the personal collection of Orlando García Martínez. I discuss this incident further in "Reclaiming Gregoria's Mule."

115. Gavin Wright observes that for the U.S. South the ownership of a mule could make a crucial difference to the terms of tenancy. See Old South, New South, 100.

116. See the anonymous report to the Chief of the Detective Bureau, Havana, titled "Report of a trip made thro Santa Clara province, by a special agent," 19 February 1901, File 1901:1209, Entry 3, RG 140, USNA.

117. See Edwin Atkins to Gen. Leonard Wood, 21 February 1900, in File 1900:504, ibid. Participants included 250 lightermen, 200 stevedores, 110 longshoremen, and 75 cartmen. See also Major Bowman to Adjutant, Rowell Barracks, Pasa Caballos, 9 March 1900, in the same file.

118. See Atkins, Sixty Years, 314–17, and Major Bowman to Adjutant, Rowell Barracks, Pasa Caballos, 9 March 1900, File 1900:504, Entry 3, RG 140, USNA. See also the letterbooks of Edwin Atkins for this period in AFP, MHS.

119. See Major Bowman to Adjutant, Rowell Barracks, Pasa Caballos, 9 March 1900, File 1900:504, Entry 3, RG 140, USNA. Also telegram from Edwin Atkins to Gen. Leonard Wood, 21 February 1900, in the same file.

120. The pioneering discussion of these debates is Alejandro de la Fuente, "Los Mitos de la Democracia Racial," forthcoming in Spanish in Martínez Heredia, García Martínez, and Scott, Espacios, and in English in Latin American Research Review.

121. See the sequence of descriptions in La Lucha for November and December 1902. The Spanish-language portion of the paper provided greater detail on the strike than the English-language one.

122. See the telegrams of Baehr to Squiers, 29 and 30 November 1902, and the draft dispatch of Squiers to Hay, 2 December 1902, in Dispatches from U.S. Ministers to Cuba, RG 59, USNA (available on Roll 4, Microfilm Publication T158). The discussion of the strike that follows draws on the reports in the Spanish-language pages of La Lucha during the period November–December 1902 and on the essay by John Dumoulin, "El primer desarrollo del movimiento obrero y la formación del proletariado en el sector azucarero. Cruces 1886–1902," Islas: Revista de la Universidad de las Villas 48 (May–August 1974): 3–66. I have also examined the strike in an essay, "Raza, Clase y Acción Colectiva en Cuba, 1895–1912: Formación de Alianzas Interraciales en el Mundo de la Caña," in El Caribe entre imperios (Coloquio de Princeton), ed. Arcadio Díaz Quiñones, Edición extraordinaria de Op. Cit. Revista del Centro de Investigaciones Históricas (Río Piedras) 9 (1997): 131–57.

123. Rich documentation on these organizations, particularly for the sugar town of Lajas, survives in the Archivo Provincial de Cienfuegos.

124. The quotation is from a letter by a correspondent from Santa Clara to the newspaper Tierra!, cited in Dumoulin, "El primer desarrollo," 15–16. For a witty portrait of the crew of anarchists associated with the newspaper, see Carlos Loveira, De los 26 a los 35 (Lecciones de la experiencia en la lucha obrera) (Washington, D.C.: Law Reporter Printing Company, 1917), 78–83. A recent study of anarchism on the island, emphasizing its Cuban as well as its Spanish roots, is Joan Casanovas, Bread, or Bullets!: Urban Labor and Spanish Colonialism in Cuba (Pittsburgh: University of Pittsburgh Press, 1998).

125. See the discussion in Dumoulin, "El primer desarrollo."

126. On the politics of José Miguel Gómez at this moment, see Dumoulin, "El primer

desarrollo." For the dispatch, see Squiers to Hay, 2 December 1902, on Roll 4, Microfilm Publication T158, USNA. Squiers seems to have thought better of this blunt statement; he penciled "omit" over the last phrase.

127. See the discussion in Dumoulin, "El primer desarrollo," 25–27.

128. See Louis A. Pérez Jr., *Cuba under the Platt Amendment, 1902–1934* (Pittsburgh: University of Pittsburgh Press, 1986), chap. 8, and Jorge Ibarra, *Cuba: 1898–1921. Partidos Políticos y Clases Sociales* (Havana: Editorial de Ciencias Sociales, 1992). For a challenge to the familiar portraits of the 1906 conflict, see Michael Zeuske, "Clientelas Regionales, Alianzas Interraciales y Poder Nacional en Torno a la 'Guerrita de Agosto' (1906)," *Illes i Imperis: Estudis d'història de les societats en el món colonial i post-colonial* (Barcelona) 2 (Spring 1999): 127–56.

129. For a full discussion of the activities of the Military Information Division, see Rebecca J. Scott, " 'The Lower Class of Whites' and 'The Negro Element': Race, Social Identity, and Politics in Central Cuba, 1899–1909," in *La Nación Soñada: Cuba, Puerto Rico y Filipinas ante el 98*, ed. Consuelo Naranjo Orovio et al. (Aranjuez, Spain: Editorial Doce Calles, 1996), 179–91.

130. See the reports from Henry Green on 20 February and 15 April 1907, Items 8 and 10 in File 68, Series 1008, Correspondence, Military Information Division, Army of Cuban Pacification (hereafter cited as Series 1008, ACP), RG 395, USNA.

131. Ross Rowell, 2nd Lieut., U.S.M.C., to Supervising Intelligence Officer, Cienfuegos, 28 July 1907, Item 29 in File 68, ibid.

132. Ibid.

133. Ross Rowell to Supervising Intelligence Officer, Cienfuegos, 10 September 1907, Item 33 in File 68, ibid.

134. See the reports in File 68, ibid. The most recent careful study of Estenoz and the Independientes is Helg, *Our Rightful Share*.

135. See the report of Ross Rowell to Chief of Military Information Division, Marianao, 28 December 1907, Item 41 in File 68, Series 1008, ACP, RG 395, USNA.

136. See papers pertaining to the Rural Guard in Santa Clara in Entry 1333, RG 395, USNA.

137. See Louis A. Pérez Jr., *Army Politics in Cuba, 1898–1958* (Pittsburgh: University of Pittsburgh Press, 1976), chaps. 2–3.

138. Author's interviews with Tomás Pérez y Pérez in Cienfuegos in 1998 and 1999, and with Leonardo Alomá at the Central Pepito Tey in 1997, 1998, and 1999. See also the payroll lists for Soledad Plantation held in the Fondo ICEA, Archivo Nacional de Cuba.

139. See Scott, *Slave Emancipation*, 260–61; Dumoulin, "El primer desarrollo," 18.

140. See *La Correspondencia* (Cienfuegos) for the months of May, June, and July 1912.

141. Cited in Louis A. Pérez Jr., "Politics, Peasants, and People of Color: The 1912 'Race War' in Cuba Reconsidered," *Hispanic American Historical Review* 66 (August 1986): 537.

142. Pérez, *Cuba under the Platt Amendment*, 151, cites a figure of 3,000 Afro-Cubans "slain in the field."

143. See the innovative and carefully documented study by Alejandra Bronfman, "Mas allá del color: Clientelismo y Conflicto en Cienfuegos, 1912," forthcoming in Martínez Heredia, García Martínez, and Scott, *Espacios*. I have also benefited from discussions of the events of 1912 with Alejandro de la Fuente, Orlando García Martínez, Michael Zeuske, and several older residents of Cienfuegos.

144. Alejandro de la Fuente explores this ideology in "With All and For All: Race,

Equality, and Politics in Cuba, 1900–1930" (Ph.D. diss., University of Pittsburgh, 1996). On the strike in Havana, see *La Correspondencia* (Cienfuegos), 18 July 1912.

145. See the pathbreaking study by John Dumoulin, *El movimiento obrero en Cruces, 1902–1912*, published as a volume of *Las clases y la lucha de clases en la sociedad neocolonial cubana*, ed. Sonia Aragón García (Havana: Editorial de Ciencias Sociales, 1981).

146. A logical urban comparison would be the New Orleans waterfront, where fragile cross-racial alliances survived for decades. See Arnesen, *Waterfront Workers of New Orleans*.

147. For the most recent general overview of the early twentieth century, see Tomás Fernández Robaina, *El negro en Cuba, 1902–1958: Apuntes para la historia de la lucha contra la discriminación racial* (Havana: Editorial de Ciencias Sociales, 1990).

148. Martí was referring specifically to intermarriage: "Por dónde empezará la fusión? Por donde empieza todo lo justo y difícil, por la gente humilde. Los matrimonios comenzarán entre las dos razas entre aquellos a quienes el trabajo mantiene juntos." These lines are from an undated manuscript by Martí, reproduced in the *Anuario del Centro de Estudios Martianos* 1 (1978): 34. I am very grateful to Ramón de Armas for having called this document to my attention, and I have used the transcription of the text cited in his essay, "José Martí: La verdadera i única abolición de la esclavitud," *Anuario de Estudios Americanos* 43 (1986): 333–51.

149. I am grateful to Louis A. Pérez Jr. for ongoing discussions of the "silence of race" in post-1912 Cuba, and to Alejandro de la Fuente for his explorations of the cracks in this silence. See de la Fuente, "With All and For All." See also Ada Ferrer, "The Silence of Patriots: Racial Discourse and Cuban Nationalism," in *José Martí's "Our America": From National to Hemispheric Cultural Studies*, ed. Jeffrey Belnap and Raúl Fernández (Durham, N.C.: Duke University Press, 1998), 228–49.

150. Nationality, however, *was* politicized, and legislation to establish preferential quotas for Cuban workers was introduced repeatedly between 1910 and 1925. Employers, backed by the United States, thwarted its passage in order to maintain their freedom of action. See Pérez, *Cuba under the Platt Amendment*, 153–64.

151. Quoted in Tunnell, *Crucible*, 173.

152. Ibid., 193–94.

153. See the deposition of Eduardo Vilar, 12 August 1904, Claim 97 (Central Teresa), Pt. 1, U.S./Spain Treaty Claims, Entry 352, RG 76, USNA.

Conditions Analogous to Slavery

1. For an example of sliding back and forth between slavery and colonialism as virtually interchangeable objects of "resistance," see James Scott, *Domination and the Arts of Resistance: Hidden Transcripts* (New Haven: Yale University Press, 1990). My account also differs from Scott's by my emphasis on the way in which the discourses of the powerful and the weak shape each other, whereas Scott tends to seal them off from each other. The resistance concept is critiqued in Sherry Ortner, "Resistance and the Problem of Ethnographic Refusal," *Comparative Studies in Society and History* 37 (1995): 173–93, and Frederick Cooper, "Conflict and Connection: Rethinking Colonial African History," *American Historical Review* 99 (1994): 1516–45.

2. Scholars invoke a variety of concepts — "discursive formation," "frame," "habitus," "epistemic community" — to point to deeply engrained boundaries in language and social convention that limit imaginable possibilities in any historical context. Nevertheless,

that which a broad community sees as normal at one time may become inconceivable at another, and that which it regards as impossible may become normal. What maintains and what transforms the limits of the politically imaginable (and the definition of the community that does the imagining) is a problem that is widely recognized, for example, in the large literature on the relationship of structure and action, as well as in framework theory, practice theory, and much of social movement theory. But it is perhaps only a bit too cynical to suggest that at the theoretical level the resolutions of this problem do not go much beyond Marx's assertion that people make their own history, but not as they wish.

3. I have dealt with the new framework of the 1940s and 1950s in detail in *Decolonization and African Society: The Labor Question in French and British Africa* (Cambridge: Cambridge University Press, 1996).

4. For an insightful study of the clashing of different visions of work, see Keletso Atkins, *The Moon Is Dead! Give Me My Money!: The Cultural Origins of an African Work Ethic, Natal, South Africa, 1843–1900* (London: Heinemann, 1993).

5. For an overview of the chronology of slavery on the African continent, see Paul E. Lovejoy, *Transformations of Slavery: A History of Slavery in Africa* (Cambridge: Cambridge University Press, 1983), and, on the nineteenth century, Robin Law, ed., *From Slave Trade to "Legitimate" Commerce: The Commercial Transition in Nineteenth-Century West Africa* (Cambridge: Cambridge University Press, 1995). The reproduction of a slave population via capture and purchase is the core of the interpretation of Claude Meillassoux, *The Anthropology of Slavery: The Womb of Iron and Gold*, trans. Alide Dasnois (Chicago: University of Chicago Press, 1991).

6. John Hanning Speke, *Journal of the Discovery of the Source of the Nile* (Edinburgh: Blackwood, 1863), xxvii. Speke made the connection to imperialism directly: "They require a government like ours in India; and without it, the slave-trade will wipe them off the face of the earth" (39).

7. David Livingstone, *Narrative of an Expedition on the Zambezi and Its Tributaries; and of the Discovery of the Lakes Shirwa and Nyassa, 1858–1864* (London: Murray, 1865), 595. The explorer Joseph Thomson, not a missionary, similarly indicted the slave trade for blocking "mutual dependence or exchange of services." Trade was too dangerous for the African, and "cut off from the outer world, he retains his primitive barbarism." Joseph Thomson, *To the Central African Lakes and Back* (1881; reprint, London: Cass, 1968), 1:162.

8. Marcel Dorigny, ed., *Les abolitions de l'esclavage de L. F. Sonthonax à V. Schoelcher, 1793, 1794, 1848* (Paris: Presses Universitaires de Vincennes et Editions UNESCO, 1995).

9. The connection of domestic upheaval and slave resistance to colonial abolition is one of the key points emphasized in Robin Blackburn, *The Overthrow of Colonial Slavery, 1776–1848* (London: Verso, 1988). See also William B. Cohen, *The French Encounter with Africans: White Response to Blacks, 1530–1880* (Bloomington: Indiana University Press, 1980); François Renault, *L'esclavage africain et l'Europe, 1868–1892* (Paris: Baccard, 1971); Dale Tomich, "Liberté ou Mort: Republicanism and Slave Revolt in Martinique, February 1831," *History Workshop Journal* 29 (1990): 85–91; and Alice Conklin, *A Mission to Civilize: The Republican Idea of Empire in France and West Africa, 1895–1930* (Stanford: Stanford University Press, 1997), 96–99.

10. The moving into and out of focus of the slavery question in French Africa emerges in a complex and textured way in Martin Klein, *Slavery and French Colonial Rule* (Cambridge: Cambridge University Press, 1998). On the adjustments of slaveowning merchants, see

Mohamed Mbodj, "The Abolition of Slavery in Senegal, 1820–1890: Crisis or the Rise of a New Entrepreneurial Class?" in *Breaking the Chains: Slavery, Bondage, and Emancipation in Modern Africa and Asia*, ed. Martin Klein (Madison: University of Wisconsin Press, 1993), 197–211.

11. Louis-Gustave Binger, *Esclavage, Islamisme et Christianisme* (Paris: Société des Editions scientifiques, 1891), 20, 80, 92, 100.

12. For a study of stereotypes, see H. Alan C. Cairns, *Prelude to Imperialism: British Reactions to Central African Society, 1840–1890* (London: Routledge and Kegan Paul, 1965).

13. These connections are discussed in Frederick Cooper, *From Slaves to Squatters: Plantation Labor and Agriculture in Zanzibar and Coastal Kenya, 1890–1925* (New Haven: Yale University Press, 1980), chap. 2, and, more generally, in David Brion Davis, *Slavery and Human Progress* (New York: Oxford University Press, 1984), 279–84, 298–306. The use of the concept of the "residuum" in metropole and colony is discussed in Gareth Stedman Jones, *Outcast London: A Study of the Relationship between Classes in Victorian Society* (Oxford: Clarendon, 1971), and Cooper, *From Slaves to Squatters*, 28–29, 38–39.

14. K. Onwuka Dike, *Trade and Politics in the Niger Delta* (Oxford: Oxford University Press, 1956); A. G. Hopkins, "Property Rights and Empire Building: Britain's Annexation of Lagos, 1861," *Journal of Economic History* 40 (1980): 777–98, and *An Economic History of West Africa* (London: Longman, 1973), 124–66.

15. Suzanne Miers, *Britain and the Ending of the Slave Trade* (New York: Africana Publishing Corporation, 1975), xi, quoting Salisbury. As Miers notes (261), King Leopold made good use of the anti-slave-trade language at the conferences to stake his claims to power in the Congo—which he was later to use in such a tyrannical and brutal way that similar rhetoric would be deployed against him.

16. For examples of the British version of the this genre, see Frederick Lugard, "Slavery under the British Flag," *Nineteenth Century* (February 1896): 335–55; Joseph Pease, *How We Countenance Slavery* (London: British and Foreign Anti-Slavery Society, 1895); and the *Anti-Slavery Reporter* throughout the 1890s and early 1900s. The French quotation is from William Ponty, Circular of 1 February 1901, quoted in Klein, *Slavery*, 127.

17. This is a schematic summary of a complex process, whose variations can most readily be charted by the studies in Suzanne Miers and Richard Roberts, eds., *The End of Slavery in Africa* (Madison: University of Wisconsin Press, 1988).

18. John Lonsdale, "The European Scramble and Conquest in African History," in *Cambridge History of Africa*, ed. Roland Oliver and G. N. Sanderson (Cambridge: Cambridge University Press, 1985), 6:723. The most comprehensive and detailed study of this process is now Klein, *Slavery*. See also Conklin, *Mission to Civilize*; Denise Bouche, *Les villages de liberté en Afrique noire française, 1887–1910* (Paris, 1968); Richard Roberts and Martin Klein, "The Banamba Slave Exodus of 1905 and the Decline of Slavery in the Western Sudan," *Journal of African History* 21 (1980): 375–94; Myron Echenberg, *Colonial Conscripts: The Tirailleurs Sénégalais in French West Africa, 1857–1960* (Portsmouth, N.H.: Heinemann, 1991); and Lovejoy, *Transformations in Slavery*, 246–68.

19. Quotations from *African Review* (1904) and Frederick Lugard, *Northern Nigeria Annual Report, 1900–01* (1901), cited in Paul E. Lovejoy and Jan S. Hogendorn, *Slow Death for Slavery: The Course of Abolition in Northern Nigeria, 1897–1936* (Cambridge: Cambridge University Press, 1993), 28, 38.

20. G. Ugo Nwokeji, "The Slave Emancipation Problematic: Igbo Society and the Colonial Equation," *Comparative Studies in Society and History* 40 (1998): 328–55.

21. The best study of the idea of abolishing the "legal status of slavery" as a means of narrowly bounding questions of power and exploitation in a colonial situation is Gyan Prakash, *Bonded Histories: Genealogies of Labor Servitude in Colonial India* (Cambridge: Cambridge University Press, 1990). The gender issue is stressed for British and French areas of Sudanic Africa by Lovejoy and Hogendron, *Slow Death*, 111, and Klein, *Slavery*, 194, 227, 250.

22. Klein, *Slavery*, 242.

23. See the studies collected in Miers and Roberts, *End of Slavery in Africa*.

24. What follows is based on Cooper, *From Slaves to Squatters*.

25. W. E. Taylor to Henry Binns, 26 July 1895, PP, 1896, LIX, 395:18; Piggott to Hardinge, 1 August 1895, Foreign Office Confidential Prints 6761, 262.

26. *District and Consular Report on Pemba* (London: Foreign Office, 1900), 12.

27. Justin Willis and Suzanne Miers, "Becoming a Child of the House: Incorporation, Authority and Resistance in Giryama Society," *Journal of African History* 38 (1997): 479–96.

28. Belfield to Harcourt, 4 May 1914, CO 533/136, PRO.

29. See also Cynthia Brantley, *The Giriama and Colonial Resistance in Kenya, 1800–1900* (Berkeley: University of California Press, 1981).

30. See also Justin Willis, *Mombasa, the Swahili, and the Making of the Mijikenda* (Oxford: Oxford University Press, 1992).

31. East Africa Commission, *Report* (London: HMSO, 1925), 37.

32. Frederick Lugard, *Instructions to Political and Other Officers* (1906), copy in Harvard University Library (other editions of this book are not so complete). On the rationales for inaction against Muslim slaveowners, see Lovejoy, *Transformations*, 261–68.

33. Louise Lennihan, "Rights in Men and Rights in Land: Slavery, Wage Labor, and Smallholder Agriculture in Northern Nigeria," *Slavery and Abolition* 3 (1982): 111–39; Lovejoy and Hogendorn, *Slow Death*.

34. Frederick Lugard, *Dual Mandate in British Tropical Africa* (London: Blackwood, 1922).

35. Parallel arguments about the sequence in East and West Africa are made in Cooper, *From Slaves to Squatters*, and Anne Phillips, *The Enigma of Colonialism: British Policy in West Africa* (Bloomington: Indiana University Press, 1989).

36. Conklin, *Mission to Civilize*.

37. Terence Ranger, "The Invention of Tradition in Colonial Africa," in *The Invention of Tradition*, ed. Eric Hobsbawm and Terence Ranger (Cambridge: Cambridge University Press, 1983), 211–62.

38. Stephen Constantine, *The Making of British Colonial Development Policy, 1914–1940* (London: Cass, 1984); Jacques Marseille, *Empire colonial et capitalisme français: Histoire d'un divorce* (Paris: Albin Michel, 1984).

39. Igor Kopytoff, "The Cultural Context of African Abolition," in Miers and Roberts, *End of Slavery in Africa*, 493.

40. The calculus of marginality, liminality, and absorption in relation to the predominant social structures in different African societies is the main contribution of Igor Kopytoff and Suzanne Miers, "African 'Slavery' as an Institution of Marginality," in *Slavery in Africa*, ed. Suzanne Miers and Igor Kopytoff (Madison: University of Wisconsin Press, 1971), 3–81. However, they write about such phenomena—described largely in terms of recent ethnographic fieldwork and sources from the colonial era—as if they were timelessly African rather than part of a messy history.

41. Edward A. Alpers, "Trade, State and Society among the Yao in the Nineteenth Cen-

tury," Journal of African History 10 (1969): 405–20; Elias Mandala, Work and Control in a Peasant Economy: A History of the Lower Tchiri Valley in Malawi, 1859–1960 (Madison: University of Wisconsin Press, 1990). More generally, on issues of slavery and gender, see Claire Robertson and Martin Klein, eds., Women and Slavery in Africa (Madison: University of Wisconsin Press, 1983).

42. This insecurity is best captured in the work of Marcia Wright, Strategies of Slaves and Women: Life-Stories from East-Central Africa (Boston: Barber Press, 1993). See also Landeg White, Magomero: Portrait of an African Village (Cambridge: Cambridge University Press, 1987), and Mandala, Work and Control. The way British missionaries and officials became entangled—in part through their antislavery policies—in the intricacies of regional politics, with often unintended consequences, is analyzed in César Solá-García, "Slave Emancipation and Colonialism: The British Missionary and Military Campaigns and African Responses in Northern Malawi, 1875–1900" (Ph.D. diss., University of Michigan, 1999).

43. Mandala, Work and Control.

44. Martin Chanock, Law, Custom and Social Order: The Colonial Experience in Malawi and Zambia (Cambridge: Cambridge University Press, 1985), 169. For another perspective on rural women in Central Africa, see Elizabeth Schmidt, Peasants, Traders, and Wives: Shona Women in the History of Zimbabwe, 1870–1939 (Portsmouth, N.H.: Heinemann, 1992).

45. Chanock, Law. Officials did not even think of allocating land rights to women, of slave origin or otherwise, for to do so would complicate what they saw as a "proper system of land tenure." Martin Chanock, "Paradigms, Policies and Property: A Review of the Customary Law of Land Tenure," in Law in Colonial Africa, ed. Kristin Mann and Richard Roberts (Portsmouth, N.H.: Heinemann, 1991), 73.

46. These issues are discussed in Cooper, Decolonization; George Chauncey Jr., "The Locus of Reproduction: Women's Labour in the Zambian Copperbelt, 1927–1953," Journal of Southern African Studies 7 (1981): 135–64; and Jane L. Parpart, " 'Where Is Your Mother?': Gender, Urban Marriage, and Colonial Discourse on the Zambian Copperbelt," International Journal of African Historical Studies 27 (1994): 241–72.

47. Ruth Slade, King Leopold's Congo (New York: Oxford University Press, 1962); Robert Harms, "The End of Red Rubber: A Reassessment," Journal of African History 16 (1975): 73–88; Adam Hochschild, King Leopold's Ghost: A Story of Greed, Terror, and Heroism in Colonial Africa (Boston: Houghton Mifflin, 1998).

48. James Duffy, A Question of Slavery (Cambridge: Harvard University Press, 1967); Ibrahim Sundiata, Black Scandal: America and the Liberian Labor Crisis, 1929–1936 (Philadelphia: Institute for the Study of Human Issues, 1980); William Gervase Clarence-Smith, "Cocoa Plantations and Coerced Labor in the Gulf of Guinea, 1870–1914," in Klein, Breaking the Chains, 150–70; Ibrahim Sundiata, From Slavery to Neoslavery: The Bight of Biafra and Fernando Po in the Era of Abolition, 1827–1930 (Madison: University of Wisconsin Press, 1996).

49. Michael Taussig, Shamanism, Colonialism, and the Wild Man: A Study in Terror and Healing (Chicago: University of Chicago Press, 1987), esp. 54.

50. One crusader against forced labor argued, "It is precisely because we accept the general and abstract justice of colonization that we desire, in the specific and concrete instance, to purify it of all that soils it." This argument for the morality of colonization, from a leading Catholic writer on social questions, hinged on the fact that God had endowed the colonies with rich resources, which it was humanity's duty to use in a productive and progressive fashion. Intervention was justified, but only in ways that served

a wide interest. Joseph Folliet, *Le travail forcé aux colonies* (Paris: Editions du Cerf, 1934), 104.

51. On segregationism as a "modernising ideology," see Paul Rich, *Race and Empire in British Politics* (Cambridge: Cambridge University Press, 1986), 56, and John Cell, *The Highest Stage of White Supremacy* (Cambridge: Cambridge University Press, 1982).

52. See, for example, John H. Harris, *Africa: Slave or Free?* (London: Student Christian Movement, 1919); André Gide, *Travels in the Congo*, trans. Dorothy Bussy (New York: Knopf, 1929); and Folliet, *Le travail forcé*.

53. Babacar Fall, *Le travail forcé en Afrique Occidentale Française (1900–1946)* (Paris: Karthala, 1993); Hilaire Babassana, *Travail forcé, exproriation et formation du salariat en Afrique Noire* (Grenoble: Presses Universitaires de Grenoble, 1978).

54. Jeanne Marie Penvenne, *African Workers and Colonial Racism: Mozambican Strategies and Struggles in Lourenço Marques, 1877–1962* (Portsmouth, N.H.: Heinemann, 1995); Clarence-Smith, "Cocoa Plantations"; Charles van Onselen, *Chibaro: African Mine Labour in Southern Rhodesia, 1900–1933* (London: Pluto, 1976); Leroy Vail and Landeg White, *Capitalism and Colonialism in Mozambique: A Study of Quelimane District* (Minneapolis: University of Minnesota Press, 1980); Kenneth Vickery, "The Second World War Revival of Forced Labor in the Rhodesias," *International Journal of African Historical Studies* 22 (1989): 423–37; L. L. Bessant, "Coercive Development: Land Shortage, Forced Labor, and Colonial Development in Colonial Zimbabwe, 1938–1940," *International Journal of African Historical Studies* 25 (1992): 39–66. As late as 1947, the Labour Party colonial secretary who had long opposed coercive labor practices was willing to compel Africans to participate in soil conservation projects, in the belief that force would save Africans from their own ignorance. Arthur Creech Jones, Circular Despatch, 22 February 1947, CO 852/1003/3, Public Record Office, London.

55. Assistant District Commissioner, Kilifi, to Provincial Commissioner, 18 October 1918, Kenya National Archives, Coast Province Deposit, 38/582. When the Kenya government in 1919 injudiciously said it would "encourage" African laborers to work for settlers, it unleashed a storm of criticism and had to withdraw the word, but not necessarily the policy.

56. See the missionary critique of Kenyan government labor policy in PP, 1920, XXXIII, 81:8–10, and a deeper one—although still within the language of antislavery ideology—in Norman Leys, *Kenya*, 4th ed. (London: Cass, 1973), and John W. Cell, ed., *By Kenya Possessed: The Correspondence of Norman Leys and J. H. Oldham, 1918–1926* (Chicago: University of Chicago Press, 1976), esp. 91–102.

57. I owe this distinction to Gillian Feeley-Harnick's comments at a colloquium at the Woodrow Wilson Center, Washington, D.C., 5 June 1986.

58. For an account by an ILO insider of the work leading to this convention and the subsequent ILO initiatives, see Jean Goudal, *Esclavage et travail forcé* (Paris: Pedone, 1929).

59. The analogy-to-slavery argument also appears in a radical indictment of imperialism written in Moscow by a South African–born Communist and his Russian collaborators. See A. T. Nzula, I. I. Potekhin, and A. Z. Zusmanovich, *Forced Labour in Colonial Africa*, ed. by Robin Cohen (London: Zed, 1979), 82–83.

60. Convention No. 29 of 1930 concerning forced or compulsory labor, International Labour Organisation, *Conventions and Recommendations, 1919–1981* (Geneva: International Labour Organisation, 1982), 29–36.

61. International Labour Conference, 1930, session of 25 June 1930, quotations from 269 (British government advisor), 276 (Portuguese government delegate), and 315 (French government delegate). See also Folliet, *Le travail forcé*, 153–62. One apologist for French use of forced labor was a leading African politician from Senegal, Blaise Diagne, who invoked his own race to show that France's heart was in the right place and that its use of forced labor was solely intended to "elevate and favor the future" of African races (International Labour Conference, 290–91).

62. René Mercier, *Le travail obligatoire dans les colonies africaines* (Paris: Imprimerie nouvelle, 1933), 198–203, 207, 217–18.

63. His argument was not unlike Marx's statement about free labor under capitalism: the worker was freed from bondage to any one landlord but was also "freed" from access to the means of production and therefore had nothing but his or her own labor power to sell. Marx's use of the word "free" was ironic; Mercier was in earnest about the absence of the second sort of freedom.

64. Before making their defense of obligatory labor for public purposes clear, top French officials solicited the opinions of officials on the scene, who invoked both the goal of advancing the African and a deep distrust of Africans' capacity to do anything on their own. The governor of Dahomey, for instance, concluded that "a certain pressure, a certain constraint are still necessary for this *work of liberation*." Letter to Governor-General, 31 December 1929, K 62 (19), Archives du Sénégal. For the debates, see Cooper, *Decolonization*, chap. 2, and contemporary statements by an ILO opponent, Mercier, *Le travail obligatoire*, and a supporter, Folliet, *Le travail forcé*.

65. Duffy, *Question of Slavery*; Sundiata, *Black Scandal*.

66. The ILO conventions regarding colonies were limited to issues within free labor ideology at the same time that that organization was coming to grips with labor in metropolitan countries in a more complex way: its proposed standards, which governments were supposed to enforce, covered such topics as the length of the work week and safety conditions for dangerous occupations. The ILO saw itself as helping to tame class conflict and ensuring that all competitors would be held to the same standards, so that brutish employers in unregulated states would not drive out progressive employers in states that enforced regulations. By contrast, the issues other than forced labor that the ILO took up in relation to colonies mainly concerned the use of penal sanctions by governments to enforce private labor contracts and the contract system itself. In both regards, contracts were seen as the temporary surrender of freedom—the worker could not exercise the option of quitting a job for the duration of the contract—and therefore in need of government regulation in the workers' interest. Only in 1944 did the ILO begin to consider workers in colonies as part of a social process that itself could be scrutinized.

67. This section is largely based on material from Archives Nationales, Section Outre-Mer (ANSOM) in France, especially from the files Affaires Politiques (AP) and Inspection Générale du Travail (IGT), and from the Archives du Sénégal (AS), file Travail (K).

68. Gilles Sautter, "Notes sur la construction du Chemin de Fer Congo-Océan," *Cahiers d'Etudes Africaines* 7 (1967): 219–99; Catherine Coquery-Vidrovitch, *Le Congo au temps des grandes compagnies concessionaires, 1898–1930* (Paris: Mouton, 1972); Fall, *Le travail forcé*.

69. Governor-General Carde, Circular to Governors, 11 October 1929, K 95 (26), AS.

70. Report of Inspecteur Maret, Ivory Coast, No. 125, 25 May 1931, AP 3066, ANSOM.

71. For an overview of Popular Front thinking, see Nicole Bernard-Duquenet, *Le Sénégal et le Front Populaire* (Paris: Harmattan, 1985).

72. Governor-General, Circular to Lieutenant Governors, 3 November 1936, K 191 (26), AS.

73. Governor-General to Minister, 25 January 1937, K 8 (1), AS. The debate over the ILO Convention, as well as the inspection reports on the Ivory Coast, opened up a little space for officials on the ground to warn about the consequences of recruitment—depopulation of recruitment areas, migration to nearby British territory to escape the labor roundups, problems with health and disease. There was also evidence that local officials were becoming demoralized with their role as mancatchers for the colons; that is clearly implied in de Coppet's letter quoted here. These reports are cited in Cooper, *Decolonization*, 37–42.

74. The Popular Front prime minister, Marius Moutet, and the leading theorist in the ministry, Robert Delavignette, were both from rural areas of France and projected a bucolic fantasy onto Africa. See, in particular, Robert Delavignette, *Soudan-Paris-Bourgogne* (Paris: Grasset, 1935). On the limits of wage labor and the peasant future, see "Pour la Commission d'Enquête. Note sur la colonisation européene et la colonisation indigène en Afrique Noire Française," 1936, Fonds Moutet, PA 28/5/152, ANSOM, and Moutet, speech to Chambre des Deputés, *Débats*, 15 December 1936, 3626.

75. Almost as soon as the new policy went into effect, the governor of the Ivory Coast began to assure a somewhat skeptical governor-general that labor was being successfully recruited without force. Reproduced in Ivory Coast, Inspection du Travail, Annual Report, 1937, AS. See also Rapport de Mission du Gouverneur Tap, Inspecteur du Travail, sur la Côte d'Ivoire, July–August 1937, K 217 (26), AS. The governor's repeated insistence that all was well gave the governor-general and minister little choice—short of confrontation—but to accept the reassurances while insisting that the free labor policy be maintained. Minister to Governor-General, 16 October 1937, K 197 (26), AS. For more detail, see Cooper, *Decolonization*, 77–88.

76. Official dispatches mix insistence that "it would be extremely annoying that a part of physically able and available manpower could remain insufficiently employed" with claims that "active propaganda" was all that was being done. Governor-General Cayla, Circular to Governors, 2 May 1940, K 186 (26), AS. Lower-level officials tried to let sympathetic senior officers in Paris know that a virtual manhunt was in progress, but even former minister Moutet could get nowhere with his inquiries. Robert Delavignette to Moutet, 28 March 1939, Moutet Papers, PA 28/5/143, ANSOM, enclosing correspondence from administrators in the Ivory Coast; Governor, Ivory Coast, to Governor-General, 20 March 1939, and Governor-General to Minister, 1 July 1939, AP 2807/3, ANSOM.

77. For Boisson's views, see his *Contribution à l'oeuvre africaine* (Rufisque: Imprimerie du Haut Commissariat de l'Afrique Occidentale Française, 1942). Some of the debate between Boisson and Vichy officials may be found in correspondence in K 277 (26) and K 296 (26), AS. An extended treatment of the labor question in French West Africa under the Vichy and Free French regimes is in Cooper, *Decolonization*, 141–66.

78. Governor-General, French West Africa, to Minister, 3 September 1945, K 324 (26), AS; Governor, Ivory Coast, speech to Conseil de Gouvernement, 20 December 1943, in *Procès Verbal du Conseil du Gouvernement de l'Afrique Occidentale Française* (Dakar, 1944), 49–53. An interesting case in point is Félix Eboué, governor-general of French Equatorial Africa, who opposed large-scale agricultural schemes depending on wage labor, saw Africans as tradition-bound peasants, and was not ready to give up forced labor. See his interventions in the Brazzaville debates, discussed below.

79. D. Bruce Marshall, *The French Colonial Myth and Constitution-Making in the Fourth Republic* (New Haven: Yale University Press, 1973). Because the legislature was politically divided, this small group could have influence. The colonial deputies also cared passionately about issues that to the majority were secondary.

80. *La Conférence Africaine Française* (Brazzaville: Editions du Baobab, 1944), 55; "Role et place des européens dans la colonisation," and "Programme général de la Conférence de Brazzaville," papers prepared for the Brazzaville conference, AP 2201/4 and 2201/7, ANSOM; transcript of session of 2 February 1944, AP 2295/2, ANSOM. The last source includes the views of Félix Eboué, as does his *La nouvelle politique indigène pour l'Afrique Equatoriale Française* (Paris: Office Française de l'Edition, 1945).

81. Frederick Cooper, "The Senegalese General Strike of 1946 and the Labor Question in French Africa," *Canadian Journal of African Studies* 24 (1990): 165–215. For more on the strike, see below.

82. Copy of Deputies' letter to Colonial Minister, 22 February 1946, AP 960/Syndicalisme, ANSOM. For the minister's reply, see below.

83. Annexe No. 565, *Documents de l'Assemblée Nationale Constituante*, session of 1 March 1946, 554.

84. Annexe No. 811, *Documents de l'Assemblée Nationale Constituante*, session of 30 March 1946, 780–83; *Débats de l'Assemblée Nationale Constituante* 2 (5 April 1946): 1514.

85. Extracts of letter of 26 July 1945, Governor-General to Minister, AP 960, ANSOM. Governors also argued as late as December 1945 that a quick transition to free labor was impossible, and the new chief labor inspector, although impressed by Houphouët-Boigny's arguments for immediate emancipation and by the extent of chaos caused by recruitment, could not bring himself at that date to press for rapid action. Inspecteur Général du Travail, French West Africa, to Inspecteur Général du Travail, Paris, 6, 17 December 1945, IGT 75/1, ANSOM.

86. When Governor Latrille tried to implement the Brazzaville plan for a five-year phaseout of forced labor later in 1944, colons insisted it was impossible. "I know the 'Negro,' " proclaimed the white planters' leader. Latrille slowed down the phaseout in exchange for a promise from planters that they would make an effort at voluntary recruitment. Secretary General Digo to Governor-General, 22 December 1944, K 321 (26), AS.

87. Testimony of Houphouët-Boigny, 31 May 1950, in *Rapport No. 11348 sur les incidents survenus en Côte d'Ivoire*, annex to the proceedings of session of 21 November 1950, Assemblée Nationale, reprinted by the Partie Democratique de la Côte d'Ivoire, 1:9; Ivory Coast, Inspection du Travail, Annual Report, 1944, AS; A. J. Lucas, "Enquête sur la condition des travailleurs en Côte d'Ivoire," n.d. [mid-1945], K 363 (26), AS.

88. "Rapport sur la Régime du Travail Indigène, par le Gouverneur Latrille," 20 February 1945, AE 576/23, ANSOM.

89. Secretary General of the Government General in Dakar, "Note relative à la main d'oeuvre en Côte d'Ivoire" (draft), n.d. [January 1946]; Governor-General to Director of Public Works, 18 March 1946, K 363 (26), AS. When Governor Latrille was on leave, his replacement criticized the SAA, thinking it was usurping administrative authority and blocking colons' efforts at labor recruitment, but the governor-general noted, "The agricultural Union is a good piece of work as long as it remains under surveillance and within fixed limits." Governor de Mauduit to Governor-General, 6 November 1945, with Governor-General's (undated) marginal note, 17G 146, AS.

90. Cooper, *Decolonization*, 196–98.

91. For official views of the crucial months of transition, see Mission Berlan, Compte Rendu, September 1946, K 363 (26), AS; French West Africa, Inspection du Travail, Annual Report, 1946, AS; French West Africa, Direction Général des Affaires Politiques, Administratives et Sociales, "La main d'oeuvre en Côte d'Ivoire," December 1946, K 363 (26), AS; Combier Report, July 1946, K 450 (179), AS; Inspection Général du Travail, Report, November 1946, AP 960, ANSOM.

92. "Inspection Côte d'Ivoire, Mission Bargues, 1946–47," AP 950, ANSOM; French West Africa, Inspection du Travail, Annual Report, 1946, AS; Directeur des Chemins de Fer de l'A.O.F. to Governor-General, 3 July 1946, K 363 (26), AS.

93. Speech to Conseil Général de la Côte d'Ivoire, 13 January 1947, from *Journal Officiel de la Côte d'Ivoire*, 15 January 1947, in Agence France Outre-Mer 393, ANSOM.

94. This break in both French and British official thinking about Africa in the 1940s is the principal subject of my *Decolonization and African Society*.

95. Such a labor system has quite different social, economic, and political implications—in the long as well as the short run—from the classic capitalist division of labor, a point made clear in Jean-Pierre Chauveau and Jacques Richard, "Une peripherie recentrée: à propos d'un système d'économie de plantation en Côte d'Ivoire," *Cahiers d'Etudes Africaines* 17 (1977): 485–523.

96. Ivory Coast, Political Report, 1946, AS. Earlier an official in the recruiting districts had commented, "One cannot say that this was purely voluntary recruitment because the chiefs used their influence and the duration of the contract was imposed at one year at the beginning; but we have observed that the contingents are returning at the end of the contract satisfied with the treatment that was given them; many declare themselves to want to return when they have, according to custom, reestablished contact with their people for a more or less long period." Report to Governor by Administrateur Supérieur, Haute Côte d'Ivoire, enclosed in Governor to Governor-General, 28 February 1946, K 363 (26), AS.

97. Ministre des Colonies to Senghor, 11 March 1946, AP 960, ANSOM.

98. Cooper, "Senegalese General Strike."

99. Citizenship in the metropole itself did not imply a universal right to vote, for France distinguished between a passive citizenship and an active one, deploying a variety of constructs to define the qualifications for active participation. It took over 150 years after the French Revolution for metropolitan women to receive the vote. See Pierre Rosanvallon, *Le sacre du citoyen: Histoire du suffrage universel en France* (Paris: Gallimard, 1992). On the constitutional debates of the late 1940s, see Marshall, *French Colonial Myth*; Rudolf von Albertini, *Decolonization: The Administration and Future of the Colonies, 1919–1960*, trans. Francisca Garvie (New York: Holmes and Meier, 1971).

100. G. Wesley Johnson, *The Emergence of Black Politics in Senegal: The Struggle for Power in the Four Communes, 1890–1920* (Stanford: Stanford University Press, 1971); Conklin, *Mission to Civilize*.

101. The willingness of the French state to engage with certain sorts of interlocutors in this period implied its refusal to engage with certain others, however. The brutality of its response to struggle that went beyond certain boundaries, including the bloody repression of the Madagascar rebellion of 1947, the harsh exclusion of a radical political party in the Cameroun in the mid-1950s, and, most painful of all, French actions in Algeria, reveals the flip side of the relatively prudent way in which the French state carried out its interactions with the French West African labor movement.

102. Doudou Thiam, *La porte de la citoyenneté française dans les territoires d'outre-mer*, thèse pour le doctorat en droit, Université de Poitiers (Paris: Société d'éditions africaines, 1951), quotes from 48, 81, 97, 130, and 174.

103. Cooper, *Decolonization*, chap. 7.

104. The ILO also acted before the war to end penal sanctions for violations of labor contracts and to regulate long-term labor contracts and migration. Both issues were seen as extensions of the ILO's position against forced labor, penal sanctions because they entailed the state's use of coercion to enforce private contracts, long-term contracts because they deprived the worker of the right to opt out of wage labor for a period of time.

105. See the published transcripts of ILO, 26th International Labour Conference, Philadelphia, 1944, and "Recommendation No. 70 Concerning Minimum Standards of Social Policy in Dependent Territories," in ILO, *Conventions and Recommendations*, 875–95. For further discussion, see Cooper, *Decolonization*, pt. 3.

106. Senghor was centrally involved in writing the definition of wage labor in the 1952 code: the worker was someone who sold his or her services to another for a wage and worked under that person's authority. Senghor wanted a definition that made no mention of the personal status of the worker and ensured that long- or short-term workers in the wage sector would be covered whenever they worked. He was content to see all other forms of labor left out. See Cooper, *Decolonization*, chap. 7.

107. Margaret E. Keck and Kathryn Sikkink, *Activists beyond Borders: Advocacy Networks in International Politics* (Ithaca: Cornell University Press, 1998); Audie Klotz, *Norms in International Politics: The Struggle against Apartheid* (Ithaca: Cornell University Press, 1995).

Afterword

1. *Le Monde*, 14 and 25 April 1998.

2. For a discussion of those households, see Rebecca J. Scott, "Reclaiming Gregoria's Mule: The Meanings of Freedom in the Arimao and Caunao Valleys, Cienfuegos, Cuba, 1880–1899," *Past and Present*, forthcoming.

Index

173 (n. 91); for freedpeople, 66, 120–21, 123; ILO on, 184 (n. 66), 188 (n. 104)
Cooper, Frederick, 27, 28, 57, 163 (nn. 47, 48)
Copper mines, 128
Coppet, Marcel de, 135, 185 (n. 73)
Corporations, multinational, 156
Corvée (hard labor), 139
Crown colony system (Great Britain), 37, 43
Cruces, Cuba: insurgency in, 89–90, 98; Centro Africano, 94; Workers' Guild, 95, 100; Workers' Congress in, 103
Cuba: emancipation in, 4, 18, 85, 86; slave trade in, 8; antislavery in, 12; transracial nationalism of, 23–26, 31, 97, 103–4, 106, 175 (n. 108); citizenship in, 24; Constitution of 1901, 25; U.S. occupation of, 25, 90–100; and sugar, 63; insurgencies in, 83–86, 87, 88, 89; nationalist leaders of, 84; modernization in, 87; and race, 91, 100–103, 174 (n. 96); unions in, 93, 103; strikes in, 93–96, 103, 176 (n. 121); working-class organizations of, 94–95, 105, 176 (n. 123); anarchists in, 95; Rural Guard of, 95, 102; Liberal Party of, 97, 99; Partido Independiente de Color, 101; politicization of nationality in, 178 (n. 150). See also Afro-Cubans; Freedpeople: in Cuba; Plantations, sugar: Cuba; Cuban war of independence
Cuban Constituent Assembly, 94
Cuban war of independence (1895–98), 23–24, 87; cross-racial alliances in, 62, 85, 87–89, 92, 94, 97; insurgent army in, 64–65, 155; counterinsurgency in, 90, 174 (n. 105); veterans of, 94, 95, 97, 98, 174 (n. 96); centenary of, 175 (n. 108)

Dahomey, 126, 184 (n. 64)
Davis, David Brion, 165 (nn. 6, 14)
DeClouet, Paul, 67, 68, 168 (n. 14), plantation of, 168 (n. 14)
Decolonization, 4
Delavignette, Robert, 185 (n. 74)

Democratic Party (La.), 70, 71, 72, 104
Diagne, Blaise, 184 (n. 61)
Discursive formation, 178 (n. 2)
Domesticity, 38
Drescher, Seymour, 164 (n. 14), 165 (n. 18)
Dubroca, C. M., 171 (n. 59)
Dymond, Florence, 82

Eboué, Félix, 185 (n. 78)
Education, industrial, 52–53, 166 (n. 47)
Ejército Libertador (Cuba), 155, 174 (n. 96)
Elgin, Lord, 50–52
Elkins, Stanley, 2; Slavery, 2
El Palmar, Cuba, 100
Emancipation, 13, 57, 158 (n. 11); in Cuba, 4, 18, 85, 86; colonial authority in, 12, 119, 179 (n. 9); in U.S., 23, 36, 65; in Brazil, 31; in classical liberalism, 38, 42–50, 61
—African, 3, 112, 118–19, 124–25, 157 (n. 2); in French Africa, 32, 108, 112–13, 114–15, 117, 139, 143, 145, 149, 151; in Nigeria, 118–19; in Zanzibar, 120–21; in Kenya, 121–22, 124; and gender, 126–29, 127; social meanings of, 126–29
—British, 36, 56, 164 (n. 8); in West Indies, 20–22, 34, 36–38; in Jamaica, 42–50, 154. See also Apprenticeship; Freedpeople: in British West Indies
Emery, Robert, 54
Esnard, J. B., 81
Esquerra, Higinio, 89
Estenoz, Evaristo, 98
Estrada Palma, Tomás, 94, 96, 99
Eyre, John, 54–55

Families: freed, 21, 52, 154–55; conjugal, 40–41; in bourgeois social order, 46; slave labor in African, 113
Ferrer, Ada, 24
Fields, Barbara Jean, 13, 165 (n. 5)
Fifteenth Amendment, 19, 161 (n. 36)
Finley, Moses, 6

Forced Labour Convention (1930), 132–33, 134, 135

Foret, Richard, 74–75

Foucault, Michel, 160 (n. 18)

France: 31, 126; colonial policies of, 31–32; legislature of, 129, 143, 144, 145, 186 (n. 79); and Forced Labour Convention, 134, 135; Popular Front government of, 135; Vichy government of, 136, 185 (n. 77); free labor ideology of, 143; colonies of, 143, 145; constituent assembly of, 145; citizenship in, 145–47, 149, 187 (n. 99); universalism of, 146, 147, 149; Fourth Republic of, 147; labor code of, 147, 148, 188 (n. 106); and French African immigrants, 152. *See also* French Africa; French Revolution

Franchise. *See* Voting rights

Fraser, Nancy, 47, 164 (n. 15), 165 (n. 20)

Freedmen's Bureau, 66, 67

Freedom, 5, 8–9, 10, 13, 18, 32, 34, 59; in African societies, 5–6

Freedpeople: societal integration of, 2, 38; under colonialism, 3; collective action by, 10; and citizenship, 14, 17, 18, 153; and voting rights, 17, 37; and work, 20–21; dispersal of from plantations, 21; economic rationality of, 21–22, 27; and resistance, 166 (n. 51)
—in Africa: 117; political participation by, 110; and land, 110, 120, 122–25; and colonial officials, 110, 125; contracts for, 120–21, 123 (*see also* Africans)
—in British West Indies, 34, 36, 42–56; emancipation contract of, 36–38; British expectations for, 44–47, 54–56; and land, 47–49; British obligations toward, 50; as bourgeois subjects, 50–56, 58–59; work ethic of, 54; and political power, 55, 163 (n. 3)
—in Cuba, 10, 91–93; and land, 92, 100, 103; strikes by, 93, 176 (n. 121) (*see also* Afro-Cubans)
—in Louisiana, 10, 63, 67, 73, 104, 168 (n. 14); strikes by, 26, 62, 69, 72–82, 170 (n. 38); and land, 66, 69–70, 92,

100, 103, 106; "labor companies" of, 66, 167 (n. 6); rights of, 71, 72. (*see also* Sugar workers, Louisiana)

Freedwomen, 17–18, 46, 58, 79, 166 (n. 59)

Free French, 31, 136–37

Free labor ideology, 22, 108, 111, 113, 120; in African, 132, 148; French, 143

Free trade legislation, 22

French Africa, 117, 136, 137, 139, 147, 179(n. 10); labor in, 4, 30–31, 110, 131, 134–43, 144, 184 (n. 61); emancipation (1946), 32, 108, 112–13, 139, 143, 145, 149; emancipation (1848), 114–15, 117, 151

French Antilles, 18–19, 114

French Equatorial Africa, 134

French Revolution, 11, 12; and citizenship, 16, 151, 165 (n. 19)

French Union, 146

French West Africa, 31, 135, 137, 141, 142, 145; labor in, 136–37; strikes in, 137, 140, 141, 143–44

Frere, A. J., 171 (nn. 59, 60)

Froude, James Anthony, 47

Fuente, Alejandro de la, 105

Fyfe, Alexander, 54

Gaines, Ernest, 173 (n. 81)

Gender, 9–10, 46, 57, 127, 129, 182 (n. 41). *See also* Marriage

Glenelg, Lord, 21, 34, 36–37, 42, 47–50; egalitarian policies of, 43, 44, 56, 57

Gold Coast, 131, 137, 140

Gómez, José Miguel, 95, 96, 176 (n. 126)

Gómez, Juan Gualberto, 88

Gómez, Máximo, 88, 90, 92

González, Zacarías, 92

González Planas, José, 88

Great Britain, 7–8, 34, 126, 148, 164 (n. 8); colonial policies of, 31–32, 33–34, 36–38. *See also* British West Indies; Colonial Office; Emancipation: British

Greece, 9, 10

Gremio de Braceros (Cruces), 95, 100

Grey, Charles, 34

Grey, Earl, 34, 36, 53, 55

Reason, universal, 12; colonization and, 159 (n. 15)
Reasoning, Enlightenment, 12, 13
Reconstruction (U.S.), 23, 26, 66–72, 157 (n. 3)
Republican Party (La.), 67, 70, 83
"Residuum," 116, 165 (n. 23), 180 (n. 13)
Resistance: by freedpeople, 65, 166 (n. 51); and livelihood, 65, 167 (n. 2); to colonialism, 178 (n. 1); to slavery, 178 (n. 1), 179 (n. 9)
Rhodesia, 128–29, 131
Richard, Jacques, 187 (n. 95)
Rodriguez, Emilia, 103
Rubber trade, 130

St. Bernard Parish, La., 72, 170 (n. 39)
St. Charles Parish, La., 170 (n. 39)
Saint Domingue. See Haiti
St. Landry Parish, La., 66
St. Mary Parish, La., 77–78
St. Thomas-in-the-East, Jamaica, 44
Salisbury, Lord, 116
San Antón (Cienfuegos), Cuba, 92
Santa Clara (Las Villas), Cuba, 84, 96, 99, 103; insurgency in, 88, 102, 104
Santa Rosalía estate (Cienfuegos), 85, 86; insurgency at, 89, 174 (n. 97); freedpersons from, 91, 92, 155
São Tomé, 130
Sarría, Claudio, 88–89
Scott, Rebecca, 10, 25, 57, 178 (n. 1)
Segregationism, 183 (n. 51)
Senegal, 114, 143
Senghor, Léopold, 142–43, 144, 145, 188 (n. 106)
Sharecropping, 2, 4
Shreveport, La., 78, 172 (n. 64)
Singletary, Otis, 169 (n. 31)
Sitios (small farms), 89, 174 (n. 98)
Slaveowners, African, 109–10, 117; Muslim, 115, 181 (n. 32); of Nigeria, 118; of Zanzibar, 120–21; of Kenya, 121, 123; merchant, 179 (n. 10). See also Planters
Slavery, 1–2, 5, 28; aftermath of, 3–4; and forced labor, 4; on plantations, 6, 119; European, 7, 27–28; as social process,

8, 9; in Greece, 9, 10; and colonialism, 10, 12, 108, 113–16, 178 (n. 1); in republican states, 13; transitions from, 20–22, 33, 34, 36–41, 120, 123–25; relation to capitalism, 22–23; Napoleon's restoration of, 151; and resources, 155; resistance to, 178 (n. 1), 179 (n. 9); "legal status" of, 181 (n. 21); and gender, 182 (n. 41)
Slavery, African, 2, 7, 8, 113, 126; and marriage, 112, 119, 126–29; and colonialism, 113–16; and British, 114, 179 (nn. 6, 7); Islamic, 115, 126, 181 (n. 32); in Nigeria, 118–19; in Kenya, 119; in Zanzibar, 119–20; chronology of, 179 (n. 5)
Slavery Convention (1926), 132
Slaves: social deprivations of, 1, 6–7, 38, 39; as property, 6; treatment of, 17; insurgencies of Cuban, 85–86, 89; runaway, 85–86, 115, 117, 119; supply system for, 113, 124; and reproduction, 179 (n. 5)
Slaves, former. See Freedpeople
Slave systems, 1, 2, 5, 22, 106
Slave trade, 10, 19, 179 (nn. 6, 9); in Africa, 2, 27, 28, 113–16; suppression of, 7, 28, 119; in Cuba, 8
"Slavish personality," 18
Sligo, Marquis of, 42–43, 50, 165 (n. 7)
Smith, Adam, 12, 40, 160 (n. 29)
Smith, Gavin, 167 (n. 2)
Social movements, theory of, 179 (n. 2); transnational, 30, 149, 155–56
Social relations: of slavery, 9; under classical liberalism, 20, 39; of free labor, 23; inequality in, 50; in Jamaica, 51
Sociéte Agricole Africaine (Ivory Coast, SAA), 140–41, 142, 186 (n. 89)
Societies, African, 5–6, 132, 181 (n. 40); colonial intervention in, 116; dependence in, 118, 119; matrilineal, 126–27
Societies, postemancipation, 3–4, 44, 57, 66; and gender, 9–10; colonial, 19–20; 126–29
Societies, slaveowning, 118, 126
Soledad Plantation (Cuba), 87, 91, 92,